DATA FLOW

VISUALIZING INFORMATION
IN GRAPHIC DESIGN

2

gestalten

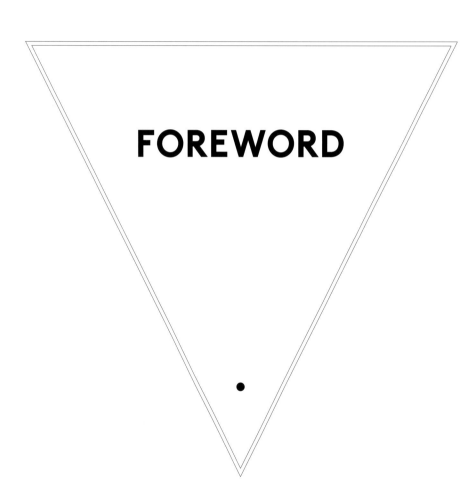

FOREWORD

Within just a few years, the once unglamorous task of giving form to abstract data has become a favorite among designers. This book serves as evidence. Published a mere 18 months after its predecessor, *Data Flow 2* is filled to the brim with interesting, innovative and inspiring examples of creative data visualization.

•

The enormous increase in interest shouldn't come as any surprise: information visualization is an ideal challenge for graphic designers. Trained to communicate precisely through visual language and experienced in creative problem solving, designers can put all their skills to use. It just did not happen earlier because large amounts of data were only available in the elitist spheres of science and business. Even if they had been easily accessible, incomprehensible scientific data sets or boring business stats are usually turn-offs for most creative folks. These days however, we have all kinds of data on our hands. We can pick almost any topic we are interested in and retrieve corresponding data. We can record our own data with GPS devices, pedometers and other sensors, access huge databases from governments and other institutions, or use the petabytes of data generated in social networks.

That is exactly what designers, programmers and even artists have been doing in the last few years. There seems to be almost nothing that has not been turned into a graph. Personal beer

PREVIOUS PAGE
ORANGE ALERT USA
Diana Cooper
/2005/Acetate, acrylic, felt, neoprene, paper, foam core,
corrugated plastic and map pins/203×168×108 inches/
Photographed by Bill Orcutt at Postmasters Gallery, NYC/

consumption, wacky film plots, emotional *Twitter* messages, there are even web applications to track and visualize our sex lives. Often beautifully designed, the purpose of many projects can be questionable, thus criticisms have often been voiced: "These are just visualizations for visualization's sake" and "There's an overemphasis on style." Indeed, we see a lot of projects that could be accused of this, and some are featured in this very book. But as legitimate as these critiques might be, we shouldn't forget that the overall quality of information visualization has leapfrogged in the last few years. We may see more visualizations that focus too much on "looks," but thanks to the sprouting interest of designers, we also see less llegible, crude diagrams, unpleasant to the eye, made by people who might know lots about the data, but don't have the means to communicate them properly.

THE PURPOSE OF VISUALIZATION IS INSIGHT, NOT PICTURES.

Experiments – be they of a visual nature or in interactive design – are vital to thriving innovation, and since information visualization is just growing out of its baby shoes, we should embrace it. As this discipline is maturing, best practice will prevail. Therefore, the selection shown here is broad by intention. From individual student projects to comprehensive commercial commissions, from amusing topics to more serious ones, from handiwork to software-based approaches, many different facets of the field are covered. Some examples do not even try to convey information in a way that is easily understandable to everyone. They use data for artistic purposes, to express and address emotions. Of course, the borders between art and design are blurry.

As important as experiments are, and without denying the merits of data-based art, we should be aware that the field of information visualization is far more than a creative playground. It is an indispensable instrument to cope with the massive amounts of data we are confronted with. Every click on a website leaves a digital trace and as soon as sensory devices are ubiquitous, even our physical movements will be translated to ones and zeros. We are just at the beginning of an era of recorded data. To make sense of it, to turn it into information which will lead to knowledge for us, and for future generations, is a tremendous call. With the urgent problems our society and our planet are facing, data visualization can be an effective tool to spur us into much-needed action. Information can change people's behavior. Making that information visible, easily understandable and enjoyable to use, is probably one of the most interesting challenges designers have ever encountered.

To live up to this task, a few things are to be considered when approaching an information visualization. /1/ A good guiding principle (which should be printed in large letters over the desk of every information designer) comes from Ben Shneiderman, a pioneer in his field: "The purpose of visualization is insight, not pictures." /2/ A visualization's function is to facilitate understanding. Form has to follow this function. This does not mean that aesthetics are not important – they are. Some researchers, among them Andrew Vande Moere, who is interviewed in this book, /see interview › PP. 28, 29/ have detected correlations between the aesthetic qualities of a visualization and how well it is understood.

2
USING VISION TO THINK (1999)
Stuart K. Card, Jock D. Mackinlay,
Ben Shneiderman

1
An interesting read is the
INFORMATION VISUALIZATION
MANIFESTO
on VISUALCOMPLEXITY.COM.
An interview with Manuel Lima,
the author of this manifesto,
can be found on page 28

EVERY VISUALIZATION
IS AN INTERPRETATION.

However, it is not only aesthetics that help to increase the information flow. Narrative is a very powerful tool as well. "I try to write stories in an appropriate and interesting way," says Joachim Sauter on his approach, /see interview › PP. 250, 251/ knowing that everyone is a sucker for a good narrative. Employing this, information can be conveyed more effectively. The relevance of storytelling hints at another important issue that should be taken into account: the designer becomes an author, not just the narrator. Every visualization is an interpretation. By selecting the data and choosing how to display it, a message is formed. This might seem trivial, but it is quite a shift for graphic designers. Previously, they worked with material which already had a message – texts or pictures. By working with data however, the designer makes the statement. The ability to misinform or even tell straight lies by the means of visualizations entails a huge responsibility.

INFORMATION VISUALIZATION IS TOO POWERFUL AND IMPORTANT TO BE LEFT ONLY TO DESIGNERS.

In this respect, designers can learn a lot from journalists. Researching, reviewing, analyzing and contextualizing facts to devise a message are part of their daily work. That is one of the reasons we interviewed Steve Duenes, who manages the graphics department at the *New York Times*. /see interview ›PP.140,141/ We also talked to Menno-Jan Kraak. /see interview ›PP.214, 215/ The Dutch cartographer also knows *How to Lie with Maps* /3/ and is well aware of his responsibility when making maps, which are used in (sometimes critical) decision making. In terms of visualizing, designers can learn from cartography. After all, this ancient discipline was using graphics to represent information long before there was such a thing as graphic design.

     These are just two examples of other disciplines which incorporate an element of visualization. There are many more – programming, science and statistic to name a few. Information designers must broaden their horizons and collaborate with these related professions. In our complex world, where everything seems to be interlinked with everything else, interdisciplinary, or even better, transdisciplinary work, is a necessity. Information visualization is too powerful and important to be left only to designers – or to any other profession for that matter.

3
HOW TO LIE WITH MAPS
is an acclaimed book
by Mark Monmonier,
demonstrating how maps can
be manipulated — for better
or worse.

DATAPROCESS

When certain phenomena or aspects of a problem are better explained by images than words, the designer has a large number of instruments at hand: flowcharts, landscape diagrams, schematics and technical illustrations – to name just a few. This chapter shows various ways to represent workflows, shed light on complex processes, demonstrate functions, and depict sequences.

•

Often the information to be visualized is not just a bunch of values in a database that can be compared or connected. As soon as time and dependencies come into play – when data follows a path – the flow chart becomes the diagram of choice. From

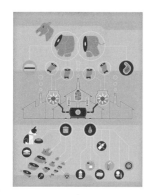

1
HERITAGE BEAST
Jude Buffum
/›P. 25 /

3
OH SNAP!
OUR STEP-BY-STEP GUIDE TO GETTING
SHOT BY THE SARTORIALIST
Joshua Covarrubias
/›P. 39 /

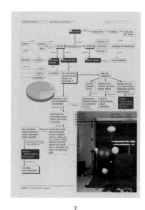

2
STANLEY
THE OPEN QUESTION MAGAZINE
Katrin Schacke
/›PP. 40, 41 /

4
ABITARE / RESEARCH
Salottobuono
/›P. 36 /

psychological processes to food production chains, from how-to instructions to anatomical studies of movements, the examples in this chapter cover a wide range of different topics, which are explained in a sequential arrangement.

A flow chart however, does not have to look like a dull gathering of bare rectangles and arrows. By flicking through the next pages, it becomes obvious that these kinds of diagrams allow lots of opportunity for representational illustrations. Take Jude Buffum's visualization about the processing of animal parts   /1/   as an example. An abstract depiction of the issue would not have the same impact. Not only do the images of a cow or pig remind us that all this is about living creatures, but they also make words obsolete. The visualization speaks the universal language of imagery, understood by everybody.

But images are not always sufficient. Some processes are better described verbally. That does not mean the flow chart cannot be designed elegantly however, as Katrin Schacke proves.   /2/ Carefully edited, it can even tell a story about the subject between the lines. With a good portion of witty humor, Joshua Covarrubias asks simple yes / no questions to determine the chances of being featured on *thesartorialist.com*.   /3/   Without spelling it out, the idiosyncrasies of this fashion blog are revealed.

Not all examples in this chapter are about sequences though. Like Salottobuono's illustration for a magazine, these visualizations dissect objects, breaking them down to their basic parts and principles.   /4/   What is usually hidden is now revealed. Information is achieved by unfolding a whole into pieces and layers. The art of these technical illustrations is to focus on the relevant details: by highlighting the important and reducing dispensable information, by amplifying the signal and fading out the noise.

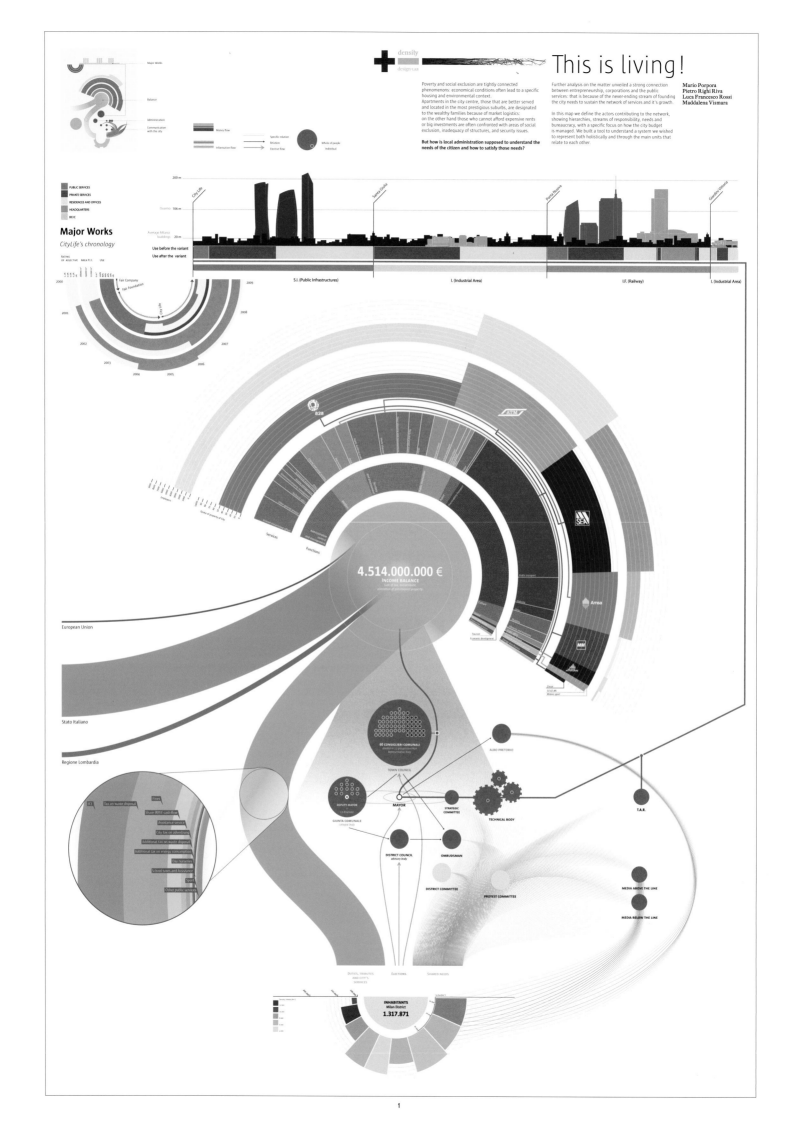

Thermohaline Belt

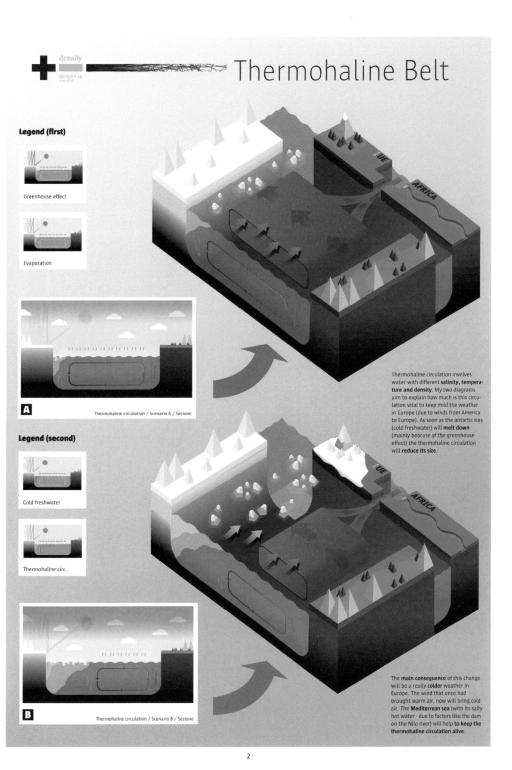

Legend (first)

Greenhouse effect

Evaporation

A Thermohaline circulation / Scenario A / Sezione

Legend (second)

Cold freshwater

Thermohaline circ.

B Thermohaline circulation / Scenario B / Sezione

Thermohaline circulation involves water with different **salinity, temperature and density**. My two diagrams aim to explain how much is this circulation vital to keep the mild weather in Europe (due to winds from America to Europe). As soon as the antartic ices (cold freshwater) will **melt down** (mainly beacuse of the greenhouse effect) the thermohaline circulation will **reduce its size**.

The **main consequence** of this change will be a really **colder** weather in Europe. The wind that once had brought warm air, now will bring cold air. The **Mediterrean sea** (with its salty hot water - due to factors like the dam on the Nilo river) will help **to keep the thermohaline circulation alive**.

2

1
HOUSING POVERTY — THIS IS LIVING!
DensityDesign
Mario Porpora, Pietro Righi Riva,
Luca Francesco Rossi
and Maddalena Vismara
Poverty and social exclusion are tightly connected phenomena: economic conditions often go along with specific housing and environmental situations. This map defines the contributing actors in urban planning and reveals the involved hierarchies, responsibilities, needs, bureaucracy and budget streams. / Scientific supervisors and academic faculty: Paolo Ciuccarelli (Associated Professor Politecnico di Milano), Marco Fattore (Prof. in Statistics, from Università Bicocca di Milano), Marco Maiocchi (Prof. in Networks, from Politecnico di Milano), Alessandro Casinovi (Graphic Designer), Salvatore Zingale (Prof. in Semiotics, from Politecnico di Milano) /

2
THERMOHALINE BELT
DensityDesign
Guido Tamino

3
BOILING OCEAN
DensityDesign
Michele Graffieti
/ → P. 22 / Scientific supervisors: Donato Ricci /

The Boiling Ocean

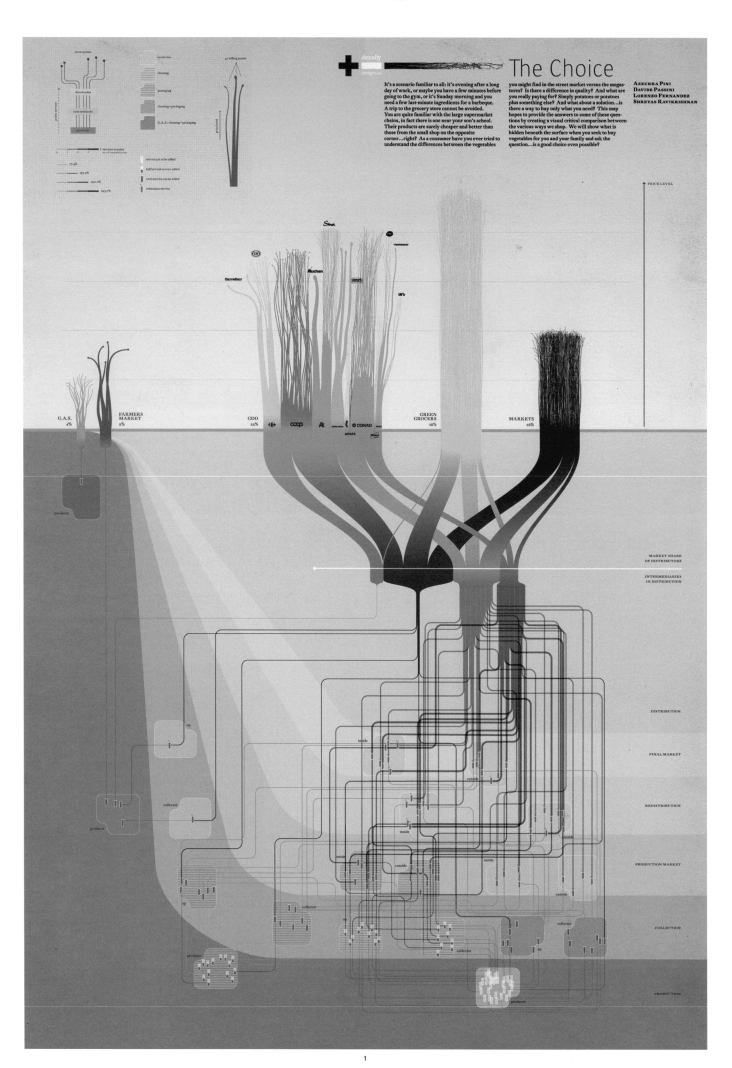

The Choice

It's a scenario familiar to all: it's evening after a long day of work, or maybe you have a few minutes before going to the gym, or it's Sunday morning and you need a few last-minute ingredients for a barbeque. A trip to the grocery store cannot be avoided. You are quite familiar with the large supermarket chains, in fact there is one near your son's school. Their products are surely cheaper and better than those from the small shop on the opposite corner…right? As a consumer have you ever tried to understand the differences between the vegetables you might find in the street market versus the megastores? Is there a difference in quality? And what are you really paying for? Simply potatoes or potatoes plus something else? And what about a solution…is there a way to buy only what you need? This map hopes to provide the answers to some of these questions by creating a visual critical comparison between the various ways we shop. We will show what is hidden beneath the surface when you seek to buy vegetables for you and your family and ask the question…is a good choice even possible?

AZZURRA PINI
DAVIDE PASSINI
LORENZO FERNANDEZ
SHREYAS RAVIKRISHNAN

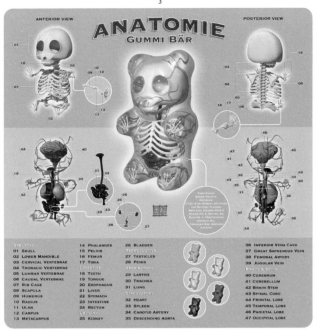

ANATOMIE GUMMI BÄR

SKELETAL
01 SKULL
02 LOWER MANDIBLE
03 CERVICAL VERTEBRAE
04 THORACIC VERTEBRAE
05 LUMBAR VERTEBRAE
06 CAUDAL VERTEBRAE
07 RIB CAGE
08 SCAPULA
09 HUMERUS
10 RADIUS
11 ULNA
12 CARPUS
13 METACARPUS
14 PHALANGES
15 PELVIS
16 FEMUR
17 TIBIA

DIGESTIVE
18 TEETH
19 TONGUE
20 ESOPHAGUS
21 LIVER
22 STOMACH
23 INTESTINE
24 RECTUM

URINARY
25 KIDNEY
26 BLADDER

REPRODUCTIVE
27 TESTICLES
28 PENIS

RESPIRATORY
29 LARYNX
30 TRACHEA
31 LUNG

CIRCULATORY
32 HEART
33 SPLEEN
34 CAROTID ARTERY
35 DESCENDING AORTA
36 INFERIOR VENA CAVA
37 GREAT SAPHENOUS VEIN
38 FEMORAL ARTERY
39 JUGULAR VEIN

BRAIN & SPINE
40 CEREBRUM
41 CEREBELLUM
42 BRAIN STEM
43 SPINAL CORD
44 FRONTAL LOBE
45 TEMPORAL LOBE
46 PARIETAL LOBE
47 OCCIPITAL LOBE

1
FOOD & POVERTY — THE CHOICE
DensityDesign
Lorenzo Fernandez, Davide Passini, Azzurra Pini and Shreyas R Krishnan
Visual communication and design can be powerful tools in effecting social change. This particular project focuses on food distribution and access in Italy — and makes us question the way we shop. / Scientific supervisors and academic faculty: Paolo Ciuccarelli (Associated Professor Politecnico di Milano), Marco Fattore (Prof. in Statistics, from Università Bicocca di Milano), Marco Maiocchi (Prof. in Networks, from Politecnico di Milano, Alessandro Casinovi (Graphic Designer) Salvatore Zingale (Prof. in Semiotics, from Politecnico di Milano) /

2
MICRO SCHEMATIC
3
ANATOMIE GUMMI BÄR
4
PNEUMATIC ANATOMICA
Jason Freeny
Jason Freeny's anatomical sketches strip the virtual flesh of tasty snacks, childhood friends and kiddie cuties for an in-depth look at the leisure industry.

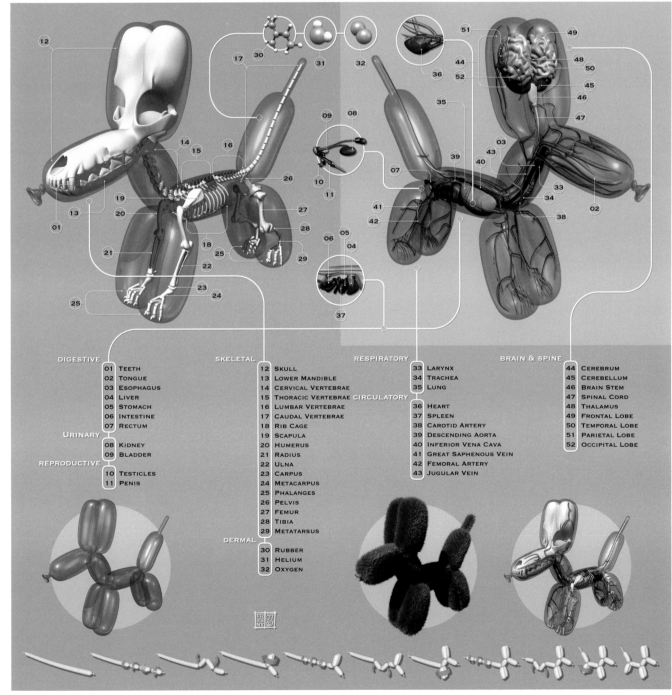

DIGESTIVE
01 TEETH
02 TONGUE
03 ESOPHAGUS
04 LIVER
05 STOMACH
06 INTESTINE
07 RECTUM

URINARY
08 KIDNEY
09 BLADDER

REPRODUCTIVE
10 TESTICLES
11 PENIS

SKELETAL
12 SKULL
13 LOWER MANDIBLE
14 CERVICAL VERTEBRAE
15 THORACIC VERTEBRAE
16 LUMBAR VERTEBRAE
17 CAUDAL VERTEBRAE
18 RIB CAGE
19 SCAPULA
20 HUMERUS
21 RADIUS
22 ULNA
23 CARPUS
24 METACARPUS
25 PHALANGES
26 PELVIS
27 FEMUR
28 TIBIA
29 METATARSUS

DERMAL
30 RUBBER
31 HELIUM
32 OXYGEN

RESPIRATORY
33 LARYNX
34 TRACHEA
35 LUNG

CIRCULATORY
36 HEART
37 SPLEEN
38 CAROTID ARTERY
39 DESCENDING AORTA
40 INFERIOR VENA CAVA
41 GREAT SAPHENOUS VEIN
42 FEMORAL ARTERY
43 JUGULAR VEIN

BRAIN & SPINE
44 CEREBRUM
45 CEREBELLUM
46 BRAIN STEM
47 SPINAL CORD
48 THALAMUS
49 FRONTAL LOBE
50 TEMPORAL LOBE
51 PARIETAL LOBE
52 OCCIPITAL LOBE

L'ELENCO DELLE SPECIE A RISCHIO

Il consumo di pesce pro capite è quasi duplicato negli ultimi cinquant'anni. Se continuassimo a pescare e a mangiare pesce al ritmo attuale rischieremmo di svuotare gli oceani. Greenpeace ha compilato un elenco delle specie a rischio: il **tonno pinna gialla** è il sorvegliato speciale più famoso. Eccone altri

Anguilla
(*Anguilla anguilla*)

Merluzzo bianco
(*Gadus morhua*)

Salmone dell'Atlantico
(*Salmo salar*)

La fattoria dei pesci

Mentre la domanda continua a crescere, le scorte di pescato diminuiscono e i mari si svuotano. Ormai quasi il 50 per cento dei consumi mondiali viene coperto da prodotti allevati. Ma l'acquacoltura è davvero una soluzione sostenibile? Tra fautori del cambiamento e ambientalisti, il dibattito è iniziato

– *di* **Francesco Franchi**
illustrazioni **Laura Cattaneo**

PESCATORI O ALLEVATORI?

La maggior parte delle specie ittiche commerciali sono state acclimatate nel Novecento: la produzione dell'acquacoltura, che nel 1950 era quasi pari a zero, ora rappresenta **più di un terzo** dei prodotti ittici globali (la maggior parte in Asia).

- ⬤ pesci d'acqua dolce
- ⬤ pesci diadromi
- ⬤ pesci marini
- ⬤ crostacei
- ⬤ molluschi
- ⬤ altri animali acquatici

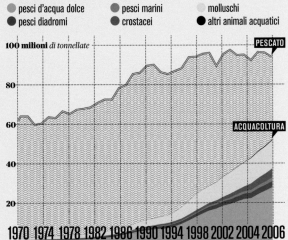

100 milioni *di tonnellate* — PESCATO

ACQUACOLTURA

1970 1974 1978 1982 1986 1990 1994 1998 2002 2004 2006

ADDIO MANDRIE E BISTECCHE

L'allevamento tradizionale di terraferma è destinato a finire. Lo sostiene Paul Roberts nel libro *La fine del cibo* (Codice Edizioni, 2009, pagg. 460, euro 28). Secondo il giornalista inglese dovremmo dunque ricavare le nostre proteine dal mare, mettendo in atto una **"rivoluzione blu"**.

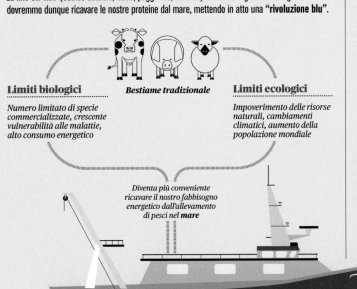

Limiti biologici

Numero limitato di specie commercializzate, crescente vulnerabilità alle malattie, alto consumo energetico

Bestiame tradizionale

Limiti ecologici

Impoverimento delle risorse naturali, cambiamenti climatici, aumento della popolazione mondiale

Diventa più conveniente ricavare il nostro fabbisogno energetico dall'allevamento di pesci nel mare

CON LA CARNE INQUINI DI PIÙ

Tra i vari parametri per calcolare la propria **impronta di CO2** (annuale) la dieta è determinante

4,8 ton CO2

Dieta a base di pesce

5,8 ton CO2

Per chi mangia carni rosse tutti i giorni

🌐 carbonfootprint.com

L'ONDA LUNGA DELL'ACQUACOLTURA NELLE DIVERSE REGIONI

Analisi dei tassi di crescita della produzione per regione: nel 2006 Medio Oriente e Sud America hanno avuto il più alto incremento

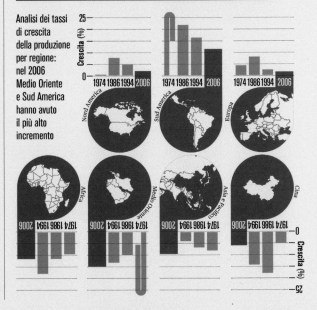

Crescita (%)
25
0

1974 1986 1994 2006
1974 1986 1994 2006
1974 1986 1994 2006

Nord America | Sud America | Europa

2006 1974 1986 1994 | 2006 1974 1986 1994 | 2006 1974 1986 1994 | 2006 1974 1986 1994

Africa | Medio Oriente | Asia e Pacifico | Cina

Crescita (%)
0
25

È L'OSTRICA GIGANTE LA PIÙ RICHIESTA IN CATTIVITÀ

I pesci consumano meno. Per vivere hanno bisogno di un apporto calorico minore rispetto alle specie di terra. Essendo a **sangue freddo** e **idrodinamici**, per far funzionare il proprio organismo bruciano poche calorie e utilizzano le rimanenti per crescere di peso. Inoltre si prestano all'**industrializzazione** meglio dei loro concorrenti terrestri: si possono **allevare in massa** e rispondono bene alla **selezione**. Ecco, nel disegno a destra, le maggiori specie allevate in acquacoltura.

01 Ostrica Gigante
Crassostrea Gigas

02 Carpa Argentata
Hypophthalmichthys Molitrix

Pesce spada
(Xiphias gladius)

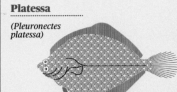

Platessa
(Pleuronectes platessa)

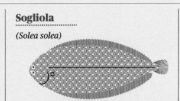

Sogliola
(Solea solea)

Razza bavosa
(Dipturus batis)

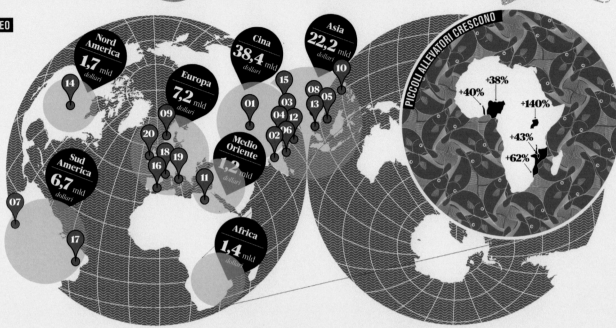

GIRO DEL MONDO SUBACQUEO IN VENTI PRODUTTORI

La mappa dell'acquacoltura mondiale. Sotto: la top 20 dei Paesi produttori. A destra, le aree di allevamento. Il mercato è dominato dall'**Asia**, con la locomotiva cinese in primo piano. Il continente orientale produce da solo l'89% del pesce del mondo (corrispondente al 77% del fatturato complessivo del settore). Sono invece in **Africa** i Paesi con i maggiori tassi di crescita. Record all'**Uganda**: dal 2004 al 2006 ha registrato un aumento della produzione del 140%. L'acquacoltura, secondo gli esperti, ha ancora **ampi margini di crescita** visto che al momento viene praticata solo vicino alla costa. L'**allevamento in acque aperte** ha tuttavia bisogno di tecnologie adeguate.

Map labels: Nord America 1,7 mld dollari · Europa 7,2 mld dollari · Cina 38,4 mld dollari · Asia 22,2 mld dollari · Medio Oriente 1,2 mld dollari · Sud America 6,7 mld dollari · Africa 1,4 mld dollari

PICCOLI ALLEVATORI CRESCONO — +38% · +40% · +140% · +43% · +62%

	Paese	tonnellate (KG)	dollari
01	Cina	34,4 mln	38 mld
02	India	3,1 mln	3,4 mld
03	Vietnam	1,6 mln	3,3 mld
04	Thailandia	1,3 mln	2,2 mld
05	Indonesia	1,3 mln	2,2 mld
06	Bangladesh	0,8 mln	1,3 mld
07	Cile	0,8 mln	4,4 mld
08	Giappone	0,7 mln	3,0 mld
09	Norvegia	0,7 mln	2,7 mld
10	Filippine	0,6 mln	0,9 mld
11	Egitto	0,6 mln	0,9 mld
12	Myanmar	0,5 mln	1,8 mld
13	Corea del Sud	0,5 mln	1,4 mld
14	Stati Uniti	0,4 mln	0,9 mld
15	Taiwan	0,3 mln	0,9 mld
16	Spagna	0,3 mln	0,4 mld
17	Brasile	0,3 mln	0,5 mld
18	Francia	0,2 mln	0,6 mld
19	Italia	0,1 mln	0,6 mld
20	Gran Bretagna	0,1 mln	0,7 mld

PAESE CHE VAI PESCE CHE TROVI

- 2-5 kg/anno
- 5-10 kg/anno
- 10-20 kg/anno
- 20-30 kg/anno
- 30-60 kg/anno
- >60 kg/anno

Non tutti mangiano pesce allo stesso modo. Vari i motivi, oltre a quelli di cultura e tradizione culinaria: disponibilità, prezzo, stagionalità. I Paesi con il **consumo di pesce pro capite** annuo più alto nel mondo (più di 60 kg) sono Groenlandia e Giappone.

SEMPRE PIÙ PESCE D'ALLEVAMENTO SULLE TAVOLE GLOBALI E IN CINA IL PESCATO NON SI MANGIA QUASI PIÙ

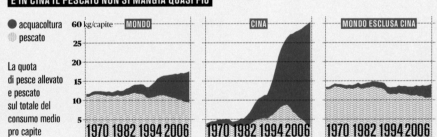

- ● acquacoltura
- ◐ pescato

La quota di pesce allevato e pescato sul totale del consumo medio pro capite

60 kg/capite

MONDO — 1970 1982 1994 2006
CINA — 1970 1982 1994 2006
MONDO ESCLUSA CINA — 1970 1982 1994 2006

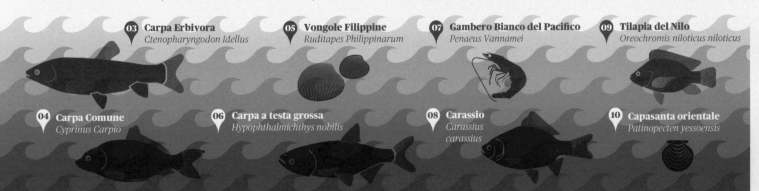

- 03 **Carpa Erbivora** *Ctenopharyngodon Idellus*
- 05 **Vongole Filippine** *Ruditapes Philippinarum*
- 07 **Gambero Bianco del Pacifico** *Penaeus Vannamei*
- 09 **Tilapia del Nilo** *Oreochromis niloticus niloticus*
- 04 **Carpa Comune** *Cyprinus Carpio*
- 06 **Carpa a testa grossa** *Hypophthalmichthys nobilis*
- 08 **Carassio** *Carassius carassius*
- 10 **Capasanta orientale** *Patinopecten yessoensis*

FONTE PRINCIPALE – *The State of World Fisheries and Aquaculture 2008* (FAO Fisheries and Aquaculture Department)

PREVIOUS PAGE
LA FATTORIA DEI PESCI
Francesco Franchi

/›PP.90,207/ What a catch: Francesco Franchi's "fish factory" explores the state of the world's oceans from a human-centric point of view. In light of intense overfishing, the diagram analyses fisheries and aquacultures according to region, utilisation and species. /Illustrator: Laura Cattaneo/

50 YEARS OF EXPLORATION
5W Infographics

"One small step for a man, one giant leap for mankind"? 50 YEARS OF EXPLORATION charts the history of humanity as a spacefaring species and also includes failed missions. /5W Infographics, Samuel Velasco, Sean McNaughton/

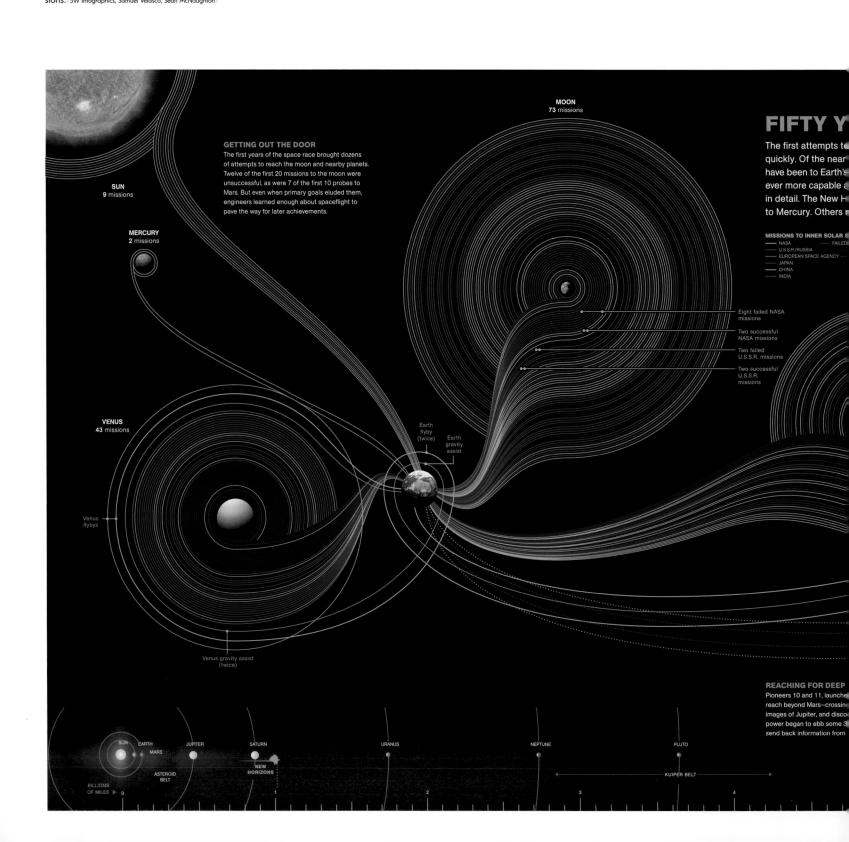

MOON
73 missions

GETTING OUT THE DOOR
The first years of the space race brought dozens of attempts to reach the moon and nearby planets. Twelve of the first 20 missions to the moon were unsuccessful, as were 7 of the first 10 probes to Mars. But even when primary goals eluded them, engineers learned enough about spaceflight to pave the way for later achievements.

SUN
9 missions

MERCURY
2 missions

VENUS
43 missions

Venus flybys

Earth flyby (twice)

Earth gravity assist

Venus gravity assist (twice)

Eight failed NASA missions

Two successful NASA missions

Two failed U.S.S.R. missions

Two successful U.S.S.R. missions

FIFTY Y

The first attempts t
quickly. Of the near
have been to Earth's
ever more capable a
in detail. The New H
to Mercury. Others

MISSIONS TO INNER SOLAR S
— NASA   — FAILED
— U.S.S.R./RUSSIA
— EUROPEAN SPACE AGENCY
— JAPAN
— CHINA
— INDIA

REACHING FOR DEEP
Pioneers 10 and 11, launche
reach beyond Mars—crossin
images of Jupiter, and disco
power began to ebb some 3
send back information from

SUN   EARTH   JUPITER   SATURN   URANUS   NEPTUNE   PLUTO
        MARS
                ASTEROID   NEW
                BELT   HORIZONS   KUIPER BELT
BILLIONS
OF MILES ▶ 0   1   2   3   4

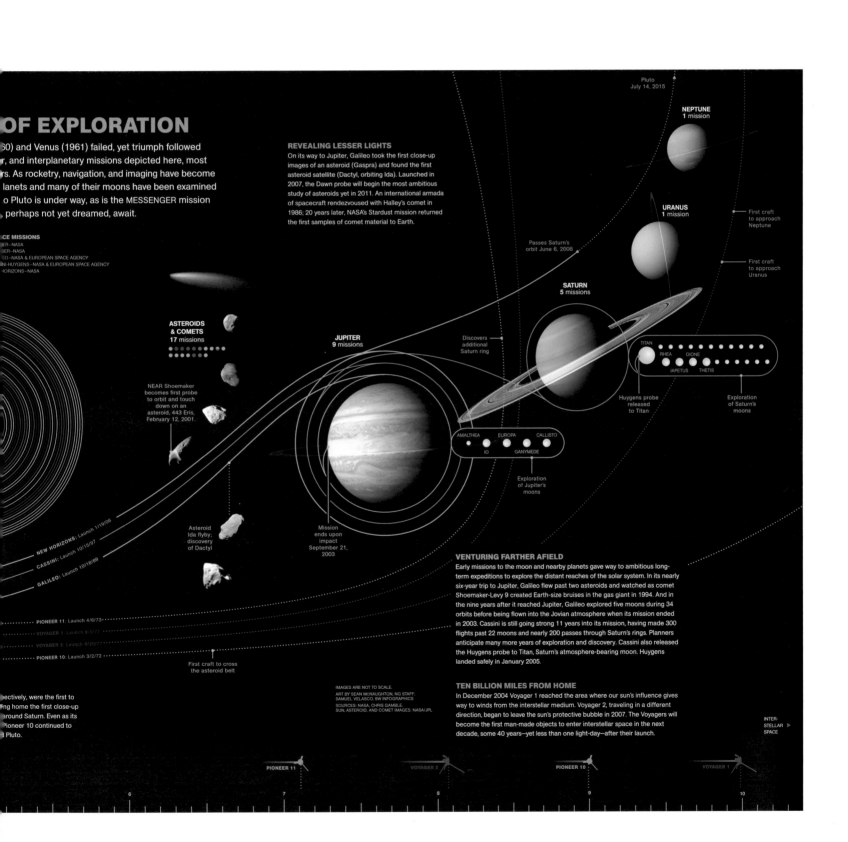

OF EXPLORATION

0) and Venus (1961) failed, yet triumph followed
, and interplanetary missions depicted here, most
s. As rocketry, navigation, and imaging have become
lanets and many of their moons have been examined
o Pluto is under way, as is the MESSENGER mission
perhaps not yet dreamed, await.

CE MISSIONS
ER–NASA
ER–NASA
EO–NASA & EUROPEAN SPACE AGENCY
NI-HUYGENS–NASA & EUROPEAN SPACE AGENCY
HORIZONS–NASA

REVEALING LESSER LIGHTS
On its way to Jupiter, Galileo took the first close-up
images of an asteroid (Gaspra) and found the first
asteroid satellite (Dactyl, orbiting Ida). Launched in
2007, the Dawn probe will begin the most ambitious
study of asteroids yet in 2011. An international armada
of spacecraft rendezvoused with Halley's comet in
1986; 20 years later, NASA's Stardust mission returned
the first samples of comet material to Earth.

Pluto
July 14, 2015

NEPTUNE
1 mission

URANUS
1 mission

First craft
to approach
Neptune

First craft
to approach
Uranus

Passes Saturn's
orbit June 6, 2008

SATURN
5 missions

Discovers
additional
Saturn ring

TITAN
RHEA   DIONE
IAPETUS   THETIS

**ASTEROIDS
& COMETS**
17 missions

JUPITER
9 missions

NEAR Shoemaker
becomes first probe
to orbit and touch
down on an
asteroid, 443 Eris,
February 12, 2001.

Huygens probe
released
to Titan

Exploration
of Saturn's
moons

AMALTHEA   EUROPA   CALLISTO
IO   GANYMEDE

Exploration
of Jupiter's
moons

Asteroid
Ida flyby;
discovery
of Dactyl

Mission
ends upon
impact
September 21,
2003

NEW HORIZONS: Launch 1/19/06
CASSINI: Launch 10/15/97
GALILEO: Launch 10/18/89

VENTURING FARTHER AFIELD
Early missions to the moon and nearby planets gave way to ambitious long-
term expeditions to explore the distant reaches of the solar system. In its nearly
six-year trip to Jupiter, Galileo flew past two asteroids and watched as comet
Shoemaker-Levy 9 created Earth-size bruises in the gas giant in 1994. And in
the nine years after it reached Jupiter, Galileo explored five moons during 34
orbits before being flown into the Jovian atmosphere when its mission ended
in 2003. Cassini is still going strong 11 years into its mission, having made 300
flights past 22 moons and nearly 200 passes through Saturn's rings. Planners
anticipate many more years of exploration and discovery. Cassini also released
the Huygens probe to Titan, Saturn's atmosphere-bearing moon. Huygens
landed safely in January 2005.

PIONEER 11: Launch 4/6/73
VOYAGER 1: Launch 9/5/77
VOYAGER 2: Launch 8/20/77
PIONEER 10: Launch 3/2/72

First craft to cross
the asteroid belt

IMAGES ARE NOT TO SCALE.
ART BY SEAN McNAUGHTON, NG STAFF;
SAMUEL VELASCO, 5W INFOGRAPHICS
SOURCES: NASA, CHRIS GAMBLE.
SUN, ASTEROID, AND COMET IMAGES: NASA/JPL

TEN BILLION MILES FROM HOME
In December 2004 Voyager 1 reached the area where our sun's influence gives
way to winds from the interstellar medium. Voyager 2, traveling in a different
direction, began to leave the sun's protective bubble in 2007. The Voyagers will
become the first man-made objects to enter interstellar space in the next
decade, some 40 years—yet less than one light-day—after their launch.

ectively, were the first to
ng home the first close-up
around Saturn. Even as its
ioneer 10 continued to
Pluto.

INTER-
STELLAR ▷
SPACE

PIONEER 11   VOYAGER 2   PIONEER 10   VOYAGER 1

6   7   8   9   10

boiling ocean

The diagrame illustrates the whole termohaline process. It compare three different period of the time to unterstand the past dynamics in the climatic system and to imagine the future.
The diagram shows all the elements that intervene in the system e the relation between them: winds, rains, ice dissolution, dams, greenhouse effect and tidal current. The diagram shows that it is not possible to assign to only an actor the cause of the climatic change, but every element with is proprierty, could influence the whole system.
The flows change colour in base of temperature and change dimension depending on airor water capacity.
Even if the diagram is abstract, it is built on the geographic place because of their relevance and characteristics.
Lucia Pugliapochi

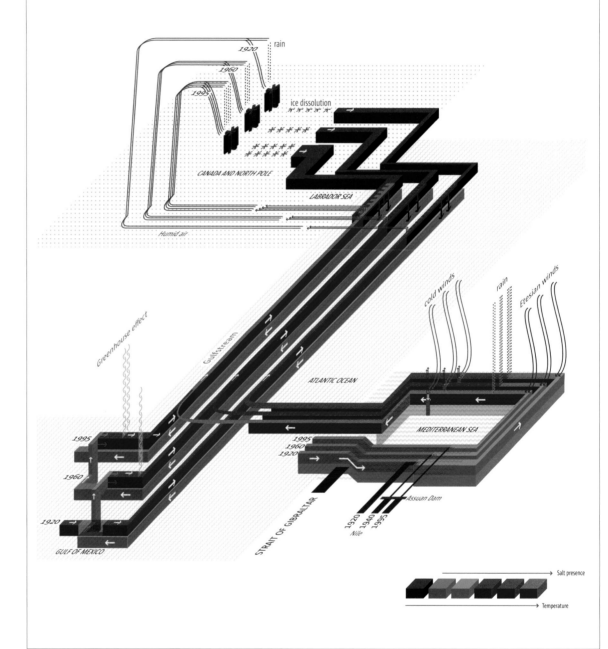

Human blood circulation

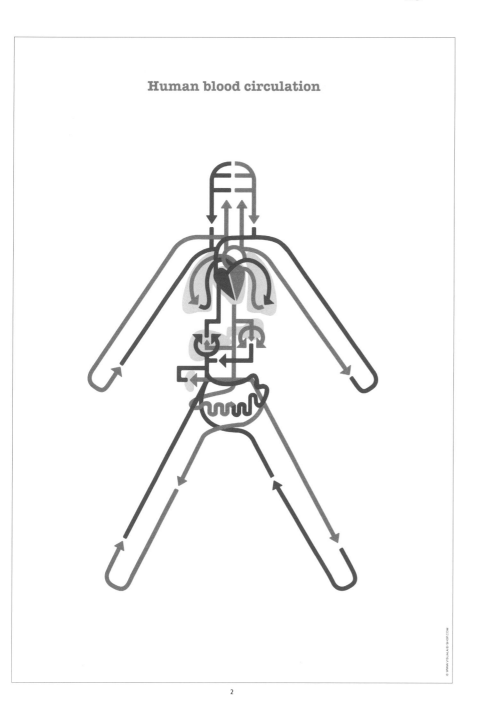

How To Please Elise

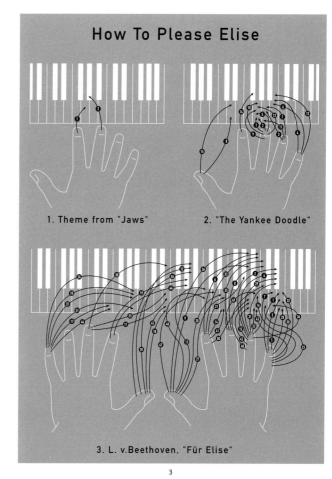

1. Theme from "Jaws" 2. "The Yankee Doodle"

3. L. v.Beethoven, "Für Elise"

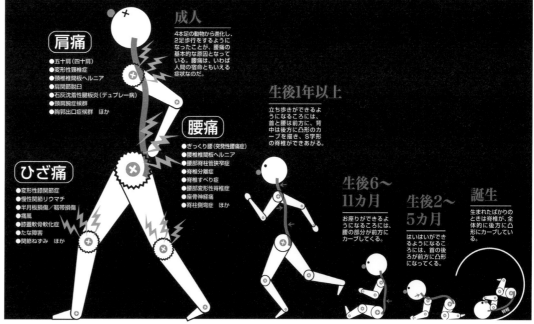

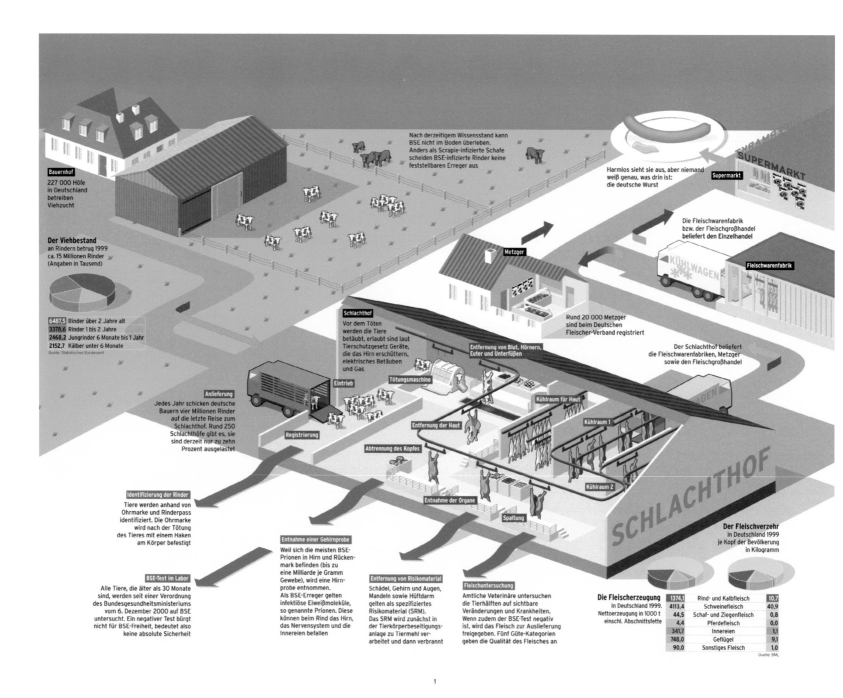

Bauernhof
227 000 Höfe
in Deutschland
betreiben
Viehzucht

Der Viehbestand
an Rindern betrug 1999
ca. 15 Millionen Rinder
(Angaben in Tausend)

6487,5 Rinder über 2 Jahre alt
3378,6 Rinder 1 bis 2 Jahre
2468,2 Jungrinder 6 Monate bis 1 Jahr
2152,7 Kälber unter 6 Monate
Quelle: Statistisches Bundesamt

Nach derzeitigem Wissensstand kann
BSE nicht im Boden überleben.
Anders als Scrapie-infizierte Schafe
scheiden BSE-infizierte Rinder keine
feststellbaren Erreger aus

Harmlos sieht sie aus, aber niemand
weiß genau, was drin ist:
die deutsche Wurst

Supermarkt

Die Fleischwarenfabrik
bzw. der Fleischgroßhandel
beliefert den Einzelhandel

Metzger

KÜHLWAGEN

Fleischwarenfabrik

Rund 20 000 Metzger
sind beim Deutschen
Fleischer-Verband registriert

Der Schlachthof beliefert
die Fleischwarenfabriken, Metzger
sowie den Fleischgroßhandel

Schlachthof
Vor dem Töten
werden die Tiere
betäubt, erlaubt sind laut
Tierschutzgesetz Geräte,
die das Hirn erschüttern,
elektrisches Betäuben
und Gas

Tötungsmaschine

Eintrieb

**Entfernung von Blut, Hörnern,
Euter und Unterfüßen**

Kühlraum für Haut

Entfernung der Haut

Kühlraum 1

Abtrennung des Kopfes

Kühlraum 2

Anlieferung
Jedes Jahr schicken deutsche
Bauern vier Millionen Rinder
auf die letzte Reise zum
Schlachthof. Rund 250
Schlachthöfe gibt es, sie
sind derzeit nur zu zehn
Prozent ausgelastet

Registrierung

Entnahme der Organe

Spaltung

SCHLACHTHOF

Identifizierung der Rinder
Tiere werden anhand von
Ohrmarke und Rinderpass
identifiziert. Die Ohrmarke
wird nach der Tötung
des Tieres mit einem Haken
am Körper befestigt

Entnahme einer Gehirnprobe
Weil sich die meisten BSE-
Prionen in Hirn und Rücken-
mark befinden (bis zu
eine Milliarde je Gramm
Gewebe), wird eine Hirn-
probe entnommen.
Als BSE-Erreger gelten
infektiöse Eiweißmoleküle,
so genannte Prionen. Diese
können beim Rind das Hirn,
das Nervensystem und die
Innereien befallen

Entfernung von Risikomaterial
Schädel, Gehirn und Augen,
Mandeln sowie Hüftdarm
gelten als spezifiziertes
Risikomaterial (SRM).
Das SRM wird zunächst in
der Tierkörperbeseitigungs-
anlage zu Tiermehl ver-
arbeitet und dann verbrannt

Fleischuntersuchung
Amtliche Veterinäre untersuchen
die Tierhälften auf sichtbare
Veränderungen und Krankheiten.
Wenn zudem der BSE-Test negativ
ist, wird das Fleisch zur Auslieferung
freigegeben. Fünf Güte-Kategorien
geben die Qualität des Fleisches an

BSE-Test im Labor
Alle Tiere, die älter als 30 Monate
sind, werden seit einer Verordnung
des Bundesgesundheitsministeriums
vom 6. Dezember 2000 auf BSE
untersucht. Ein negativer Test bürgt
nicht für BSE-Freiheit, bedeutet also
keine absolute Sicherheit

Der Fleischverzehr
in Deutschland 1999
je Kopf der Bevölkerung
in Kilogramm

Die Fleischerzeugung		
in Deutschland 1999.	1374,1 Rind- und Kalbfleisch	10,7
Nettoerzeugung in 1000 t	4113,4 Schweinefleisch	40,9
einschl. Abschnittsfette	44,5 Schaf- und Ziegenfleisch	0,8
	4,4 Pferdefleisch	0,0
	341,7 Innereien	1,1
	748,0 Geflügel	9,1
	90,0 Sonstiges Fleisch	1,0
		Quelle: BML

1

2

3

4

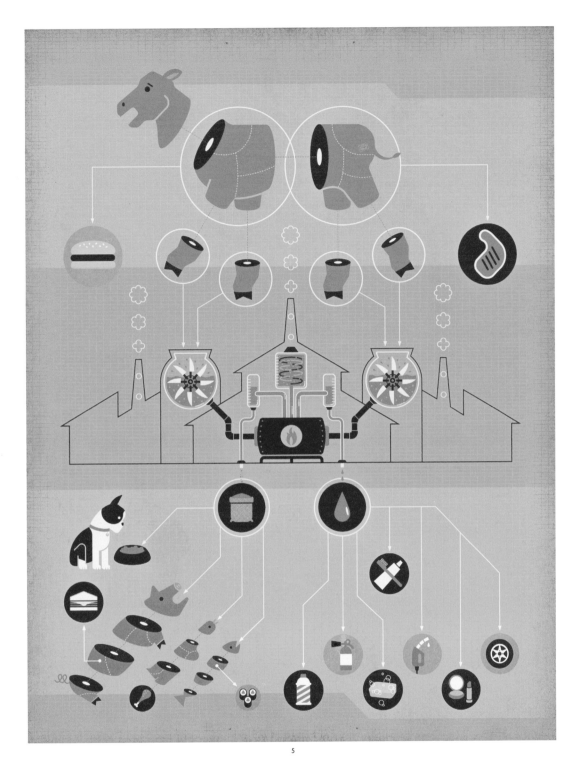

5

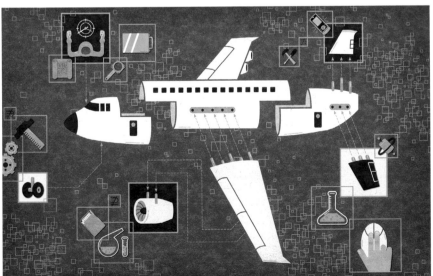

6

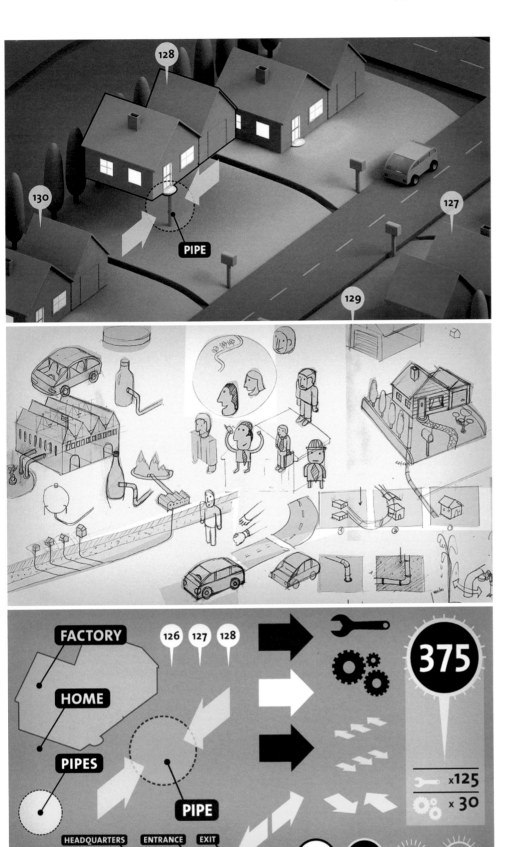

2

1
MODERN INDUSTRY
Adam Hancher
MODERN INDUSTRY highlights the importance of effective communication through the analogy of a circuit diagram. In industry and electronics, once a single connection breaks, the entire circuit — or productivity chain — will fail.

2
SPRINT/NEXTEL
Rafaël Macho
The things that connect us: SPRINT/NEXTEL explains how telecommunications networks send mobile communications through the airwaves or pipe data to our homes. Superfad: Kevin Batten, Justin Leibow

ANDREW VANDE MOERE

was born in Belgium, trained in Switzerland and now lectures at the University of Sydney in Australia. He maintains the popular blog *infosthetics.com*. As this beautiful neologism suggests, Vande Moere's main interest lies in the exploration of "information aesthetics," a domain only few are researching as thoroughly as he is.

●

MANUEL LIMA

works as a senior user experience designer at Nokia's NextGen Software & Services in London. Like Vande Moere, he is also diligently observing and documenting the field of information visualization on his website *visualcomplexity.com*. Again, "nomen est omen": the visualization of complex networks is a topic Lima frequently talks about at conferences around the world.

●

How do you explain the popularity that information visualization has gained recently? /AVM/ I think there are many different reasons for the increase in popularity which seem somehow to have resonated in a synchronous way in the last years. In particular, I believe that because designers have become engaged in the topic, the field of data visualization has become both more approachable for developers as well as for end-users, convincing others of its true potential.   With this movement, the field has become less reserved for experts, and has been opened up as a medium in its own right. This seems trivial but it is quite a revolution to change the claim that data visualization is solely for finding valuable patterns in highly specialized, colossal, complex, multi-dimensional datasets, towards a more medium-oriented function of democratizing the access and exploration of socially relevant data for a large but lay audience. /ML/ In my view there are a couple of key reasons for the current outburst of information visualization. First, computing storage: in the face of contemporary technological accomplishments, our ability to generate and acquire data has by far outpaced our ability to make sense of that data. Meaningful information is not a given fact, and particularly now, when our cultural artifacts are being measured in terabytes and petabytes, organizing, sorting and displaying information in an efficient way is a crucial measure for intelligence, knowledge, and ultimately wisdom.   Secondly, data has never been so widely accessible at such a minimal cost. We see more and more companies, governments, and institutions opening up their datasets to the general public, allowing

for a growing number of people to depict them in whatever way they feel appropriate. Social networks, with their complex structures and abundance of shared content, are another driver for information visualization. As is mainstream media: the *New York Times*, *WIRED*, *CNN*, just to name a few, have embraced an assortment of new methods for displaying information, contributing to a conscientious awareness for the extended reach of the discipline, far beyond the familiar pie charts. Another important factor is the democratization of visualization tools. Ten years ago the retrieval, analysis and visualization of large complex datasets were only at the reach of a few. Now we observe a profusion of open-source initiatives that are contributing to a wider accessibility of the field, bringing people from many other areas without requiring a deep knowledge of programming. All this, combined with our unprecedented greed for factual data, and an immense appetite for the universally quantifiable entity, has led to the massive increase of popularity of information visualization. /AVM/ I'd like to add a few more reasons: We have seen much more cross-disciplinary education in the last years – designers learning computing skills and IT students using design-oriented approaches. The immediateness of visualizations is also an important stimulus. Developing a visualization nowadays has a direct result that is potentially understandable for a large audience. Also, the many visualization challenges that are still open and require urgent attention – such as visual search, visual shopping, smart energy metering displays and so on – are stirring interest in the field.

> OUR ABILITY TO GENERATE AND ACQUIRE DATA HAS BY FAR OUTPACED OUR ABILITY TO MAKE SENSE OF THAT DATA.
> Manuel Lima

Manuel, on your blog you published the *Information Visualization Manifesto*, consisting of 10 aspects to consider when approaching a visualization project. What prompted you to write this manifesto? /ML/ There were several motivations behind the manifesto, but the two main ones relate to the broad overuse of the term "visualization" and the lack of a theoretical framework able to accommodate the field's recent growth. Even though some might argue this is a time for flourishing unguided innovation, some direction can still be pursued. This manifesto can be seen as a simple step in that path.

You are proposing to differentiate between "information visualization" and "information art." /ML/ Information visualization and information art already exist as separate fields of practice. Having proposed a set of 10 considerations on the context of information visualization, I simply considered the use of a different term for those projects that didn't pursue any of them, hence the suggestion of "information art."

But aren't some of the most interesting visualizations we've seen lately somewhere in the middle between those two categories? /ML/ It depends on your definition of "interesting" and "visualization". If by interesting you imply emotional appeal, astounding beauty, or an inclination for popularity, these are all qualities that can be embraced by information visualization, but they are not the only ones. The field's central aspiration resides on explanation and unveiling, which in turn leads to discovery and insight. /AVM/ There is no question that there is a need to differentiate between different ways of representing abstract data, to set the expectations with users, but also to determine more usable criteria of good and bad visualization. However, I feel the distinction between "information visualization" and "information art" is too much along the already much-debated lines of utility versus art. Instead, I believe the real innovation is happening in the combination of the two, which I have named "information aesthetics." Ultimately, such information-aesthetic applications use aesthetic engagement to increase the information flow, and thus make the visualization – when seen as a tool – more useful, more memorable, more engaging, or more educational. In fact, I think it is exactly those visualizations that accomplish this equilibrium, that are currently receiving the media attention mentioned in your first question.

"Information overload" is an expression we often hear these days. Is there such a thing as "too much information"? /ML/ Although the same worry has recurrently emerged in different stages of civilization, there is unquestionably something unique to our day and age. Some might say that information overload is foremost a problem of design. But how will design cope with the prospect of an ordinary laptop storing every book ever written or every song ever produced? While new methods will need to be devised, and old paradigms shifted, information visualization will still be one of the best-equipped disciplines to answer the call. /AVM/ The notion of "too much" or "too little" is too relative to the actual context to make a useful observation about. What we find useless today might be of invaluable significance tomorrow for someone else. It is one of the characteristics of intelligence to store gathered knowledge for later generations, which by itself is based on data in some way.

Is information visualization just another drug that feeds our information addiction, or the cure to cope with it? /AVM/ It can be both. It can solve our data hunger by allowing us to discover exactly what we were seeking or wondering about. But at the same time, and actually mostly while using the visualization itself, it can provoke completely new questions we were not aware of before. /ML/ I like to think of it as an addictive cure to data glut, which might explain why so many people have become enamored with this realm.

Where do we need more information, especially in the form of visualization? /AVM/ We have an urgent need to use visualization for socially relevant purposes, ranging from making people aware of world problems to helping people to eat healthier: putting information in people's hands when and where it counts, with the purpose of helping. For instance, it has been scientifically proven that providing people with a simple, direct visualization tool like a pedometer helps them become more aware of their activity, and ultimately motivates people to be more physically active than any other traditional method. Similarly, one can only imagine when real-time, smart energy displays would go beyond simply displaying numbers, and become more compelling and insightful about revealing our sustainable usage patterns. /ML/ I also believe that information visualization can be an instrumental part of changing people's behavior. It can ultimately advance our ability to persuade government officials and lawmakers, while also contributing to a responsive public awareness for sustainability. Our tools are not only a source of discovery and insight, but also conscientious actions.

> WE HAVE AN URGENT NEED TO USE VISUALIZATION FOR SOCIALLY RELEVANT PURPOSES.
> Andrew Vande Moere

PROZESS   ← MAL VOM TROPFEN DES WASSERS   ⬤ GESCHWINDIGKEIT (SEK.)

KONZEPTEN

Visuelle Programme / Visual Codes
Gruppenseminar Martin Grothmaak
Student: Liu, Xuejing / Zwanzig Minuten Zeit
Sommersemester 2008 Studienbereich Kommunikationsdesign
Staatliche Hochschule für Gestaltung Karlsruhe
www.visuelle-programme.de

WERKZEUGE UND MATERIALIEN

— 001
⬤ 00:04:50.91

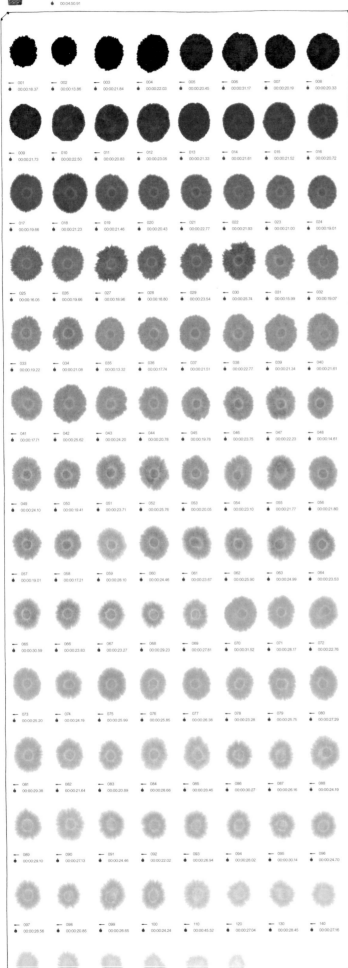

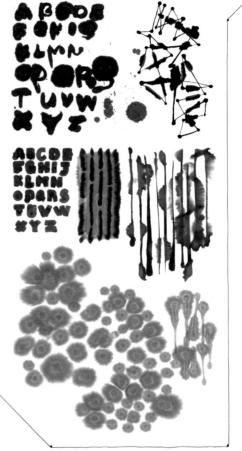

TUSCHE   CHINESISCHE PINSEL

MESSGLAS   GLÄSER

PIPETTEN

STOPPUHR   REISPAPIER (20 METER)

TUSCHTROPFEN

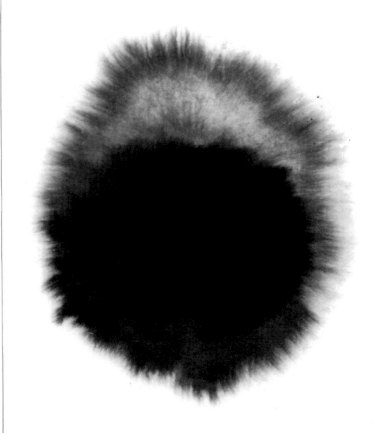

1

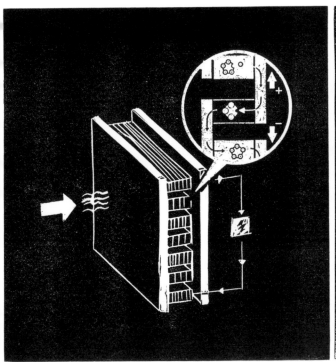

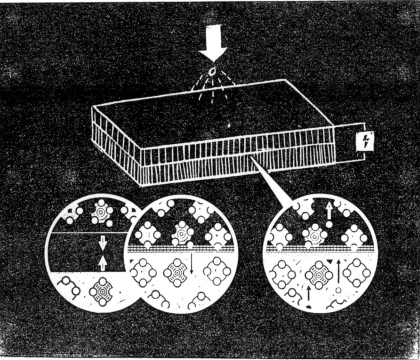

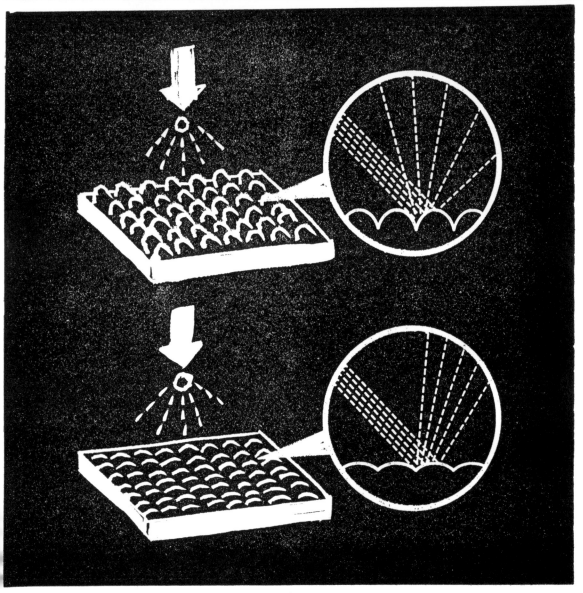

2

1
VISUELLE PROGRAMME 2.0
projekttriangle
Liu Xuejing
Hochschule für Gestaltung Karlsruhe
Martin Grothmaak's seminars at HfG
Karlsruhe pursue the creation of programmes
and rules for the generation of new visual
means of expression. Student projects include taxonomy of text messaging in the
guise of fern fronds or the dilution and dispersal of calligraphy ink over time. / Lecturer:
Martin Grothmaak / Course Title: Visuelle Programme 2.0 / Visual Codes 2.0 / www.visuelle-programme.de

2
**SMART SURFACES AND THEIR APPLICATION
IN ARCHITECTURE AND DESIGN**
onlab
Self-cleaning windows, light-emitting wallpaper, curtains that generate electricity: the
latest developments in material engineering
suggest a wealth of new applications for
smart surfaces in architecture and design.
Yet what goes on below the surface of those
complex new technologies? While the scientific explanations might go over our collective heads, Onlab's linocut schematics take
the black box magic out of the equation
and peel back the layers to reveal the components, processes and production methods
at work underneath.   In their strict simplification — due to the linocuts' inevitable
crudeness — the images focus on the core
principles and demystify the patented fine
print for a clear, no-nonsense explanation
of the materials' future potential for designers and architects alike. / Art direction: onlab, Nicolas
Bourquin, Thibaud Tissot / Illustrations and linocuts: onlab, Nicolas Bourquin, Marte Meling Enoksen, Maike Hamacher, Matthias Hübner / Project coordination: onlab, Judith Wimmer /

NEXT PAGE (LEFT)
I HATE MOSQUITOES
Christoph Niemann
/ › PP. 85, 107 / A quick flowchart on those pesky
creatures.

NEXT PAGE (RIGHT)
**CRYONICS POCKET GUIDE: SIGN UP,
CRYOPRESERVATION AND VITRIFICATION**
Tutu
Canned human, anyone? Tutu's handy CRY-
ONICS POCKET GUIDE investigates the idea
of cryonics and its place in modern science,
culture and society.

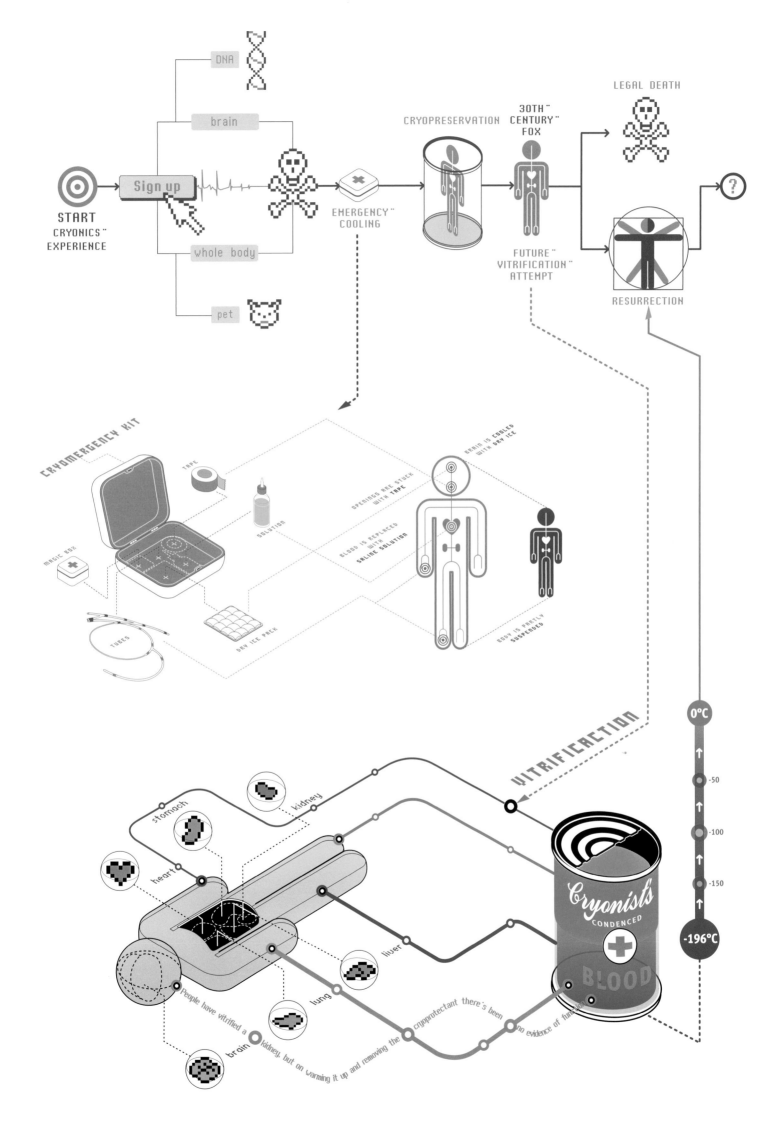

START
CRYONICS™
EXPERIENCE

Sign up

DNA

brain

whole body

pet

EMERGENCY™
COOLING

CRYOPRESERVATION

30TH™
CENTURY™
FOX

LEGAL DEATH

FUTURE™
VITRIFICATION™
ATTEMPT

RESURRECTION

?

CRYOMERGENCY KIT

TAPE

SOLUTION

MAGIC BOX

TUBES

DRY ICE PACK

BRAIN IS COOLED
WITH DRY ICE

OPENINGS ARE STUCK
WITH TAPE

BLOOD IS REPLACED
WITH SALINE SOLUTION

BODY IS PARTLY
SUSPENDED

VITRIFICATION

stomach

kidney

heart

liver

lung

brain

kidney

People have vitrified a kidney, but on warming it up and removing the cryoprotectant there's been no evidence of function

Cryonist's
CONDENCED

BLOOD

0°C

-50

-100

-150

-196°C

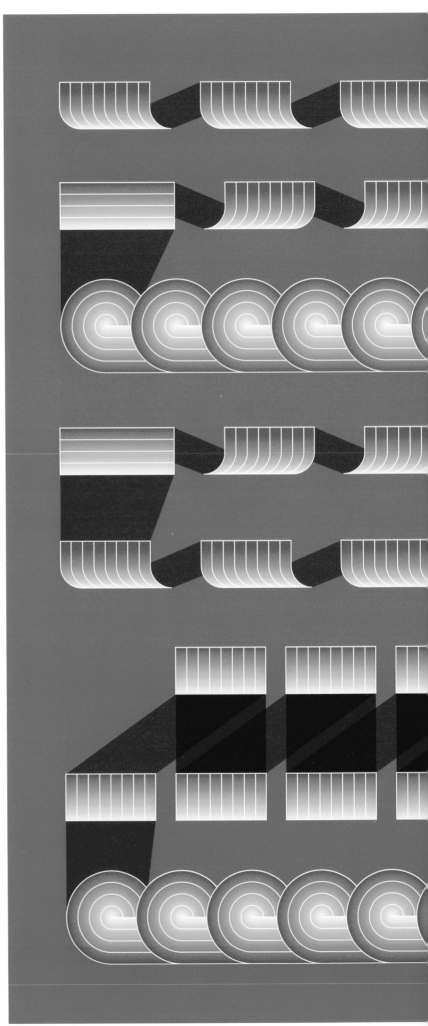

1

2

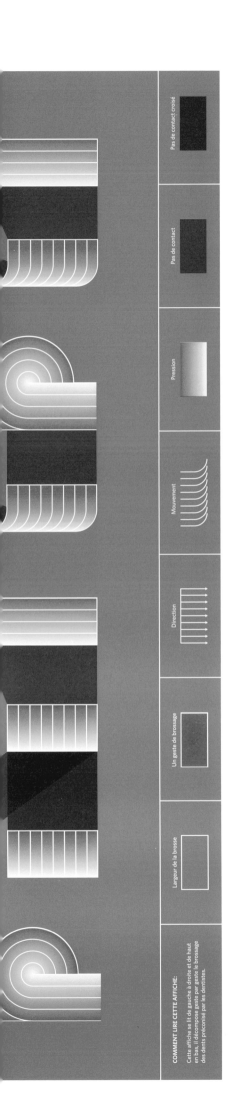

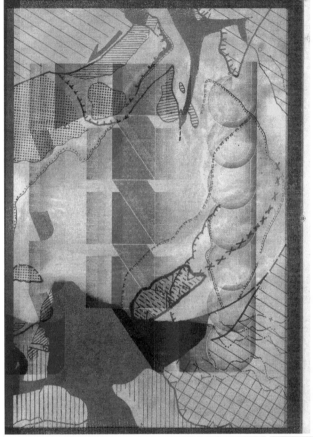

1
THE SEED
Johnny Kelly

From tiny pip to flowering tree and juicy fruit, THE SEED follows the trials and tribulations of a humble apple seed on its two-minute animated voyage through the human food chain and nature's life cycle. Commissioned by Adobe, the short film blends stop-motion papercraft with illustrated 2D animation and a healthy dose of software wizardry. /Story and direction: Johnny Kelly / Production manager: Jo Bierton / 2D animation: Michael Zauner / 3D animation: Eoin Coughlan / Paper modeler: Elin Svensson / Assisted by: Anna Benner / Stop frame DOP: Micolaj Jarosewicz / Stop frame animation: Matthew Cooper / Compositing: Alasdair Brotherston / Music: Jape Sound / Supervisor: Mike Wyeld Foley / Artist: Sue Harding / Executive producers: Charlotte Bavasso, Chris O'Reilly / Producer: Christine Ponzevera / Agency: Goodby, Silverstein & Partners / Creative director: Keith Anderson Associate / Creative Director: Tony Stern / Associate Creative Director: Frank Aldorf / Art director: Johan Arlig / Copywriter: Steve Payonzeck / Art director: Karishma Mehta / Copywriter: Gregory Lane / Interactive Producer: Stella Wong / Art Buyer: Jenny Taich /

2
BRUSHING TEETH POSTER
3
HOW TO USE IT ?
Benjamin Dennel

A colourful manual on the use of a toothbrush, Benjamin Dennel's "How to" blueprint investigates both the human learning process and the representation of movement in space. His methodology of brushing transforms the ups and downs of a dentist's recommendation into a linear timeline of the proposed motions. Beautifully executed — in the colour of healthy gums and teeth — Dennel's newly minted visual nomenclature translates the various swoops and swishes into a new, universal language and to a number of different media.

1
ABITARE / RESEARCH
Salottobuono

Italian architects Salottobuono are experts at taking things apart — and breaking them down into their basic parts and principles. Their unwavering diagrammatical analysis exposes weak points, critical nodes and discontinuities in products and structures.

As co-editors of the research segment of Italian architecture and design review ABITARE, they now take a peek behind the scenes and below the hood of innovative projects and techniques developed in their native country. Stripped down all the way, layer by layer, these true-to-scale, no-nonsense depictions throw new light onto the latest creations and reveal the structure and machinations beneath.

2
MANUAL OF DECOLONIZATION
Salottobuono

Salottobuono designed several "strategies of subversion" for Israeli residential settlements in the West Bank and included them in their MANUAL OF DECOLONIZATION: a generic toolbox for post-occupation scenarios. The manual investigates to what extent evacuated structures could be adapted to new usage scenarios and provides a detailed architectural representation of possible solutions. Rather than a single unified proposal of urban planning, the project suggests thorough transformations on an architectural scale. Although there are hundreds of thousands of Israeli built structures in the West Bank, the number of typologies are limited to variations on single-family settlement dwellings and concrete prefab military barracks. The portrayed "fragments of possibility" constitute a semi-generic approach that could be modified to other evacuated areas./ Decolonizing Architecture, Barbara Modolo, Pietro Onofri, Armina Pilav, Manuel Singer, Alessandro Zorzetto /

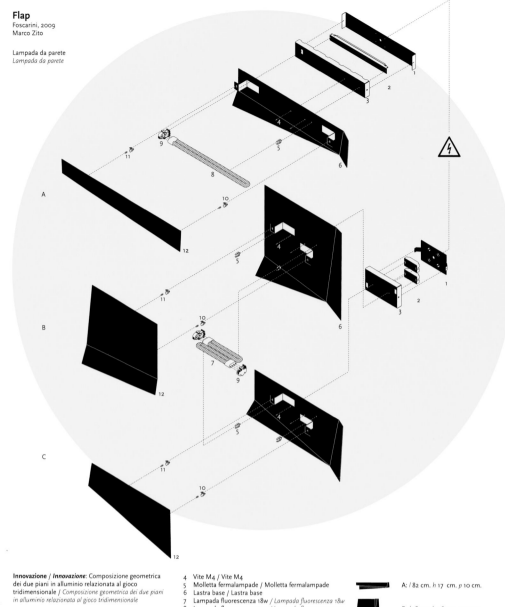

Flap
Foscarini, 2009
Marco Zito

Lampada da parete
Lampada da parete

Innovazione / *Innovazione*: Composizione geometrica dei due piani in alluminio relazionata al gioco tridimensionale / *Composizione geometrica dei due piani in alluminio relazionata al gioco tridimensionale*

Legenda / *Legenda*
1 Piastra a muro / *Piastra a muro*
2 Alimentatore elettronico / *Alimentatore elettronico*
3 Scatola per cablaggi / *Scatola per cablaggi*
4 Vite M4 / *Vite M4*
5 Molletta fermalampade / *Molletta fermalampade*
6 Lastra base / *Lastra base*
7 Lampada fluorescenza 18w / *Lampada fluorescenza 18w*
8 Lampada fluorescenza 55w / *Lampada fluorescenza 55w*
9 Portalampade 2g11 / *Portalampade 2g11*
10 Snap di fissaggio / *Snap di fissaggio*
11 Perno di fissaggio / *Perno di fissaggio*
12 Schermo / *Schermo*

A: l 82 cm. h 17 cm. p 10 cm.

B: l 58 cm. h 46 cm. p 10 cm.

C: l 66 cm. h 28 cm. p 10 cm.

Flywire & Lunarlite
Design Nikelab
Nike, 2008

Scarpa LunaRacer
LunaRacer Shoe

R **Ricerca / *Research*:** Flywire è una tecnologia rivoluzionaria in cui i filamenti ad alta resistenza lavorano come i cavi di un ponte sospeso, con rinforzi ingegnerizzati precisamente dove il piede lo richiede. Ciò permette di ridurre al minimo la quantità di materiale necessaria per la parte superiore della scarpa. Lunarlite è una schiuma leggerissima e morbida che distribuisce uniformemente le forze sulla pianta del piede, in modo da permettere agli atleti di non scaricare il peso su un unico punto / *Flywire is a revolutionary technology whose high-strength threads work like cables on a suspension bridge with support engineered precisely where a foot needs it. It reduces the amount of material required for the upper of a shoe to the bare minimum. Lunarlite is an extremely lightweight and soft foam that spreads out force more evenly over a larger area so athletes aren't pounding all their pressure in one place.*

Legenda / *Legenda*
1 Schiuma Lunarlite contenuta in Phylon / *Lunarlite foam embedded in Phylon*
2 Suola foam pillow waffle / *Foam pillow waffle outsole*
3 Flywire: Vectran® fibres / *Flywire: Vectran® fibres*

6% A 155

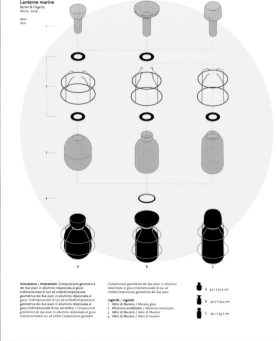

Lanterne marine
Barber & Osgerby
Venini, 2009

Vaso
Vaso

Innovazione / *Innovazione*: Composizione geometrica dei due piani in alluminio relazionata al gioco tridimensionale di luci ed ombreComposizione geometrica dei due piani in alluminio relazionata al gioco tridimensionale di luci ed ombre / *Composizione geometrica dei due piani in alluminio relazionata al gioco tridimensionale di luci ed ombreComposizione geometrica dei due piani*

Legenda / *Legenda*
1 Vetro di Murano / *Murano glass*
2 Alluminio anodizzato / *Alluminio anodizzato*
3 Vetro di Murano / *Vetro di Murano*
4 Vetro di Murano / *Vetro di murano*

A 42,1 x 57,2 cm
B 52,0 x 38,0 cm
C 59,1 x 35,7 cm

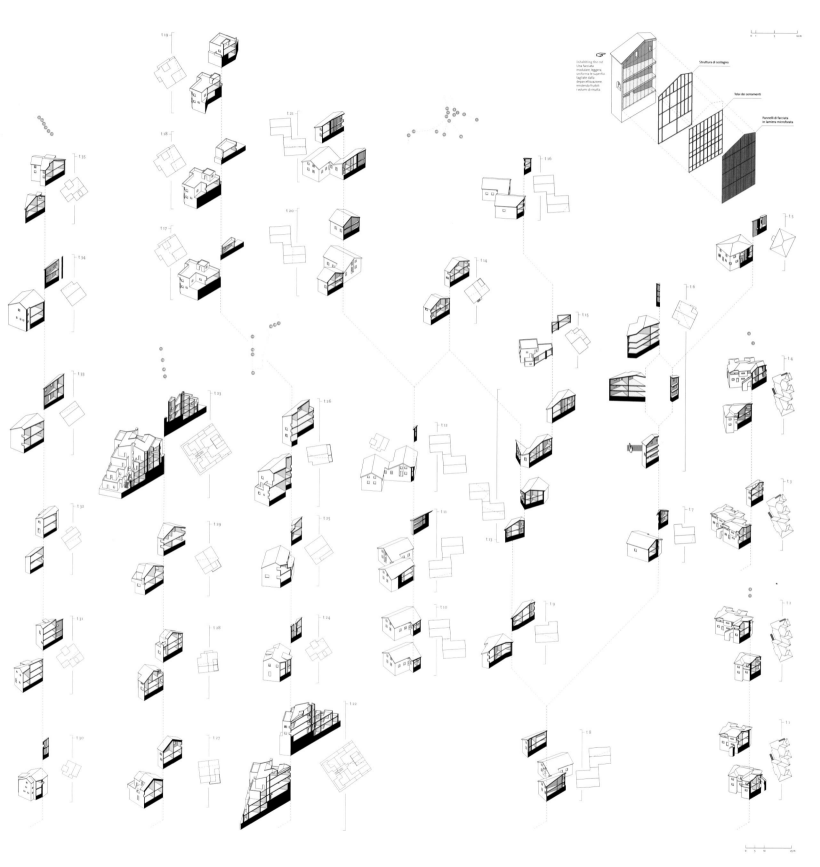

MONOPOLY GAME
LUNCH CRUNCH
WHERE DOES FOOD CRISIS COME FROM?

START

START AGAIN?

GAME OVER

20% OF WORLD'S RICHEST **20%** POOREST **PEOPLE** ACCOUNT FOR CORRESPONDINGLY

MOREOVER

0.13% OF THE WORLD'S **POPULATION** CONTROLS OVER A **QUARTER** OF ALL GLOBAL **FINANCIAL ASSETS**

SO WHAT?

HALF OF THE WORLD'S **100 BIGGEST** BODIES ARE **CORPORATIONS** DESTROYING

THIRD WORLD'S DEVELOPING ECONOMIES

MEANWHILE

TODAY OF THE WORLD'S **ONE BILLION STARVING PEOPLE** A THIRD LIVE IN **INDIA** YET LAST YEAR INDIAN GOVERNMENT HAD **100 MILLION TONS** OF SURPLUS **FOOD GRAINS** INCLUDING **RICE&WHEAT**

MOST OF THEM **WERE LEFT** IN THE GRANARIES **TO ROT** BECAUSE THE **GOVERNMENT** WAS HOPING TO **EXPORT GRAIN** TO MAKE MONEY **IT ALSO STOPPED** BUYING GRAIN FROM **LOCAL FARMERS** LEAVING THEM **DESTITUTE**

WHAT'S NEXT?

SO WE'RE BACK AT THE **VERY START OF THE GAME** AND WHO IS THE **WINNER?**

45% 5% OF WORLD **MEAT&FISH**
58% 4% OF TOTAL WORLD **ENERGY**
84% 1.1% OF ALL CONSUMED **PAPER**
87% <1% OF ALL WORLD'S **VEHICLES**
74% 2% OF WORLDWIDE **TELEPHONE LINES**
ALL THAT SUMS UP TO **86%** 1% OF TOTAL GLOBAL **CONSUMPTION**

AND THESE ARE **TOP BIOFUEL PRODUCTION** CROPS **GROWN IN POOR** COUNTRIES TO FEED **VEHICLES** NOT HUNGRY PEOPLE

AT THE SAME TIME GOVERNMENT OF INDIA WAS BUYING GRAIN FROM AMERICAN CORPORATIONS BECAUSE THEY HAVE TO DO SO IN ACCORDANCE TO CONDITIONS **OF RECEIVING AID FROM WORLD BANK**

GO ON...

THE FARMERS HAVE GONE INTO DEBT **TO PURCHASE EXPENSIVE CHEMICAL FERTILISERS** ON THE ADVICE OF THE GOVERNMENT **AND WERE FORCED TO BURN THEIR CROPS** IN THEIR OWN FIELDS

REALLY?

WHICH MEANS THAT **TODAY INDIA IS THE LARGEST IMPORTER** OF THE SAME GRAIN IT **EXPORTS**

WELL...

AND INCREASED **FOOD DEMAND** FOR COUNTRY'S **OWN NEEDS** RESULTED IN **SUSPENDED RICE EXPORTS**

HOW DOES IT AFFECT YOU?

PALM OIL RAPE SEEDS OIL CORN SUGAR CANE RICE
WHEAT SOYA BEETROOT CHOCOLATE

HOW ABOUT ALL THOSE FUELS?

AND ON TOP OF ALL **MEAT & DAIRY FARMING** PRODUCES MORE **CLIMATE CHANGING GASES** THAN ALL OF THE **WORLD'S CARS PLANES AND LORRIES**

MILK SHORTAGE

WOULD YOU NOTICE **MILK SHORTAGE** IN INDIAN REGION IF YOU'RE MILES AWAY? ACTUALLY, YES

CHEESE BUTTER MILK MILK POWDER
4 p MORE EXPENSIVE 3 p MORE EXPENSIVE 2.5 p MORE EXPENSIVE 2 p MORE EXPENSIVE

IN DEVELOPED COUNTRIES **1 IN 4 TEENS IS OBESE** COMPARED TO **1 IN 4 UNDERNOURISHED** IN DEVELOPING REGIONS

ANOTHER FOOD FOR THOUGHT

YES YOU WILL HAVE TO **PAY 1 PENNY MORE** FOR YOUR FAVOURITE **CHOCOLATE**

MILK CHOCOLATE
1 p MORE EXPENSIVE

HOW ABOUT YOUR FAVOURITE LOCAL **INDIAN CURRY DELI** GOING BANKRUPT AND **SHUTTING ITS DOORS?**

YOU DON'T FANCY RICE? WELL WHAT ABOUT **MEET AND DAIRY?** OR CHOCOLATE BAR?

IN REALITY EVERY COW BREEDED FOR MEAT **REQUIRES AN ENTIRE** OLYMPIC SWIMMING POOL OF WATER EVERY WEEK

THAT IS OVER 10 TIMES MORE THAN AN AVERAGE **INDIAN FAMILY COULD USE** OVER THE SAME PERIOD

500L
5000L
50L

DO YOU KNOW THAT **BOTTLED WATER** COSTS YOU 1,900 TIMES **MORE THAN TAP WATER?**

WHILE FOR YOUR **99 p SUPERMARKET SALAD** AFRICA PAYS **50 L** OF FRESH WATER?

£0.99 = 50L

LET'S SEE...

JUST A FEW MORE **EXAMPLES WHY IT MIGHT** CONCERN YOU **PERSONALLY** NOT ONLY OTHERS

ANYTHING ELSE?

FURTHERMORE, EVENTUALLY ALL THIS **WATER AND MEAT** ENDS UP ON THE PLATES **IN ONE OF THE MAJOR FAST FOOD CHAINS** OWNED BY THOSE 0.13% **OF THE RICHEST**

NO WAY!

ONE AVERAGE BRITISH FAMILY WEEKLY USES UP TO **10 SWIMMING POOLS** WHICH IS 180 L PER PERSON A DAY

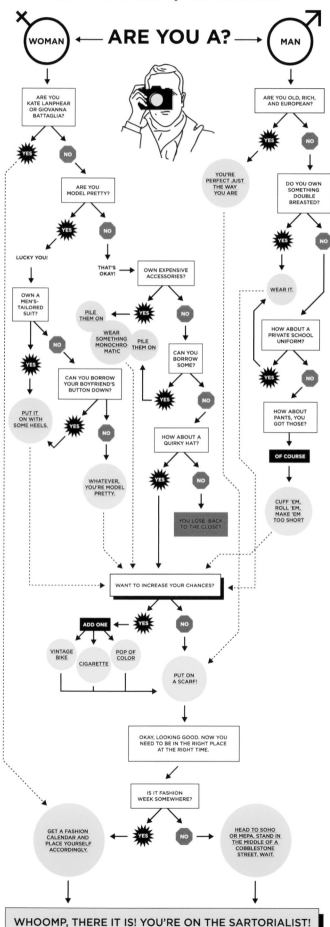

WHOOMP, THERE IT IS! YOU'RE ON THE SARTORIALIST!

2

1
LUNCH CRUNCH:
WHERE DOES THE FOOD CRISIS
COME FROM?
Tutu
An information-rich overview of the food industry, LUNCH CRUNCH explores the lesser-known facts around the global food crisis.

2
OH SNAP!
OUR STEP-BY-STEP GUIDE
TO GETTING SHOT BY THE SARTORIALIST
Joshua Covarrubias
Famous New York street fashion photographer and overall style maven Scott Schuman — aka The Sartorialist — snaps the latest trends on the public catwalk. So how do people attract his eye? Covarrubias' tongue-in-cheek flowchart takes us through the recurring themes and predictable hot buttons of this suave global trend hunter. / Written by Christene Barberich & Piera Gelardi /

3
HOW TO TRY A TERRORIST
Fogelson-Lubliner
All paths lead to prison? Find out for yourself and pick your own route in this op-ed illustration and flowchart diagram for the NEW YORK TIMES. / Art Direction: Brian Rea (The NEW YORK TIMES) /

THE NEW YORK TIMES **OP-ED** THURSDAY, NOVEMBER 1,

CRIME → INVESTIGATION
CHARGES FILED — ARREST
INITIAL APPEARANCE — PRELIMINARY HEARING
DETENTION — BAIL HEARING
TRIAL — ARRAIGNMENT
CONVICTION — SENTENCING
APPEAL — PRISON

GARY FOGELSON

How to Try a Terrorist
By John C. Coughenour

SEATTLE
MICHAEL B. MUKASEY, President Bush's nominee to be attorney general, is coming under increasing

strates that our courts can protect Americans from terrorism. Through the commendable efforts of law enforcement authorities in 1999, Mr. Ressam was captured before he was able to carry out his plan to bomb the airport. For two years after his conviction, thanks in part to the fairness he was shown by the court, Mr.

3

100% UNIVERSUM —begann als→ SINGULARITÄT —im→ URKNALL —vor→ 15 MILLIARDEN JAHREN

UNIVERSUM —beinhaltet→

—seitdem→ EXPANSION DES UNIVERSUMS

ATOME ←speziell— PARTIKEL ←besteht aus— MATERIE —ist transformierbar in→ ENERGIE → POTENZIELLE E / KINETISCHE E / NUKLEAR E

PARTIKEL / MASSE ←besitzt—

ATOME —verbinden sich zu→

MATERIE —bekannt→ **4%** SICHTBARE MATERIE
MATERIE —unbekannt→ **23%** DUNKLE MATERIE
ENERGIE —unbekannt→ **73%** DUNKLE ENERGIE ←Folge von— BESCHLEUNIGUNG ←dessen— EXPANSION DES UNIVERSUMS

MOLEKÜLE ←→ ELEMENTE ←— SICHTBARE MATERIE

MOLEKÜLE —können sein→ FEST / FLÜSSIG / GASFÖRMIG

SICHTBARE MATERIE —besitzt→ 3 ZUSTÄNDE → FEST / FLÜSSIG / GASFÖRMIG

DUNKLE MATERIE —ist→ 95% DER MATERIE IN JEDER GALAXIE ÜBERALL IM UNIVERSUM !!! —→ MÖGLICHE KANDIDATEN

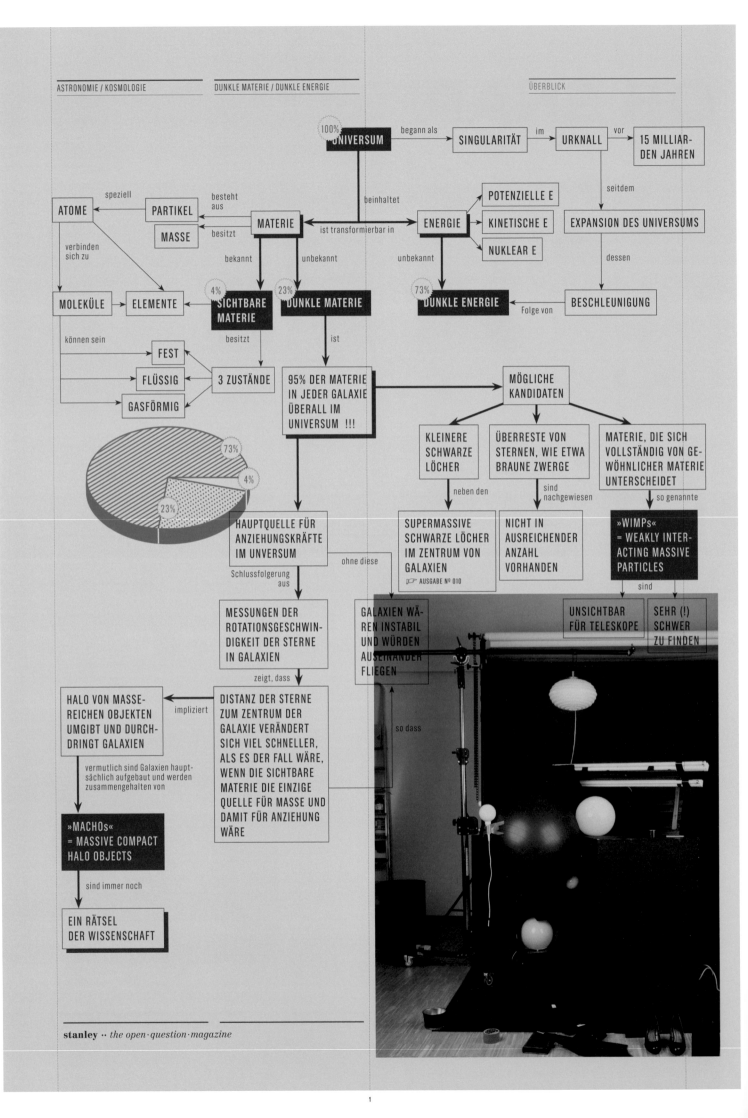

MÖGLICHE KANDIDATEN →
- KLEINERE SCHWARZE LÖCHER —neben den→ SUPERMASSIVE SCHWARZE LÖCHER IM ZENTRUM VON GALAXIEN ☞ AUSGABE N° 010
- ÜBERRESTE VON STERNEN, WIE ETWA BRAUNE ZWERGE —sind nachgewiesen→ NICHT IN AUSREICHENDER ANZAHL VORHANDEN
- MATERIE, DIE SICH VOLLSTÄNDIG VON GEWÖHNLICHER MATERIE UNTERSCHEIDET —so genannte→ »WIMPs« = WEAKLY INTERACTING MASSIVE PARTICLES —sind→ UNSICHTBAR FÜR TELESKOPE / SEHR (!) SCHWER ZU FINDEN

95% DER MATERIE... →
HAUPTQUELLE FÜR ANZIEHUNGSKRÄFTE IM UNVERSUM —ohne diese→ GALAXIEN WÄREN INSTABIL UND WÜRDEN AUSEINANDER FLIEGEN

HAUPTQUELLE FÜR ANZIEHUNGSKRÄFTE IM UNVERSUM —Schlussfolgerung aus→ MESSUNGEN DER ROTATIONSGESCHWINDIGKEIT DER STERNE IN GALAXIEN —zeigt, dass→ DISTANZ DER STERNE ZUM ZENTRUM DER GALAXIE VERÄNDERT SICH VIEL SCHNELLER, ALS ES DER FALL WÄRE, WENN DIE SICHTBARE MATERIE DIE EINZIGE QUELLE FÜR MASSE UND DAMIT FÜR ANZIEHUNG WÄRE

DISTANZ DER STERNE... —so dass→ GALAXIEN WÄREN INSTABIL UND WÜRDEN AUSEINANDER FLIEGEN

DISTANZ DER STERNE... —impliziert→ HALO VON MASSEREICHEN OBJEKTEN UMGIBT UND DURCHDRINGT GALAXIEN —vermutlich sind Galaxien hauptsächlich aufgebaut und werden zusammengehalten von→ »MACHOs« = MASSIVE COMPACT HALO OBJECTS —sind immer noch→ EIN RÄTSEL DER WISSENSCHAFT

1

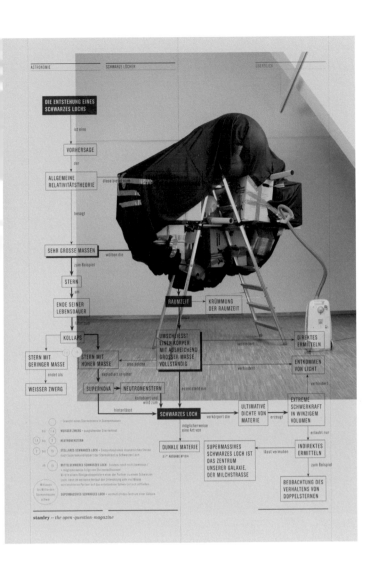

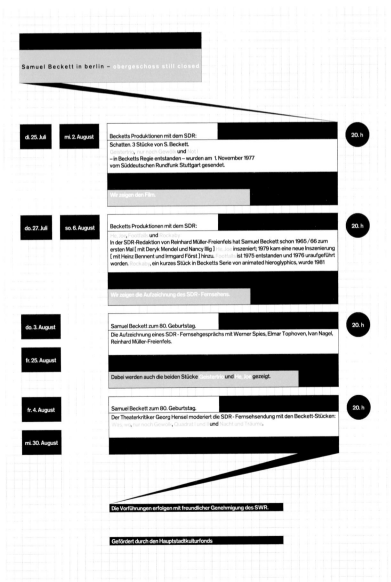

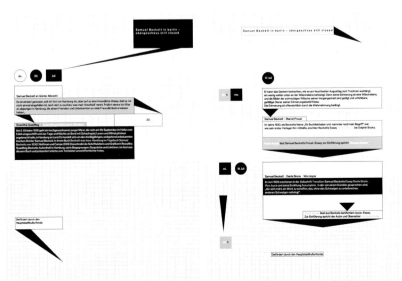

1
STANLEY
THE OPEN QUESTION MAGAZINE
Katrin Schacke
/›PP. 182, 183/ STANLEY — THE OPEN QUESTION MAGAZINE aims to fill in the blank spots of human knowledge, and highlight those left to be explored. Focusing on the 100 most significant unanswered questions in the realm of science, every issue summarises the current state of knowledge or ignorance on one particular remaining mystery. In her overview of STANLEY topics, Katrin Schacke attempts to draw a landscape of knowledge — an undertaking at least as ambitious as the quest for answers itself. Divided into major disciplines, from astronomy to medicine, the diagram visualises their interrelations and emphasises those elusive moments of wonder that continue to act as sharpening stones for human ingenuity.

2
SAMUEL BECKETT — OBERGESCHOSS
STILL CLOSED
jung + wenig
Promotional posters for a series of SAMUEL BECKETT IN BERLIN — OBERGESCHOSS STILL CLOSED (upstairs still closed) performances at Literaturhaus Berlin.

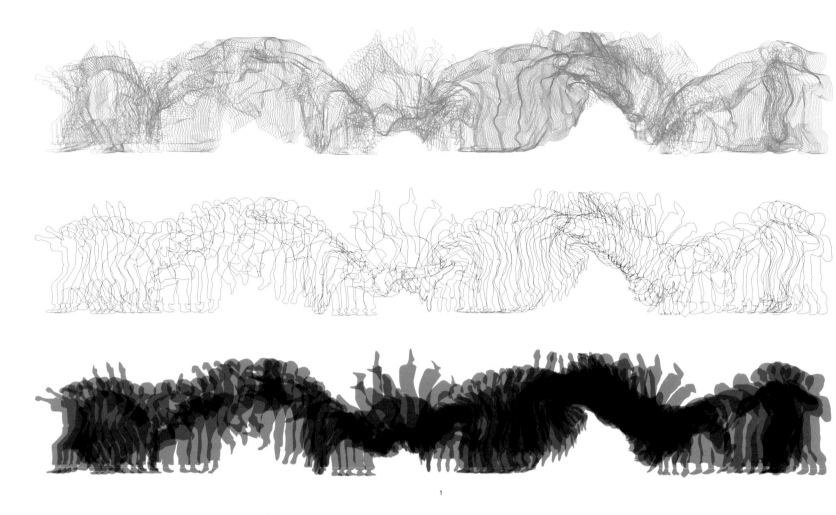

1

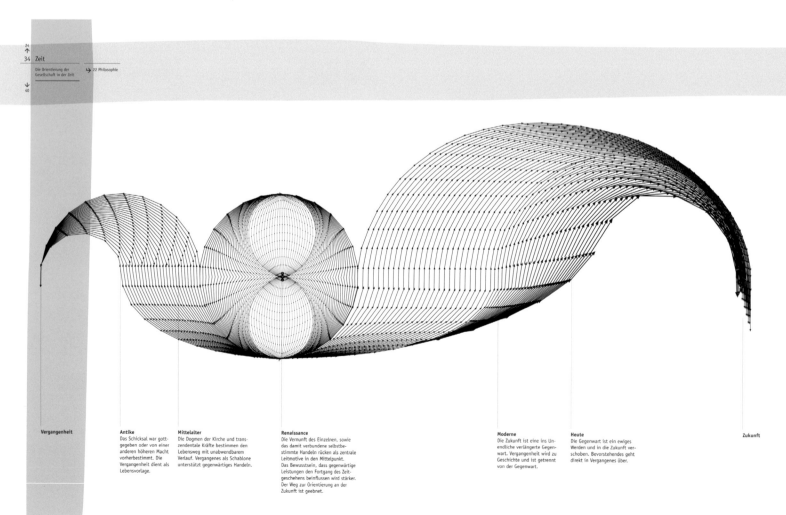

24 ↑
34 Zeit
Die Orientierung der
Gesellschaft in der Zeit   ↳ 22 Philosophie
↓
40

Vergangenheit

Antike
Das Schicksal war gott-
gegeben oder von einer
anderen höheren Macht
vorherbestimmt. Die
Vergangenheit dient als
Lebensvorlage.

Mittelalter
Die Dogmen der Kirche und trans-
zendentale Kräfte bestimmen den
Lebensweg mit unabwendbarem
Verlauf. Vergangenes als Schablone
unterstützt gegenwärtiges Handeln.

Renaissance
Die Vernunft des Einzelnen, sowie
das damit verbundene selbstbe-
stimmte Handeln rücken als zentrale
Leitmotive in den Mittelpunkt.
Das Bewusstsein, dass gegenwärtige
Leistungen den Fortgang des Zeit-
geschehens beinflussen wird stärker.
Der Weg zur Orientierung an der
Zukunft ist geebnet.

Moderne
Die Zukunft ist eine ins Un-
endliche verlängerte Gegenwart. Vergangenheit wird zu
Geschichte und ist getrennt
von der Gegenwart.

Heute
Die Gegenwart ist ein ewiges
Werden und in die Zukunft ver-
schoben. Bevorstehendes geht
direkt in Vergangenes über.

Zukunft

2

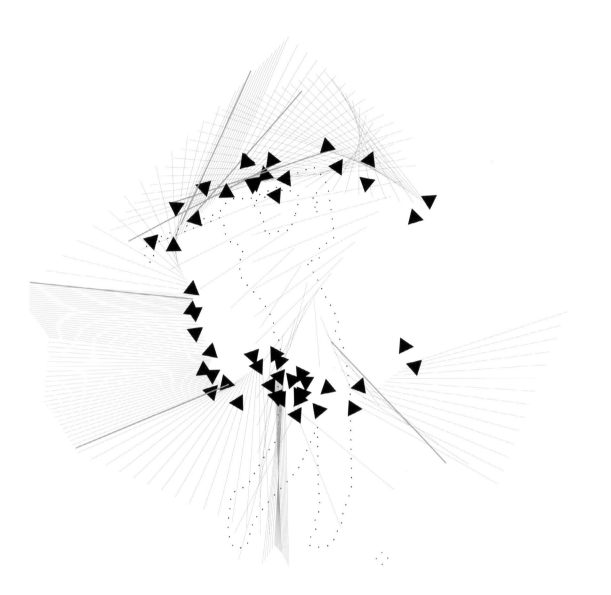

1
STATIC MOVEMENTS
Piero Zagami

Lightning-fast and lethal! With just a quick kick or flick of the wrist, a martial artist can defeat his opponent.   As part of his conceptual study of human movements, London-based graphic designer Piero Zagami reveals the tricks of the trade in this frame by frame dissection of a master's fluid motions. Printed on transparent paper, his aesthetic experiment freezes the powerful movements of seasoned performers into a tangible series of incremental actions.

At the same time, Zagami invites the user to experiment with layers, adding complexity to these discrete states of being. Taken to the extreme and overlaid to excess, the separate, dissected movements re-merge into organic shapes and dissolve in a web of tangled abstraction.

2
NEU
WEGE ZUM FORTSCHRITT
Martin Gorka

/ P. 96 / NEU — WEGE ZUM FORTSCHRITT (new — paths to progress) uses a street atlas format to reconstruct how new thoughts and inventions have spread through the world. TIME, for example, maps society through different ages while a chapter on networking depicts the proliferation of internet hosts between 1981 and 2006.

3
GESTURE
Élodie Mandray

Dispensing with unnecessary flourishes, Élodie Mandray's "gestural graphics" reduce a range of sports to their bare essentials — and from four dimensions (space / time) to the two of a page or screen.   To this end, Mandray picks apart high-speed footage of professional athletes frame by frame, and plots the pertinent positions of hand, feet and sporting equipment (i.e. golf club, discus, tennis racket) over the course of the discipline's defining moment.

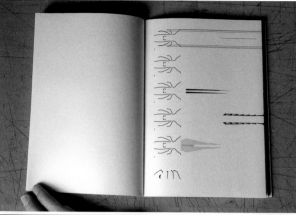

1
SALTICUS SPIDER'S COURTSHIP DISPLAY
Clio Chaffardon

Some animals go wild during mating season. Take the salticus spider for example, its frenzied courtship dance is a thing to behold — and hard to document in a scientific manner.   Clio Chaffardon took it upon herself to record and "re-transcribe" the spider's mating ritual in a series of separate booklets. Subdivided into the dimensions of sound (blue triangles), ground contact or "leg work" (black dots and lines) and air vibrations that amplify the sound (yellow and orange shapes), the dance becomes a thing of severe beauty, stripped of its original meaning.   An accompanying poster reunites the elements of arachnid seduction in a colourful, yet formalised notation devised by the artist.

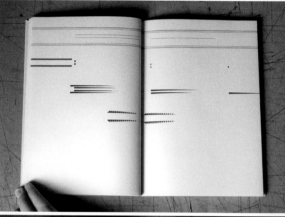

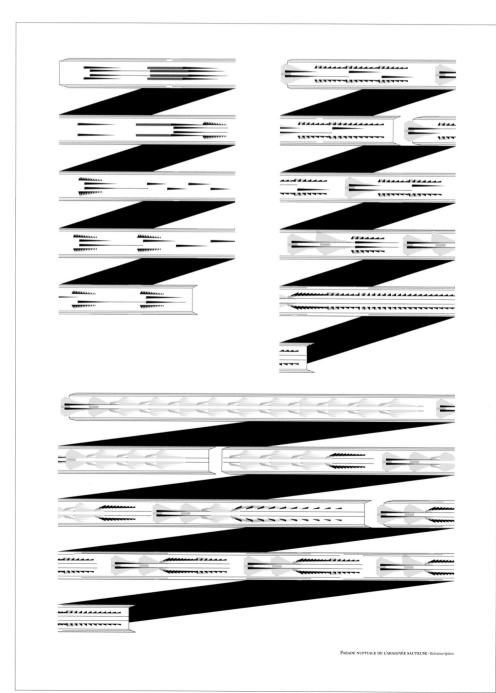

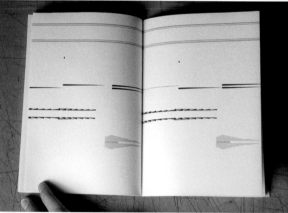

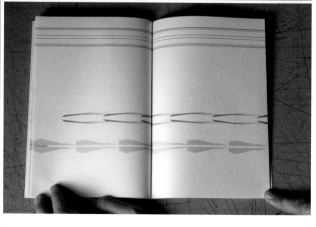

PARADE NUPTIALE DE L'ARAIGNÉE SAUTEUSE · *Retranscription*

2
METROPOLIS
Twopoints.Net
More and more designers take cues from nature — the original blueprint of successful design. Expanding on this important trend, a feature in New York-based design magazine METROPOLIS explores examples of great design in the world that surrounds us, including the evolution of behavioural pathways.

Whether single file, amorphous swarm or arrow-shaped flight pattern, the article's illustrations highlight examples of tried and tested crowd formations and the underlying design principles of a swarm, flock or trail. Following the lines of least resistance, natural elegance and efficiency prevails.

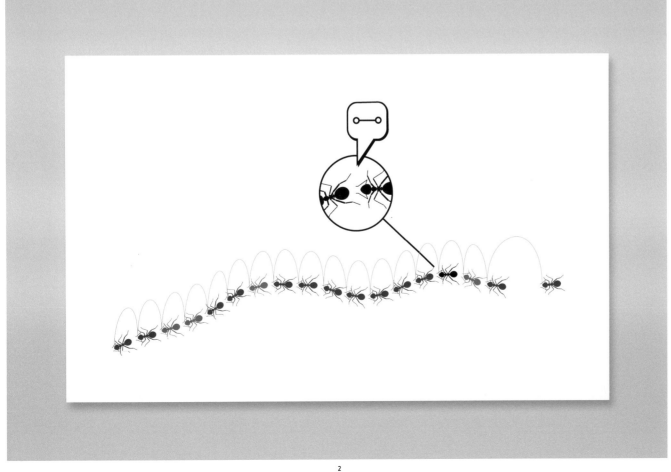

1
POKER DRAWINGS II (3ᴿᴰ PLACE)
2
POKER DRAWINGS I (8ᵀᴴ PLACE)
Torgeir Husevaag

The winner takes it all? In the case of Torgeir Husevaag's poker drawings, it is the process that matters. Here, victory becomes just another aspect of overall group and game dynamics. Based on an online poker tournament where ten players vie for the pot, these sketches play to their own set of rules. In order to visualise the group dynamics between bold, strong chip leaders and more timid participants, Husevaag draws the path of bets and calls, losses, victories and eliminations, colour-coded by type/amount and connected by dotted lines.

Governed by this self-imposed index of signs and symbols, Husevaag's illustrations plot the interactions and interdependencies of the different player nuclei — including that of the designer himself. / POKER DRAWINGS II (3ᴿᴰ PLACE) / 2008 / Ink on paper / 52×48 cm / POKER DRAWINGS I (8ᵀᴴ PLACE) / 2006 / Ink on paper / 50×63 cm /

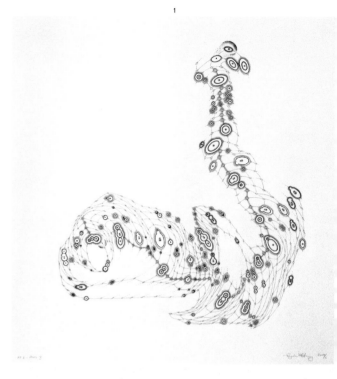

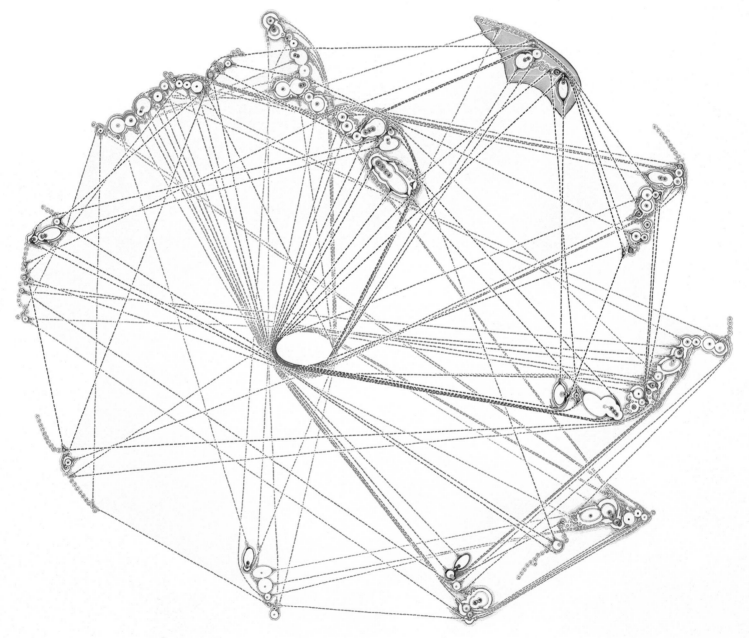

3

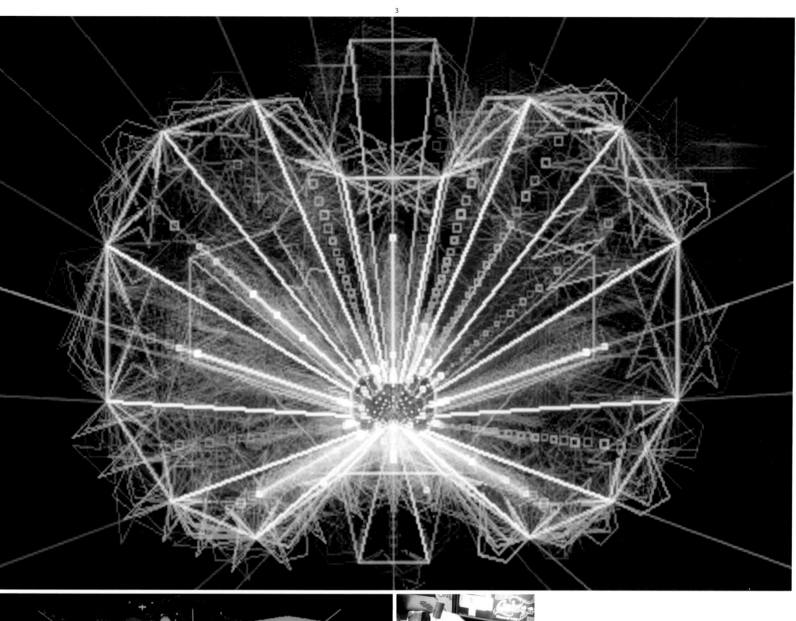

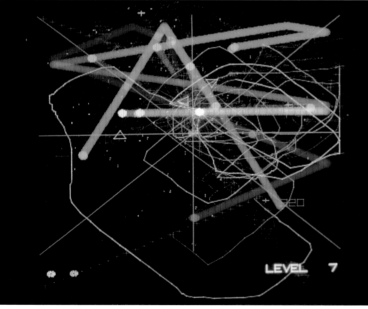

LEVEL 7

4

5

3
TEMPEST 1
4
QUANTUM 1
5
LONG EXPOSURE PHOTOGRAPHS
OF 80'S ERA ARCADE GAMES
Rosemarie Fiore

A labour of love and hands-on documentation, New York-based artist Rosemarie Fiore
decided to play several popular 1980s arcade
games (Tempest, Quantum and Gyruss) all
the way through to their final level. By recording each complete game in a single,
long-exposure photograph, she created a
number of discrete kinematic maps of the
games' governing structure and play.
Still resonating with their era's characteristic,
pixelated video game aesthetics, Fiore's one-
frame documentations of an entire game distil
the overall process, the hours of play required
to complete each level, into a single representation that exposes the games' hidden
logic like a digital Rorschach test. / TEMPEST 1 /
2001 / Digital C-print 48 × 72 in. (122 × 183 cm) / QUANTUM 1 /
2002 / Digital C-print 36 × 40 in. (91.5 × 101.5 cm) / LONG EX-
POSURE PHOTOGRAPHS OF 80'S ERA ARCADE GAMES /
2004 / Photo: Michael Ferris Jr. / Courtesy of Priska C. Juschka
Fine Art /

1

2

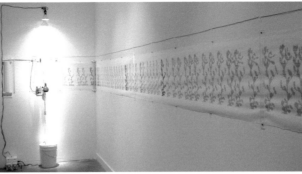

3

1
PERPETUAL STORYTELLING APPARATUS
Benjamin Maus and Julius von Bismarck

The plot thickens and the story unravels: Julius von Bismarck's and Benjamin Maus' PERPETUAL STORYTELLING APPARATUS transforms forgotten patents into a never-ending flow of associative serendipity.

Their customised drawing machine parses popular bestsellers into patent drawings by analysing a database filled with information on seven million patents, linked by more than 22 million references.   To this end, the artists' algorithm eliminates "filler words" in the novel (i.e. "and", "to", "for" etc.) and uses the remaining phrases — in chronological order — as the basis for patent searches. Once key patents have been identified, the programme establishes relevant links, based on references to older patents — so-called "prior art", to construct a linear storyline.

In this printed chain of ideas, new visual connections and narrative layers emerge from the blend of contemporary plot and technological achievements. The result is a beautifully meandering tale that evolves all the way down the paper scroll — yet remains as cryptic and impenetrable as many of the patents themselves. / 2009 / Customized drawing machine, custom software, roll paper /

2
REMOTE SONAR DRAWING DEVICE
David Bowen

A wave of friendship across the world or an exercise in (mis)understanding? Bowen's multinational telepresence robotic installation sparks interaction and interpretation.

At the Laboral Centro de Arte y Creación Industrial, Gijón-Asturias (Spain) and the Visualization and Digital Imaging Lab, University of Minnesota (USA) identical sonar sensor arrays and drawing arms chart the movements of people through (gallery) space. All sensory information is transmitted in real time to the opposite location's drawing device, where a piece of charcoal attached to the machine translates the visitors' recorded actions into a set of skittish gestures.   From passive passers-by to deliberate hand waves, the experiment thrives on the interplay of movement and dynamics, but most of all the mutual exchange of interest and attention between both locations. / 2008 /

3
GROWTH RENDERING DEVICE
David Bowen

In David Bowen's closed system of growth and emulation, nature and technology, each element "feeds" on the other. While the systemic set-up provides the plant with light and nutrition, the plant in turn responds by growing. As a reaction to this growth, the device takes measure of the plant's development and produces a faint shadow — a rasterised inkjet drawing — of its latest progress. Ever-moving and unconnected to the outside world, the system automatically shifts the ream of paper after each drawing and thus signals a new growth and measurement cycle.   The project itself is open-ended and the final outcome not predetermined. / 2007 /

1

2

LEFT PAGE
TREE DRAWING
HAWTHORN ON EASEL#1
1
OAK ON EASEL#1
2
LARCH ON EASEL [FOUR PEN]#1
Tim Knowles

TREE DRAWING is a series of sketches produced by tying drawing implements to tree branches and then letting nature (and the breeze) take its course. Just like our own signatures, each drawing reveals a lot about the qualities and characteristics of its "author": from the light touch of a willow's relaxed, flowing line to a hawthorn's stiff, scratchy and neurotic marks. / Copyright the Artist / TREE DRAWING HAWTHORN ON EASEL#1 / 2005 / C-type print and ink on paper 790×620 mm + 790×620 mm / OAK ON EASEL#1 / 2005 / Detail Diptych C-type Print & Ink on paper 790×620 mm + 790×620 mm / LARCH ON EASEL [FOUR PEN]#1 / 2005 / Drawing Detail Diptych C-type Print and Ink on Paper 780×980 mm + 780×590 mm /

3
WINDWALK #2
SEVEN WALKS FROM SEVEN DIALS
Tim Knowles

"The answer, my friend, is blowing in the wind ..."   A lesson in direction and misdirection: Tim Knowles looks to the elements for an element of chance in our increasingly regulated lives. Akin to scientific experimentation, guided by external forces, his projects seek to reveal the invisible powers in the world around us and the nature of hidden systems. To this end, he relies on devices, mechanisms, systems or processes beyond the artist's own control.   In his series of windwalks for example, it is a helmet-mounted sail that points the way and serves as a guiding arrow for seven perambulations through Central London, recorded by GPS and a device-mounted camera. Starting from the city's historic Seven Dials structure — the starting point of seven streets — Knowles repeats his chance-driven experiment until each of the Dials had been walked down. / 2009 / Copyright the artist /

3

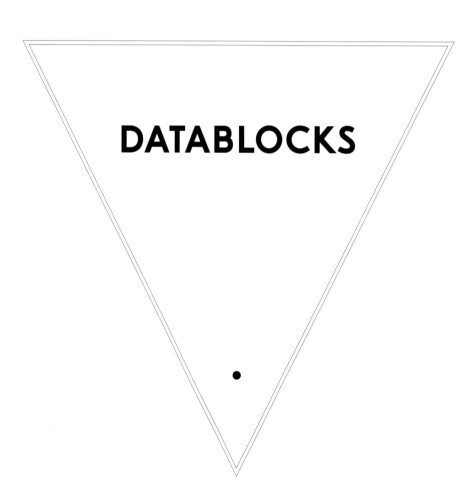

DATABLOCKS

Rectangles are the most popular shape in information visualization. They are not just applied in the classic bar chart or in sophisticated tree diagrams, but also in many other ways, as this chapter shows. From bars to squares to cubes, the next pages are filled with diagrams that use areas, elements or masses to divide and compare data – in all their rectangular glory.

•

Everywhere we look, we see rectangular structures. In windows, doors, floor tiles, tables, cereal boxes, *Lego* bricks, and buildings. The rectangle is the most used shape in numerous domains, because of its many good qualities. One that makes it a perfect match for information visualization is its efficient use of space. When stacking blocks, nothing is wasted. Every millimeter, every pixel (also a rectangle) can be used to the utmost. Many projects featured on the following pages are extremely dense, showing lots of information in a compact space, without losing clarity. Haohao Huang's mammoth project of mapping his family's history is just one example. /1/ A myriad of numbers are put into a tight grid, before being color-coded by hand, resulting in an impressive mesh of compressed information.

A titan of efficiency is the treemap. This rather new method in the history of information visualization is enjoying increasing popularity and has even found its way into mainstream media. By definition, no space is wasted. Tiles fill the whole area, covering everything with datablocks. A broad overview is provided at a glance, as can be seen in Moritz Stefaner's visualization of information flow in science. /2/ Rectangles also play nicely within the grids imposed by their surroundings. Sheets of paper have right angles, monitors do too. Within the screen estate, on most websites for example, HTML and CSS put content into boxes. Bars and squares align to those outer borders – and to each other – suggesting harmony, stability, and clarity. Caroline Fabès's color-coded typeface system /3/ makes perfect use of that.

In their poster for the art and culture award of Lucerne, Cybu Richli and Fabienne Burri add another dimension by placing blocks of data in a 3D grid. /4/ Different but related datasets are visualized, forming an intriguing, intricate structure, while the rigid, rectangular grid gives the viewer orientation. This points at another quality of the rectangle: its clear geometry guides our eyes and suggests simplicity on complex issues.

1
MAPPING TIME BASED ON GENEALOGY
AND HISTORICAL STUDY
COLORING STAGE
Haohao Huang
/ › PP. 74, 75 /

3
L'AVENTURE DES ÉCRITURES
Caroline Fabès
/ › P. 61 /

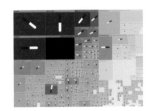

2
WELL-FORMED. EIGENFACTOR
VISUALIZING INFORMATION FLOW
IN SCIENCE
Moritʒ Stefaner
/ › P. 66 /

4
DATEN DES KUNST-
UND KULTURPREISTRÄGERS
UND DER ANERKENNUNGSPREISTRÄGER
DER STADT LUZERN 2009
C2F: Cybu Richli & Fabienne Burri
/ › PP. 68, 69 /

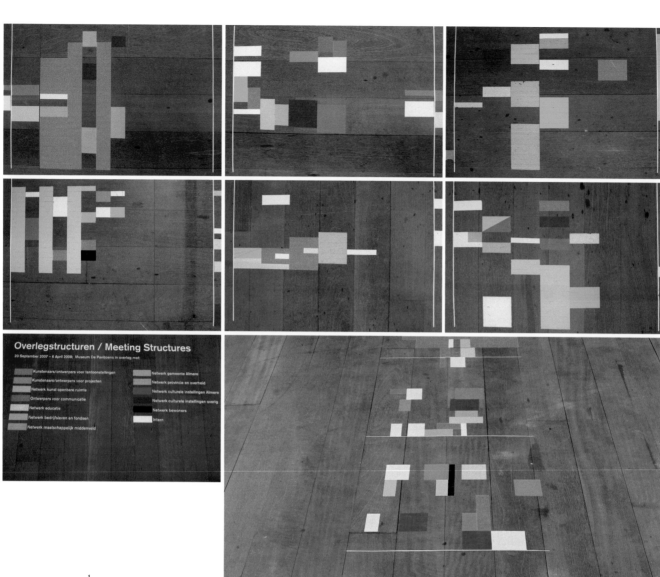

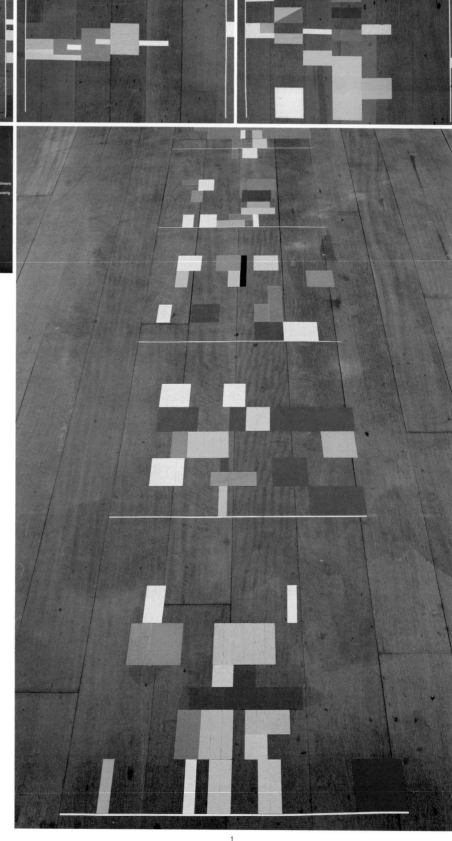

1

MEETING STRUCTURES
(OVERLEGSTRUCTUREN)
Luna Maurer

MEETING STRUCTURES (Overlegstructuren) allows a peek behind the scenes of gallery routines and administration. Over the course of six months, the museum's meeting agenda took over the public floor in the guise of colour-coded strips of tape.   Charting the progress of art and bureaucracy across time and space in a walkable floor installation, the exhibit reveals the multi-faceted organisational constellations between artists and funding, local government and communication designers at play in a medium-sized art institution.

2

ILLINOIS:
VISUALIZING MUSIC
VOCAL ALBUM GRID
Jax de León

/›P.170›/ In a further facet of his ILLINOIS: VISUALIZING MUSIC project, Jax de León translates Sufjan Stevens' songwriting gems into a colourful notation.   Akin to the booking system of a theatre, de León's method reflects the nerdy pleasure of colouring predefined spots on a grid. Here, each square represents a single second, colours indicate lyric subjects and grey areas vocal-free passages. Squares are split into sections for multiple voices, while other marks refer to backing singers or non-word expressions like "ooh" and "ahh".   Although the pixelated outcome cannot convey the song's subtext, the emotions carried by each individual note, it provides an overview of the singer's performance — his rhythm, cadences and moments of silent contemplation.

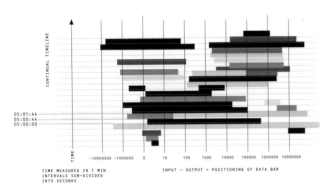

INPUT DISPLAYED USING COLOUR

100000000->
1000000-10000000
100000-1000000
10000-100000
1000-10000
100-1000
10-100
0-10

INPUT IN MB

OUTPUT DISPLAYED USING BAR DISTANCE

CONTINUAL TIMELINE

TIME

05:01:44
05:00:44
05:00:00

-10000000 -1000000 0 10 100 1000 10000 100000 1000000 10000000

TIME MEASURED IN 1 MIN
INTERVALS SUB-DIVIDED
INTO SECONDS

INPUT − OUTPUT = POSITIONING OF DATA BAR

OUTPUT
IN MB

0-10
10-100
100-1000
1000-10000
10000-100000
100000-1000000
1000000-10000000
100000000->

1

1
THE SHARP PROJECT
four23

A long-standing Manchester landmark, the monolithic cuboid of the Sharp Building stood empty for a number of years. With a £5m refurbishment on the horizon, the city wanted to transform the retro behemoth into a brand new digital media production hub for the city and beyond.   Tasked with creating a visual identity, four23 joined forces with local legend Peter Saville to develop a suitable reflection of the new life in this stern structure. Inspired by the world of computer-generated arts, they alit on a logo in flux, an encrypted representation of the building's real-time buzz.   The resulting visual identity — generated from parameters like creative throughput in megabyte or output mapped against distance from bar — shifts and develops over time to represent a creative community that never stays still or remains the same.

2
CINEMA REDUX
Katy Foster

A tricky brief asked Katy Foster to condense an entire film into a single image. Her chosen favourite, rock epic ALMOST FAMOUS, features almost 50 different songs. Foster's visual representation distils the movie's entire soundtrack into one colourful diagram where each shade represents a specific song and white space denotes music-free passages.

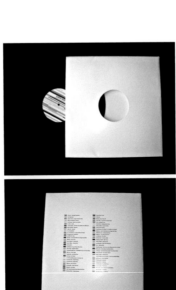

ALMOST FAMOUS
Cinema Redux: Movie Soundtrack

2

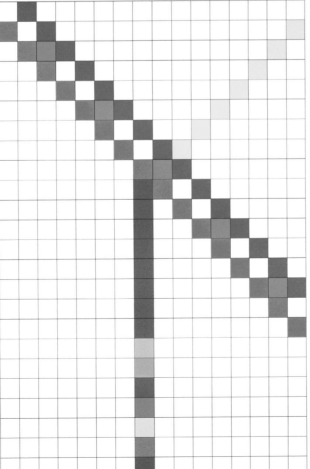

THE BROKEN WINDMILL

HOAGY HOUGHTON

3
ALEATORY COMPOSITIONS
Hoagy Houghton
ALEATORY COMPOSITIONS is a book of sheet music — written by people unaware of this fact. Houghton's involuntary allies created their pieces by filling a blank grid with seven colours, shading the squares whichever way they liked. A colour scale translated their visual compositions into musical notes, resulting in a wide range of random chords and abstract melodies.

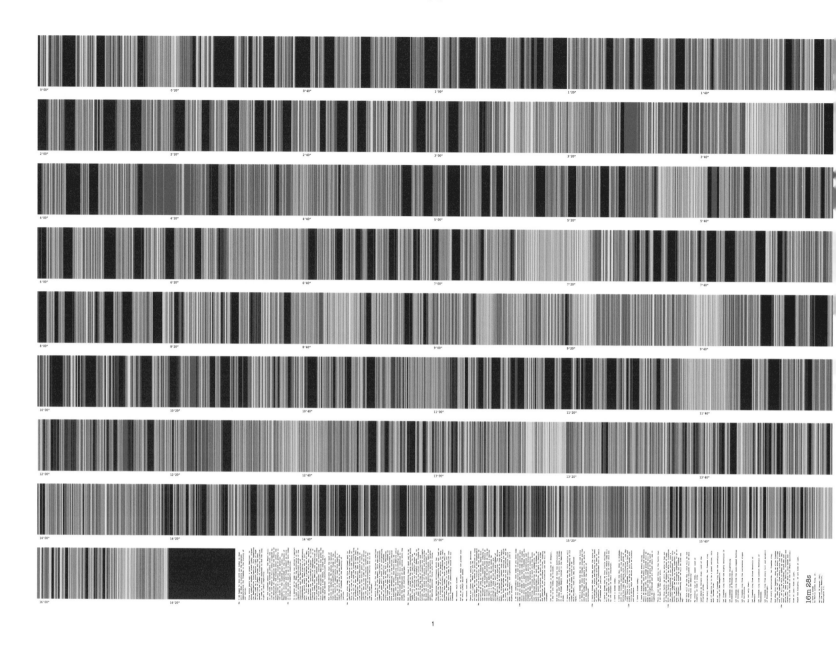

1

1
16M 28S
why not smile
Hoon Kim
16M 28S calls time on inequality. Named after the length of Martin Luther King, Jr.'s seminal "I Have a Dream" address, it untangles the rhythm and melody of the human rights champion's stirring speech. Transposed into a colour spectrum (from red = loud through to purple = silent) to reflect King's evocative intonation, 16M 28S facilitates interpretation by adding a supplementary layer of sensory input to the text.   Thus, even a paper copy of King's speech moves beyond the pure, written content — and into the realms of passion and rhetoric.

2
POÉSIE DE SUPERMARCHÉ
Caroline Fabès
In her exploration of the mundane "poetry of supermarkets", Caroline Fabès processed photographic evidence from the stores into graphics. Deleting all text references, she focussed on the dominant colours of product packaging and then retranslated this visual information into words according to her own L'AVENTURE DES ÉCRITURES colour code.

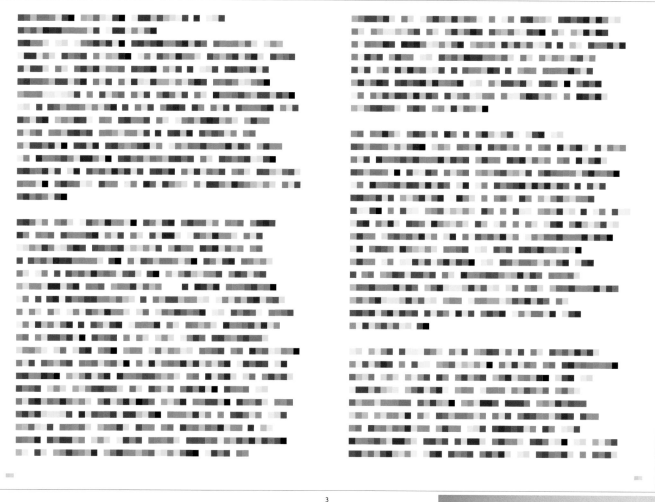

3

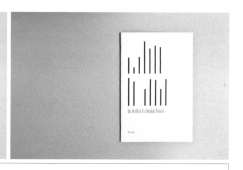

3
L'AVENTURE DES ÉCRITURES
Caroline Fabès
In Caroline Fabès' "typeface adventure",
each letter is replaced with a differently
coloured square, while punctuation marks
cover the greyscale spectrum. This particular
example applies the code to a pedagogic
text found in the National Library.

4
L'IMAGE DU TEXTE
Caroline Fabès
L'IMAGE DU TEXTE is a code based on un-
folding each letter of the Zofage typeface.
The resulting font is applied to an article on
the image of text by Emmanuel Souchier.

1
CONVERSATION + SYNESTHESIA
Shaheena Pooloo
Synaesthesia — in this case the colour variety — causes a brain to associate colours with specific letters or numbers. CONVERSATION + SYNAESTHESIA recreates the exchange between Pooloo and a synaesthetic friend in a map of corresponding colours.

2
POETRY ON THE ROAD 2007
Boris Müller and one/one
Since 2002, Boris Müller has been putting POETRY ON THE ROAD with a range of visual themes for an annual international literature festival. The only rule: all graphics are generated by a computer programme that turns text into image. Once you have cracked the code, the piece of poetry is yours! /Team: Boris Müller, Florian Pfeffer, Andrea Schaffors/

CONVERSATION + SYNESTHESIA

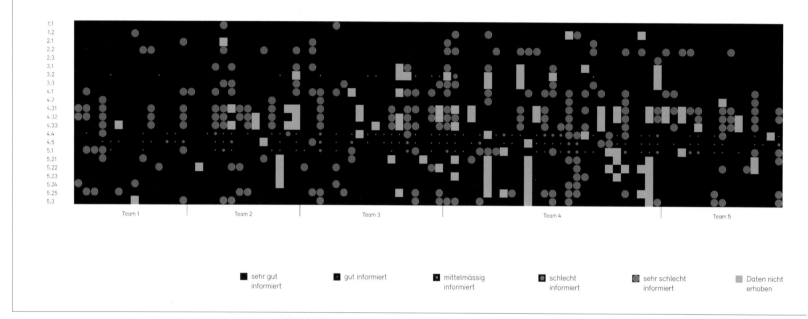

Gesamtansicht

B5 Patientenaustritt

| | Team 1 | Team 2 | Team 3 | Team 4 | Team 5 |

■ sehr gut informiert   ■ gut informiert   ■ mittelmässig informiert   ● schlecht informiert   ■ sehr schlecht informiert   ■ Daten nicht erhoben

1

VISUELLER ATLAS DES SPITALALLTAGS
VISUALISIERUNG ORGANISATORISCHER
UND KOMMUNIKATIVER ABLÄUFE
IM PATIENTENPROZESS
Hahn und Zimmermann

The research project VISUELLER ATLAS DES SPITALALLTAGS (visual atlas of hospital routines) visualises four typical patient interactions at Inselspital Bern in order to facilitate the analysis of these organisational and communicative processes. / Project management: Barbara Hahn, Christine Zimmermann, Hochschule der Künste Bern, Forschungsschwerpunkt Kommunikationsdesign / Cooperation partner: Inselspital Bern, ärztliche Direktion, Fachstelle für Qualitätsmanagement, Annekäthi Bischoff /

2

STATISTICS STRIP IN THE EXHIBITION
"WORK. MEANING AND WORRY"
ART+COM AG

/ › P. 106 / As part of the exhibition WORK. MEANING AND WORRY at the German Hygiene-Museum Dresden, ART+COM turned graphs, charts and diagrams into wall-mounted strips of statistics. Protruding out into physical space and our personal comfort zones, these facts and figures refuse to be ignored.   As a continuous theme, the long black aluminium thread guides visitors through the exhibition. At strategic points along the way, it opens up into pertinent graphs and charts. The greater the numbers, the bigger the display on the wall — some charts reach over three metres in height.
The data strip is complemented by several interactive media stations where visitors can get involved and see for themselves how changed parameters create different outcomes. 100 interviews add a personal perspective to these naked figures. / Curating: Praxis für Ausstellungen und Theorie / Concept and Design: ART+COM /

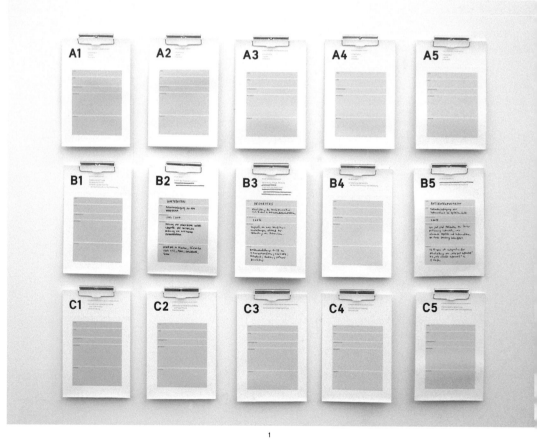

1

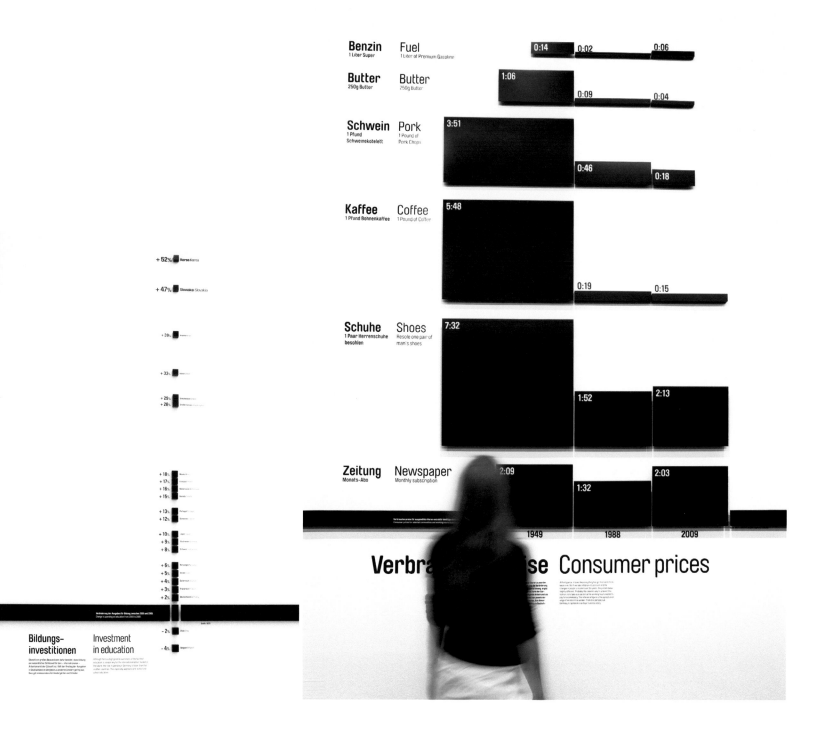

		1949	1988	2009
Benzin 1 Liter Super	Fuel 1 Liter of Premium Gasoline	0:14	0:02	0:06
Butter 250g Butter	Butter 250g Butter	1:06	0:09	0:04
Schwein 1 Pfund Schweinekotelett	Pork 1 Pound of Pork Chops	3:51	0:46	0:18
Kaffee 1 Pfund Bohnenkaffee	Coffee 1 Pound of Coffee	5:48	0:19	0:15
Schuhe 1 Paar Herrenschuhe besohlen	Shoes Resole one pair of man's shoes	7:32	1:52	2:13
Zeitung Monats-Abo	Newspaper Monthly subscription	2:09	1:32	2:03

Bildungs-investitionen Investment in education

+ 52% Korea Korea
+ 47% Slowakei Slovakia
+ 39%
+ 33%
+ 29%
+ 28%
+ 18%
+ 17%
+ 16%
+ 15%
+ 13%
+ 12%
+ 10%
+ 9%
+ 8%
+ 6%
+ 5%
+ 4%
+ 3%
+ 2%
− 2%
− 4%

Verbra... se Consumer prices

Zeitverwendung Use of time

13 % 15 % 34 %
12 %
17 % 9%

17 h 25 h

Bezahlte und unbezahlte Arbeit Paid and unpaid work

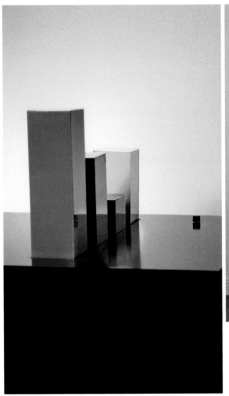

1

1
WABLE
Physical Interaction Lab
See the writing on the wall? Akin to a physical bar chart, the web table or WABLE mirrors personal feeds from web applications such as FACEBOOK, FLICKR or LAST.FM and changes according to the user's internet activity. / Photo: Joel Stockman / Illustration: Linn Granlund /

2
WELL-FORMED.EIGENFACTOR
VISUALIZING INFORMATION FLOW
IN SCIENCE
Moritz Stefaner
WELL-FORMED.EIGENFACTOR presents interactive visualisations of emerging patterns in scientific citation networks. To this end, Stefaner measures the importance of individual journals — their Eigenfactor score — as well as citation flow and hierarchical clustering. The resulting information highlights different aspects of scientific reporting.

3
LIFEMAP
Ritwik Dey
Tasked with mapping his own life, this example of healthy navel gazing takes us through the artist's life, education and ever-broadening interests. / Created at Parsons The New School for Design, New York / Teacher: Dmitry Krasny /

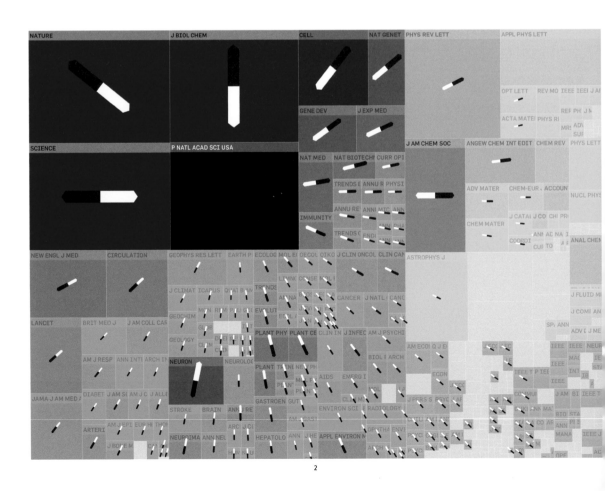

2

LifeMap_{1.1}

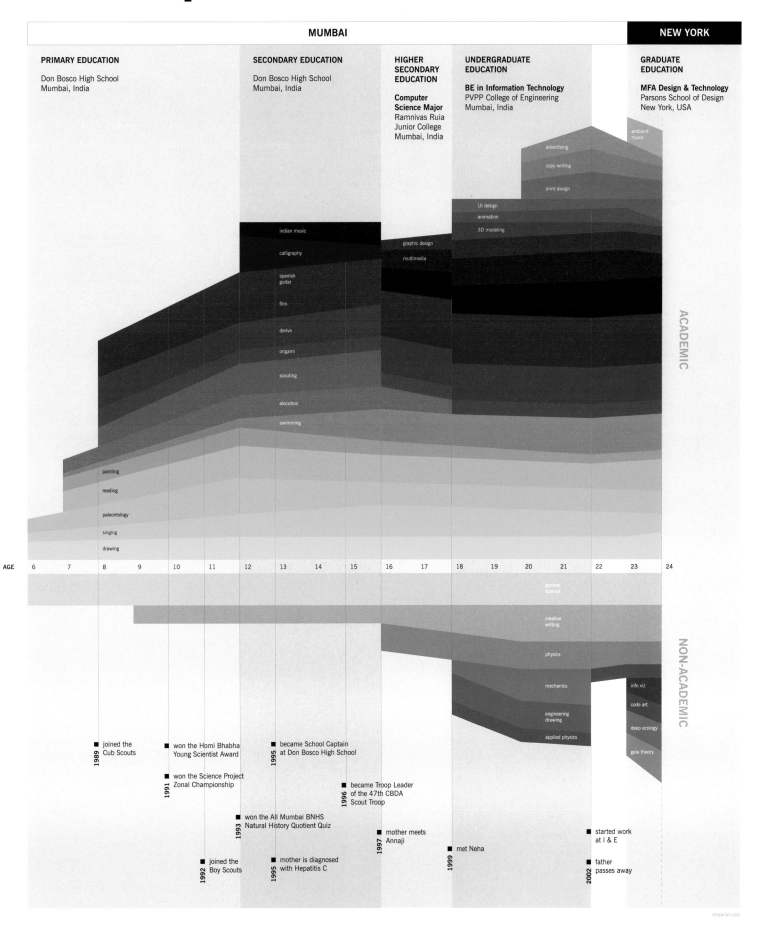

	MUMBAI				NEW YORK

PRIMARY EDUCATION

Don Bosco High School
Mumbai, India

SECONDARY EDUCATION

Don Bosco High School
Mumbai, India

HIGHER SECONDARY EDUCATION

Computer Science Major
Ramnivas Ruia
Junior College
Mumbai, India

UNDERGRADUATE EDUCATION

BE in Information Technology
PVPP College of Engineering
Mumbai, India

GRADUATE EDUCATION

MFA Design & Technology
Parsons School of Design
New York, USA

ambient music
advertising
copy writing
print design
UI design
animation
3D modeling
graphic design
multimedia

indian music
calligraphy
spanish guitar
film
derive
origami
scouting
elocution
swimming

painting
reading
paleontology
singing
drawing

ACADEMIC

AGE 6   7   8   9   10   11   12   13   14   15   16   17   18   19   20   21   22   23   24

general science
creative writing
physics
mechanics
engineering drawing
applied physics

info viz
code art
deep ecology
gaia theory

NON-ACADEMIC

1989 ■ joined the Cub Scouts

1991 ■ won the Science Project Zonal Championship

■ won the Homi Bhabha Young Scientist Award

1993 ■ won the All Mumbai BNHS Natural History Quotient Quiz

1992 ■ joined the Boy Scouts

1995 ■ became School Captain at Don Bosco High School

1995 ■ mother is diagnosed with Hepatitis C

1996 ■ became Troop Leader of the 47th CBDA Scout Troop

1997 ■ mother meets Annaji

1999 ■ met Neha

2002 ■ started work at I & E

■ father passes away

3

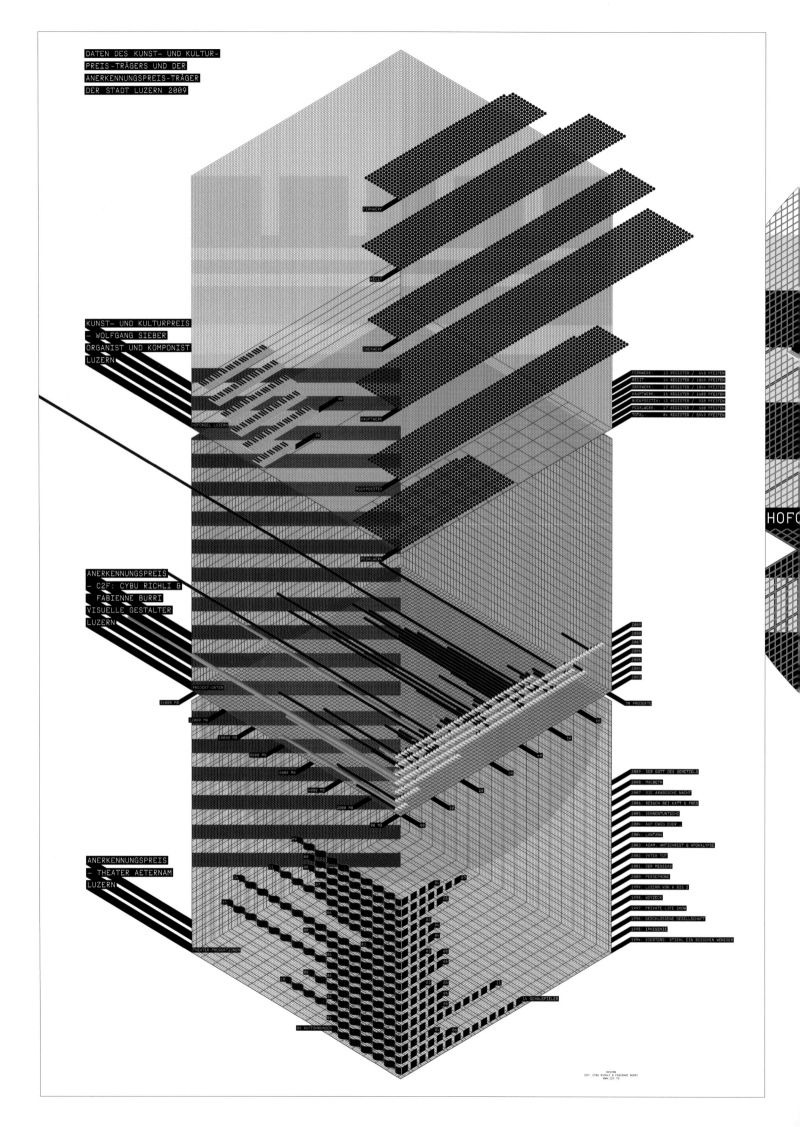

DATEN DES KUNST- UND KULTUR-
PREIS-TRÄGERS UND DER
ANERKENNUNGSPREIS-TRÄGER
DER STADT LUZERN 2009

KUNST- UND KULTURPREIS
- WOLFGANG SIEBER
ORGANIST UND KOMPONIST
LUZERN

ANERKENNUNGSPREIS
- C2F: CYBU RICHLI &
FABIENNE BURRI
VISUELLE GESTALTER
LUZERN

ANERKENNUNGSPREIS
- THEATER AETERNAM
LUZERN

FERNWERK: 13 REGISTER / 648 PFEIFEN
RECIT: 14 REGISTER / 1069 PFEIFEN
OBERWERK: 12 REGISTER / 1044 PFEIFEN
HAUPTWERK: 16 REGISTER / 1600 PFEIFEN
RUCKPOSITIV: 12 REGISTER / 928 PFEIFEN
PEDALWERK: 17 REGISTER / 660 PFEIFEN
TOTAL: 84 REGISTER / 5949 PFEIFEN

FERNWERK

RECIT

OBERWERK

HAUPTWERK

HOFORGEL LUZERN

RUCKPOSITIV

PEDALWERK

PROJEKT-DATEN

14000 MB

12000 MB

10000 MB

8000 MB

6000 MB

4000 MB

2000 MB

10 MB

THEATER-PRODUKTIONEN

86 AUFFUHRUNGEN

2009
2008
2007
2006
2005
2004
2003

70 PROJEKTE

2009: DER GOTT DES GEMETZELS
2008: MACBETH
2007: DIE ARABISCHE NACHT
2006: BESUCH BEI KATT & FRED
2005: SENNENTUNTSCHI
2004: AUF EWIG EUER -
2004: LANTANA
2003: ADAM, ANTICHRIST & APOKALYPSE
2002: VATER TUT
2001: DER MESSIAS
2000: PERSEPHONE
1999: LUZERN VON A BIS Z
1998: WOYZECK
1997: PRIVATE LIFE SHOW
1996: GESCHLOSSENE GESELLSCHAFT
1995: IPHIGENIE
1994: SIEBTENS: STIEHL EIN BISSCHEN WENIGER

14 SCHAUSPIELER

DESIGN
C2F: CYBU RICHLI & FABIENNE BURRI
WWW.C2F.TO

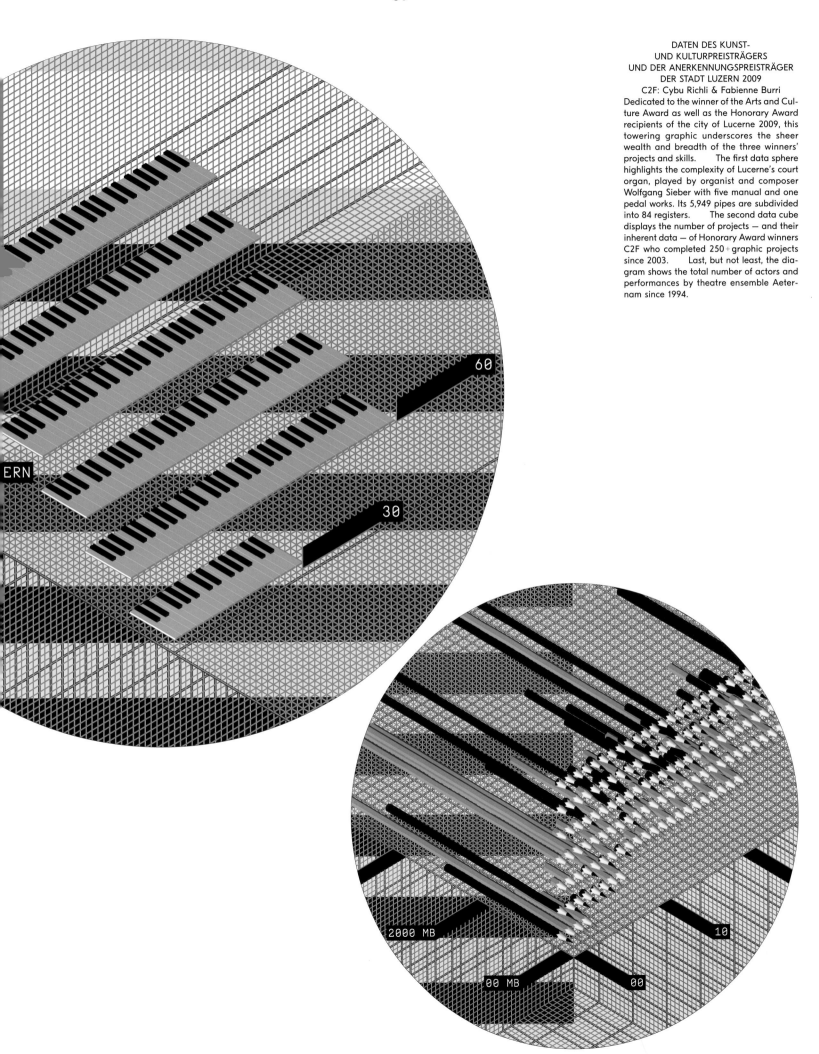

DATEN DES KUNST-
UND KULTURPREISTRÄGERS
UND DER ANERKENNUNGSPREISTRÄGER
DER STADT LUZERN 2009
C2F: Cybu Richli & Fabienne Burri
Dedicated to the winner of the Arts and Culture Award as well as the Honorary Award
recipients of the city of Lucerne 2009, this
towering graphic underscores the sheer
wealth and breadth of the three winners'
projects and skills.   The first data sphere
highlights the complexity of Lucerne's court
organ, played by organist and composer
Wolfgang Sieber with five manual and one
pedal works. Its 5,949 pipes are subdivided
into 84 registers.   The second data cube
displays the number of projects — and their
inherent data — of Honorary Award winners
C2F who completed 250+ graphic projects
since 2003.   Last, but not least, the diagram shows the total number of actors and
performances by theatre ensemble Aeternam since 1994.

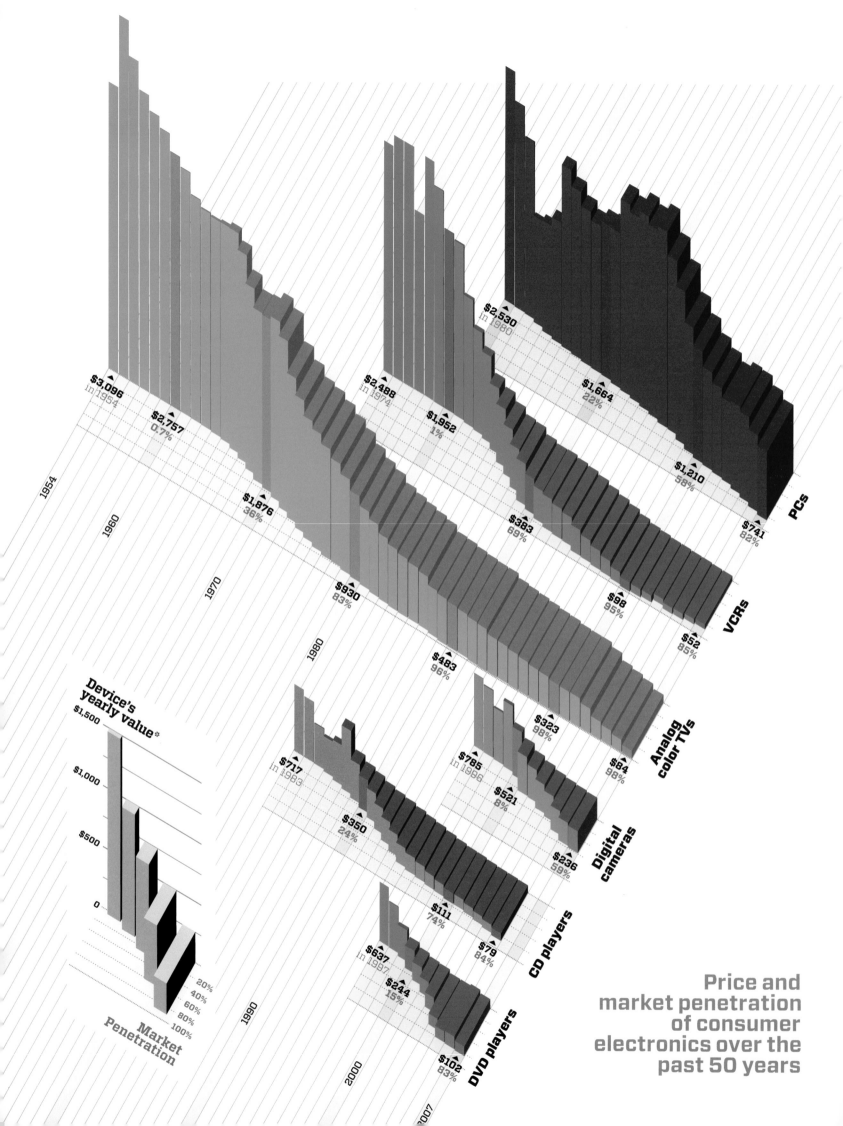

Price and market penetration of consumer electronics over the past 50 years

Device's yearly value*

$1,500
$1,000
$500
0

Market Penetration

20%
40%
60%
80%
100%

PCs

$3,096 in 1954
$2,757 0.7%
$1,876 36%
$930 83%
$483 96%

VCRs

$2,488 in 1974
$1,952 1%
$383 69%
$98 95%
$52 85%

Analog color TVs

$2,530 in 1980
$1,664 22%
$1,210 58%
$741 82%

Digital cameras

$717 in 1983
$350 24%
$111 74%
$79 84%

CD players

$785 in 1986
$521 8%
$236 59%
$323 98%
$84 98%

DVD players

$637 in 1997
$244 15%
$102 83%

1954
1960
1970
1980
1990
2000
2007

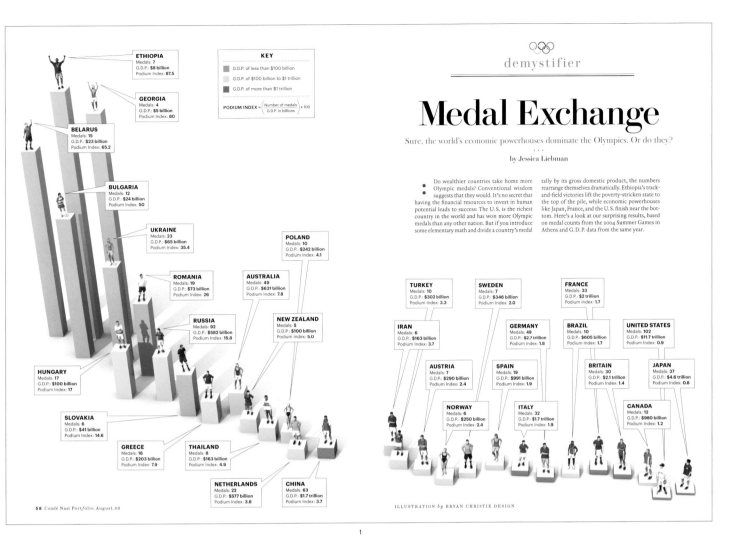

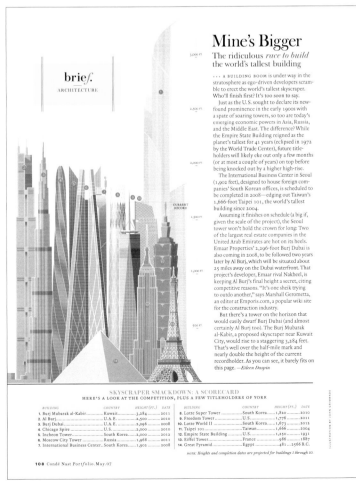

LEFT PAGE
GEEKINESS AT ANY PRICE
Arno Ghelfi
This diagram — or gadget meter — for tech bible WIRED MAGAZINE illustrates the time it takes for specific consumer electronics to drop in price (vertical scale) and penetrate the US market (depth).

1
MEDAL EXCHANGE
John Grimwade
An exercise in demystification, Grimwade's MEDAL EXCHANGE explores the correlation — or lack thereof — between a country's overall wealth and its international sporting success (measured in number of medals divided by GDP).

2
MINE'S BIGGER
John Grimwade
The title says it all. In their race to scrape the sky and build the world's tallest building, nations vie for the highest vanity structures. From Old World to New, MINE'S BIGGER delivers a handy score card for the next game of Top Trumps.

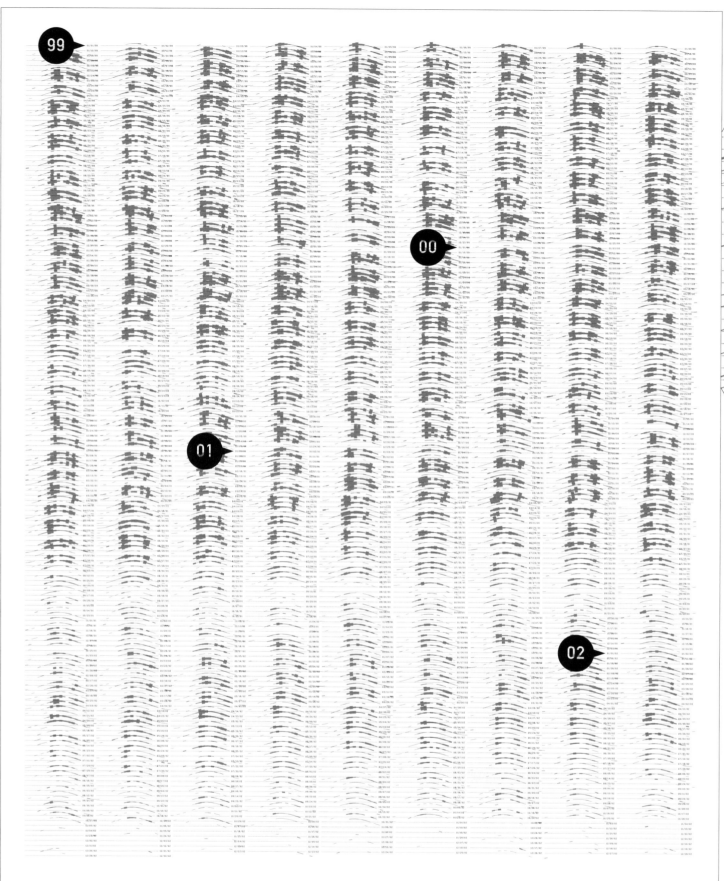

**FLOCKING
DIPLOMATS NYC
1999 – 2002**

// VIOLATIONS/HOUR

Parking Violations by Diplomats / Hour in 1999 to
2002 in New York City. The violations are plotted in
relation to the sun-position as seen from Central
Park (LATITUDE 40° 47' N / LONGITUDE 73° 58' W).

ANNUAL TOTALS (YEAR: TOTAL (MAX / DATE)

1999: 42.542 (65 / 09-24) -- Security Council /
Fifty-fourth Year, 4048th Meeting, Small Arms.
Friday, 24 September 1999, 9.30 a.m.

2000: 38.338 (62 / 02-24) -- Security Council /
Fifty-fifth Year, 4104th Meeting, The situation
concerning the Democratic Republic of the Congo.
Thursday, 24 February 2000, 11.30 a.m.

2001: 25.390 (56 / 02-12) -- Security Council /
Fifty-sixth Year, 4276th Meeting, The situation
along the borders of Guinea, Liberia, Sierra Leone.
Monday, 12 February 2001, 3 p.m.

2002: 12.703 (33 / 04-23) -- Security Council /
Fifty-seventh year, 4517th Meeting, The situation
in Angola. Tuesday, 23 April 2002, 10.30 a.m.

SOURCES

- Based on data from: Ray Fisman and Edward Miguel,
  "Corruption, Norms and Legal Enforcement: Evidence
  from Diplomatic Parking Tickets", forthcoming,
  December 2007, Journal of Political Economy.
- Daylight Saving Time: http://sunearth.gsfc.nasa.gov/
  eclipse/SEhelp/daylightsaving.html
- Sun-position (method of calculation): http://answers.
  google.com/answers/threadview?id=782886 (L. Flores)
- Time of sunrise and dawn: http://aa.usno.navy.mil/
  data/docs/RS_OneYear.php
- New York City Department of Finance

DATA MINING / SCRIPTING / DESIGN

Catalogtree, january 2008

printed at Plaatsmaken, Arnhem

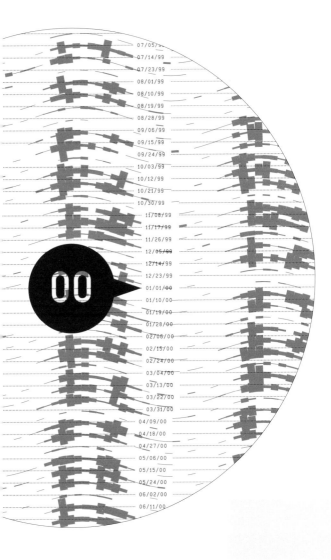

1
FLOCKING DIPLOMATS 1
Catalogtree
/ › PP. 94, 168, 224 / A different representation of rampant illegal parking practices among diplomatic staff in New York City; FLOCKING DIPLOMATS anchors their collective parking violations (registered between 1998 and 2005) in the metropolitan landscape.
Of all 143,702 violations committed during this particular period, 141,369 were suitable for geocoding, resulting in 16,355 unique locations. / Geocoding: Lutj Issler, Aachen, Germany / Thanks to Ray Fisman and Edward Miguel for kindly permitting us to use their data /

2
GLOCAL SIMILARITY MAP
Jer Thorp
Similarity maps illustrate the complex relationships that exist between a single image and the rest of the Glocal image pool. Starting from one central image (the seed), compositionally similar pictures are connected by a series of lines. This in turn triggers a second "generation" of related images, resulting in more and more branches radiating away from the central seed. / Glocal Project artists: M. Simon Levin, Sylvia Grace Borda, and Jer Thorp / The Glocal Project was a residency at the Surrey Art Gallery's TechLab.a /

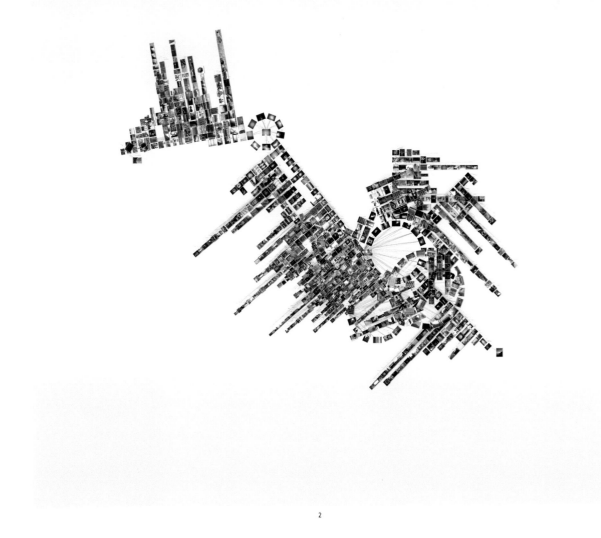

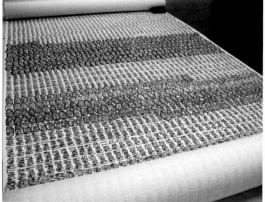

MAPPING TIME BASED ON GENEALOGY
AND HISTORICAL STUDY
COLORING STAGE
Haohao Huang

Haohao Huang's MAPPING TIME offers cryptic insights into a national and family history — and the artist's own place within it. Based on an extensive study of past events and genealogy, Huang's 25-metre scroll of codified history is a labour of love and journey back in time that covers the entire floor.

Juxtaposing landmark events in politics, war and the natural environment with his own personal heritage, the artist visualises pertinent facts on the timeline in painted colours and handwritten numbers, with cold shades indicating "official" facts and warmer colours alluding to personal events.

1
LIFETIME
Kerstin Ballies
Life is short and linear — no matter how
hard we try, we cannot relive those fleeting
moments. So how do we spend those long
mundane stretches between birthdays, vaca-
tions and public holidays? LIFETIME splits the
average German lifespan into 847 months
(or sheets of paper), colour-coded by activity
to visualise the more mundane, and probably
no less enjoyable aspects of our lives.

2
AT RANDOM?
NETWORKS AND CROSS-POLLINATIONS
LUST
AT RANDOM? NETWORKS AND CROSS-POL-
LINATIONS focused on the workshop character of exhibitions to explore creativity's
non-linear nature and associative and unpredictable properties.   A prime example
of "work in progress" and interdisciplinary
cross-fertilisation, Lust's paper exhibit invited
artists and visitors alike to get involved. To
this end, all of the paper required before
and during the exhibition — 80,000 sheets
in total — received a re-invented Iris print
and became a dwindling in-gallery paper
sculpture.   Besides all posters, invitations
and gallery info material, the paper was also
used for the exhibition catalogue — printed
by the visitors themselves on an adjacent
copier. / Photo: Nadine Stijns /

1

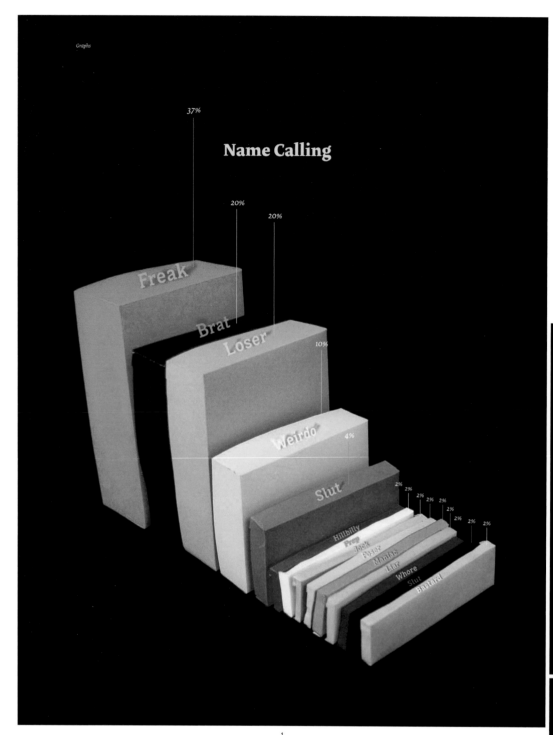

Graphs

Name Calling

37%

20%

20%

10%

4%

2% 2% 2% 2% 2% 2% 2% 2%

Freak

Brat

Loser

Weirdo

Slut

Hillbilly
Prep
Jock
Poser
Maniac
Liar
Whore
Slut
Bastard

1

Graphs

Swear Words

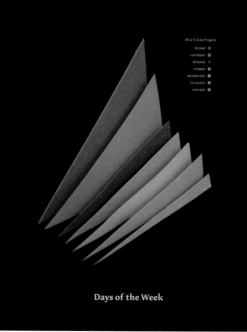

Most To Least Frequent
FRIDAY
SATURDAY
MONDAY
SUNDAY
WEDNESDAY
THURSDAY
TUESDAY

Days of the Week

1
DEAR GRETCHEN,
Gretchen Nash
DEAR GRETCHEN, investigates almost 200
letters tucked away and forgotten since the
artist's childhood. In this confrontation with
her former self, Nash categorises all missives
by word and phrase frequency, sender, date
and personal reflections.

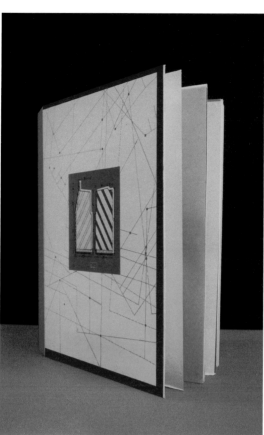

2
POP-UP BOOK
Mariano Sidoni
From 2D to 3D and back again, this pop-up book translates data to less predictable shapes than tried and tested bars or charts. Sidoni's objective was an atmospheric/emotional analysis of his big screen favourite ARTIFICIAL INTELLIGENCE, brought to life in a range of complex paper models.

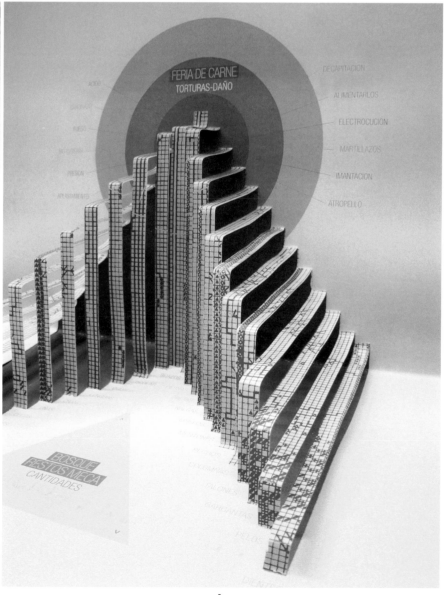

DATACIRCLES

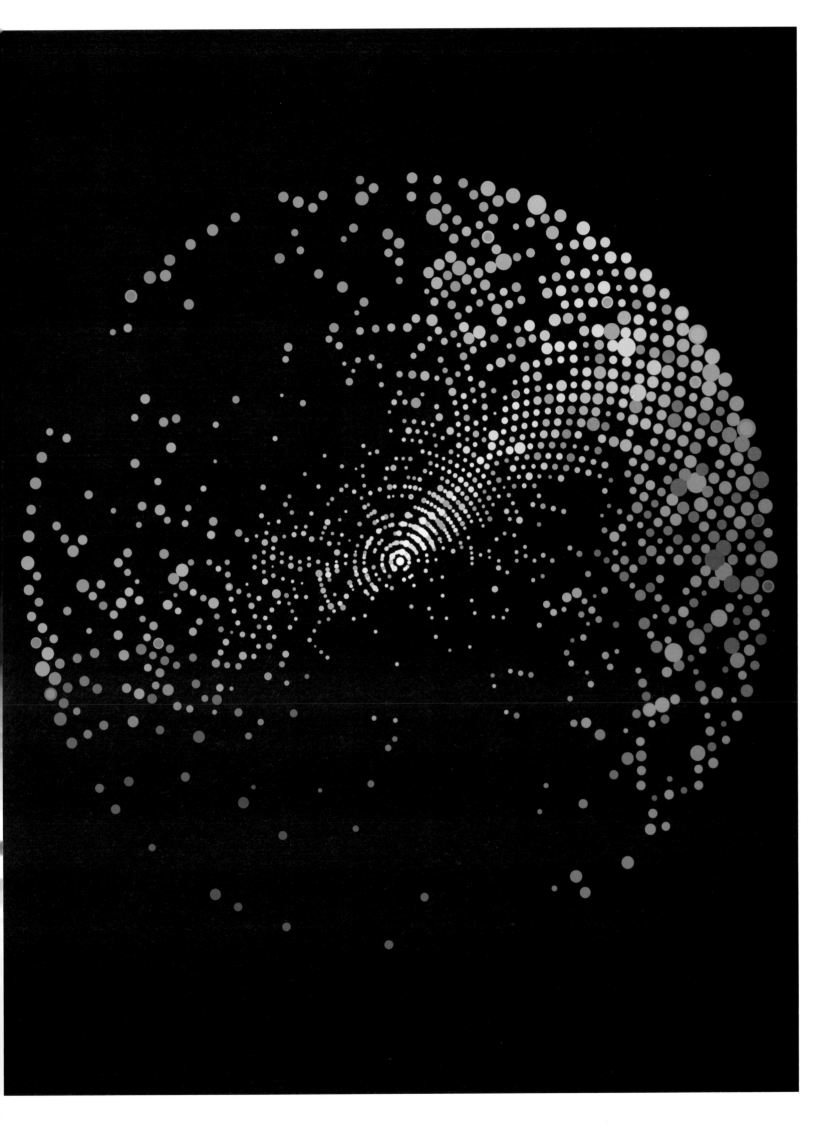

A circle represents a whole. Slicing it into parts by moving outwards from the center, we get shares of that entity. That's a piece of cake. Because this principle is so easy to understand, the pie chart has become widely used for displaying fractions and percentages. This chapter however, has more to offer than pie charts in their typical variations. We also see clever use of concentric grids and other circular arrangements. A well-rounded affair.

•

Circles may not have the best standing in contemporary information visualization due to their dull incarnation – the ubiquitous pie chart. Often crudely rendered in Microsoft Excel, pie charts are not only associated with regional managers presenting boring sales projections, they are also regarded as a poor visualization method for displaying information because it is harder to compare areas than lengths (as in a bar chart, for example). Aesthetically however, the circle is an irresistible asset in the designer's repertoire. Its perfect rotundity and unique geometry make it the most

PREVIOUS PAGE
ADOBE KULER COMMUNITY PULSE
stamen
COMMUNITY PULSE visualizes preferred color schemes on Adobe KULER, a web-hosted application for color-theme generation.

fascinating of all shapes. It seems that designers are fighting hard to re-establish the reputation of their favorite. As if to prove that a circle has more potential than ending up as a pie chart, we see numerous projects using nifty circular arrangements that go far beyond splitting a whole into slices.

Design studio Stamen decided on a concentric array to visualize the popularity of colors. /see ›P.81/ Thanks to the spherical layout, much more information than just the frequency of color use is conveyed. It also shows which colors are complimentary (those opposite) and which have the same saturation (those which are equidistant to the centre). The round shape in *Germany's Top 20* /1/ was obviously chosen as a visual reference to the topic: record sales. These illustrations however, show that the circle is capable of more than just looking like a vinyl record. A polar area diagram – with sectors of equal angle but different extensions from the centre – indicates when a song was in the charts and how successful it was in each month. This makes it easy to spot if an artist was popular throughout the year, or just produced summer hits.

When it comes to representation of time, circular arrangements are very familiar to us. At least, they were in pre-digital times, when a clock ticked round and round in a circle. Maybe Rodrigo Machado had that in mind when he visualized the crazy, complex plot of the movie *Adaptation*. /2/ By showing the action of the different characters on multiple layers of time, the intricate structure of the movie (and the wackiness of screenwriter Charlie Kaufman) becomes apparent. Illustrator Christophe Niemann on the other hand, likes it more straightforward. To demonstrate how bad his dreams are, he chose the much-berated pie chart /3/ in its most simplistic form. He proves that it can indeed be charming, at least if done with water-color and a sense of humor.

1
GERMANY'S TOP 20
Christopher Adjei
& Nils Holland-Cunz
/›P.89/

2
ADAPTATION — INADAPTADO
Rodrigo Machado
/›P.98/

3
I HAVE A DREAM
Christoph Niemann
/›P.85/

1
LIBERTÉ EGALITÉ FRATERNITÉ
Xavier Barrade
LIBERTÉ EGALITÉ FRATERNITÉ replaces well-worn stereotypes with pie charts to expose popular misconceptions about France and its political system.

2
I HAVE A DREAM
Christoph Niemann
/ ›P. 107 /

liberté   égalité   fraternité

1

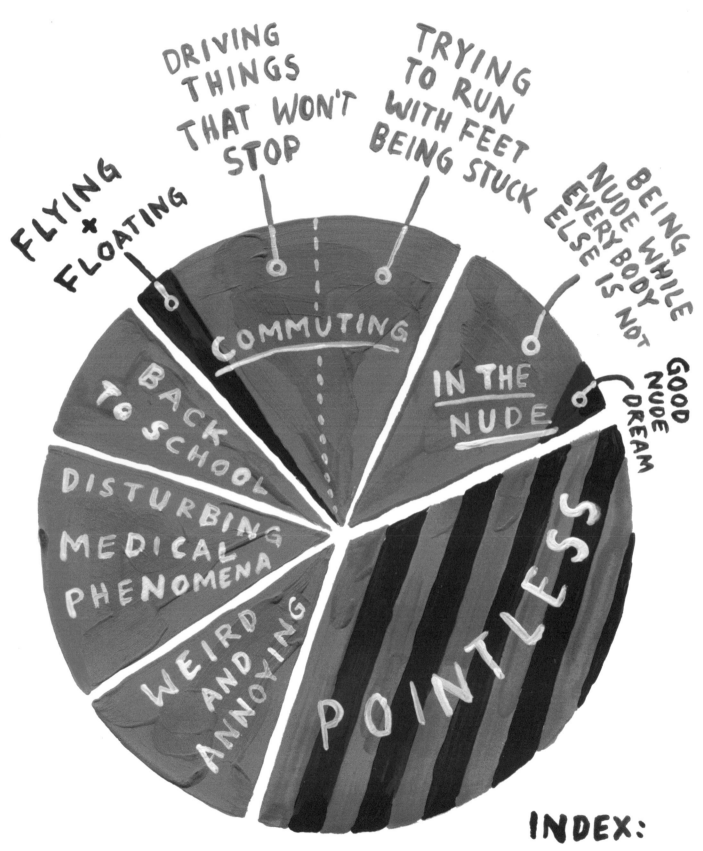

1
LONDON (ETHNI)CITY
Matt Willey
An A1 poster to celebrate London's cultural diversity, its unique and vibrant ethnic mix, using only two colors.

2
LINAGE OF SIN IN THE BIBLE
Anna Filipova
Anna Filipova's diagram provides a graphic representation of time — measured in sin. From the biblical "original" to latter day saints and sinners, her work explores the correlation between longevity and wrongdoings among characters of the bible. While lifespan decreases from Adam to Moses, sin appears to be on the rise.

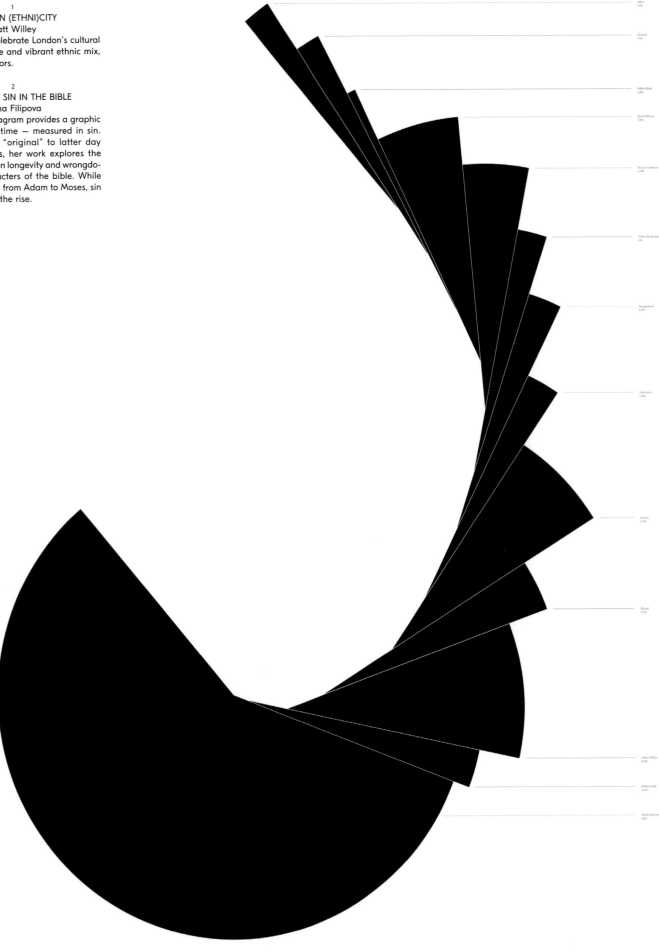

London is unique in it's great cultural mix, it's ethnic diversity. It is what makes this city so vibrant, so vital, so wonderful.

LINAGE OF SIN IN THE BIBLE

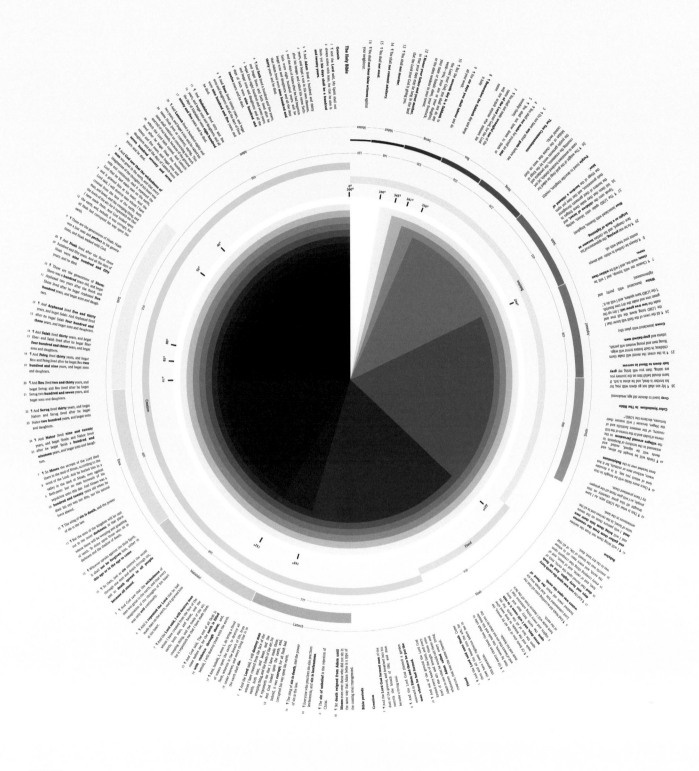

Value of age | sin

| Noah 950 years | Adam 930 years | Set 912 years | Enos 905 years | Mahalalel 895 years | Lamech 777 years | Shem 600 years | Arphaxad 438 years |

| Salah 433 years | Peleg 239 years | Reu 236 years | Serug 230 years | Nahor 148 years | Moses 120 years |

Historic periods

Creation

Flood

Babylon

Value of sin

+ −

DINING

TWO THOUSAND AND EIGHT

Selected findings from meals at 81 restaurants, 13 homes and four events.

NEW YORK DINING OUT WITH COMPANY

140

LEAST KOSHER MEAL

MOMOFUKU SSAM

WHOLE PORK BUTT WITH OYSTERS

SOCIAL MEALS BY WEEK

JAN — DEC

TAKAHACHI, AVE A (15), TAKAHACHI, DUANE ST (8), EDWARD'S (5), LIL' FRANKIES (5), SPRING ST NATURAL (5), BARRIO CHINO (4), LES HALLES (4), RUBY'S (4), SPITZER'S CORNER (4), BACK FORTY (3), CHIPOTLE (3), HOME (3), MEXICAN RADIO (3), PRUNE (3), WARREN'S HOUSE (3), AMADOR & SARA'S HOUSE (2), DO HWA (2), DRESSLER (2), EL PORTAL (2), JENN & JENN'S HOUSE (2), LOBO (2), MOLÉ (2), PINCHÉ TAQUERIA (2), AURORA (1), BAR TABAC (1), BEDOUIN TENT (1), BLACK MOUNTAIN WINEHOUSE (1), BLAUE GANS (1), BLUE RIBBON, 5TH AVE (1), BLUE RIBBON, SOHO (1), BREAD (1), BRICK LANE (1), CABRERA (1), CORNER BISTRO (1), DIM SUM GO GO (1), FAMIGLIA PIZZERIA (1), FESTIVAL MEXICANO (1), FETTE SAU (1), GORDON RAMSAY AT THE LONDON (1), HANA'S MOTHER'S HOUSE (1), HILL COUNTRY (1), HUNDRED ACRES (1), IKK (1), IN VINO (1), ISABELLA'S OVEN PIZZERIA(1), JACQUES (1), JEAN GEORGES (1), LA FALAPA (1), LI HUA (1), LITTLE GIANT (1), LOVELY DAY (1), LUCKY STRIKE (1), LURE (1), MAGGIE'S HOUSE (1), MAT HOUSE (1), MARIANA & GLENN'S HOUSE (1), MAS FARMHOUSE (1), MATSURI (1), MAX (1), MOMOFUKU NOODLE BAR (1), MOMOFUKU SSAM (1), MOTTSU (1), NHA TRANG I (1), NHA TRANG 2 (1), PACIFICO (1), PEASANT (1), PERSIMMON (1), SARAH'S HOUSE (1), SOBA NIPPON (1), SOBA-YA (1), SPLASHLIGHT STUDIOS CAFETERIA (1), SUSHI YASUDA (1), SUPPER (1), TACO BITE (1), 'WICHCRAFT (1)

MEALS COOKED AT HOME

17

LEAST EXPECTED MENU ITEM

FLYING FISH

PRESENTED WITH WINGS

MOST AMBITIOUS COOKING EXPERIMENT

SOUS VIDE SALMON

SOCIAL MEALS BY TYPE

HOME COOKED 28%
OTHER ASIAN
VARIOUS 7%
ITALIAN 7%
MEXICAN
JAPANESE
AMERICAN 26%

CULINARY HIGHLIGHTS

FUGU, FROG LEGS & GOAT

AT TAKAHACHI, JEAN GEORGES AND PIERRE'S IN TAMARIU

NYC STREET HOT DOGS

ONE

AT LAFAYETTE & CANAL

MOST ILLICIT-SEEMING FOODSTUFF

MIRACLE FRUIT

SYNSEPALUM DULCIFICUM

DRINKING

TWO THOUSAND AND EIGHT

Regarding the beverages consumed at 73 restaurants, 52 bars, 25 homes, seven events and two offices.

DRINKS ENJOYED WITH COMPANY

573

BLOODY MARYS

SEVEN

SOCIAL DRINKS BY WEEK

JAN — DEC

STELLA ARTOIS (170.5), RED WINE (64.5), ASSORTED BEERS (56.5), SIERRA NEVADA PALE ALE (23.5), MARGARITA (23), SAPPORO (22.5), SAKE (20), GUINNESS (16), ASAHI (14), CORONA (14), BROOKLYN LAGER (13), HOEGAARDEN (13), SIERRA NEVADA ESB (12.5), WHITE WINE (11), DOS EQUIS (9), NEGRA MODELO (9), BLOODY MARY (7), JAMESON (6), NEWCASTLE (6), PEAK ORGANIC NUT BROWN ALE (6), PERONI (6), BLUE POINT TOASTED LAGER (5), BROOKLYN IPA (5), DESSERT WINE (4.5), BECK'S (4), CHAMPAGNE (4), LAGUANITAS IPA (4), VODKA BEVERAGES (4), TSING TAO (3.5), ASSORTED WHISKEYS (3), BROOKLYN WINTER ALE (3), DARK AND STORMY (3), ESTRELLA DAM (3), GROLSCH (3), PACIFICO (3), PRESIDENTE (3), ANCHOR LIBERTY ALE (2), CAIPIRINHA (2), BLUE MOON (2), BLUE POINT SUMMER ALE (2), BUDWEISER (2), CENTURION (2), CUTTHROAT PALE ALE (2), MOJITO (2), MOSCOW MULE (2), SAM ADAMS (2), SIX POINTS IPA (2), SIX POINTS WHEAT BEER (2), STONE ARROGANT BASTARD (2), TEQUILA COCKTAILS (2), GIN COCKTAIL (1), GRAPPA (1), SPARKLING WINE (1), TEQUILA SHOT (1), ADAM'S WASABI-INFUSED VODKA (1)

BEER BRANDS

ASSORTED 50%
BROOKLYN 5%
SAPPORO 6%
SIERRA NEVADA
STELLA 30%

FAVORITE BEER

SIERRA NEVADA ESB

STRANGEST COCKTAIL

FIG, MINT & TEQUILA

COURTESY OF CHARLIE

BEERS ENJOYED SOCIALLY

408

THANKSGIVING TEQUILA SHOTS

ONE

DISCLAIMER

THE FACULTY-IMPAIRING QUALITIES OF ALCOHOL MAKE THESE FIGURES IMPOSSIBLE TO COLLECT WITH COMPLETE CONFIDENCE.

PLEASE ASSUME A MARGIN OF ERROR OF PLUS OR MINUS TWO PERCENT FOR ALL DRINKING STATISTICS.

DRINK OF THE YEAR

STELLA ARTOIS

WITH ELISE AT PUFFY'S

BEER PURCHASED FOR BIRTHDAY

2.9

GALLONS OF ASAHI

MUSIC

TWO THOUSAND AND EIGHT

The verdict on 12 months of listening habits as recorded at last.fm/user/feltron.

ITUNES TRACKS PLAYED

33,817

UP 34% FROM 2007

ARTISTS PLAYED

511

SONGS PLAYED BY WEEK

TOP 10 ARTISTS | OTHER ARTISTS

CDS PURCHASED

2

DIPLO & SANTOGOLD
DEERHUNTER

ALBUMS DOWNLOADED

46

BLEEP (22)
OTHER MUSIC (13)
AMAZON (6)
ITUNES (5)

GENRE DISTRIBUTION OF TOP 100 ARTISTS

ELECTRONIC 23%
POST-ROCK 8%
HIP-HOP 15%
INDIE 14%
IDM 9%
ALL OTHER 26%
EXPERIMENTAL 5%

TRACKS PLAYED BY TOP 10 ARTISTS

BRADFORD COX
(ATLAS SOUND & DEERHUNTER) 36%
THE NOTWIST
VAMPIRE WEEKEND 4%
THOM YORKE
ETANA
ELLIOTT SMITH
FLYING LOTUS
DAEDELUS
RADIOHEAD 15%

BEST ALBUM

ATLAS SOUND

"LET THE BLIND LEAD THOSE WHO CAN SEE BUT CANNOT FEEL"

BEST MIXTAPE

DIPLO & SANTOGOLD

"TOP RANKING MIXTAPE"

CONCERTS ATTENDED

8

DEERHUNTER
GLEN EDEN QUAY
LE LOUP/RUBY SUNS
THE NOTWIST
SIGUR RÖS
VAMPIRE WEEKEND
WEST DAKOTA (TWICE)

NIGHTS DJ'D

EIGHT

5X LAPTOP & 3X VINYL

READING

TWO THOUSAND AND EIGHT

A set of determinations drawn from the reading of 2,440 book and 1,079 magazine pages.

BOOKS READ (WHOLLY OR PARTIALLY)

FOURTEEN

ABSURDISTAN (333 PAGES), THE BLACK SWAN (20 PAGES), COLLECTIONS OF NOTHING (76 PAGES), DRY STOREROOM NO. 1 (16 PAGES), DOWN AND OUT IN PARIS AND LONDON (228 PAGES), THE END OF OIL (270 PAGES), FROM HEAVEN LAKE (192 PAGES), IN DEFENSE OF FOOD (205 PAGES), IN PATAGONIA (199 PAGES), IT MUST'VE BEEN SOMETHING I ATE (54 PAGES), KING RAT (479 PAGES), THE MARTIAN CHRONICLES (182 PAGES), THE MEZZANINE (144 PAGES), THE VILLAGE UNDER THE SEA (60 PAGES)

NEW YORKER READING BY ISSUE

MAGAZINES READ

76

FAST COMPANY (26 PAGES), GOOD (35 PAGES), NEW YORK (64 PAGES), NEW YORKER (455 PAGES), NY TIMES MAGAZINE (9 PAGES), WIRED (46 PAGES)

JAN — DEC

BEST FICTION

THE MEZZANINE

BY NICHOLSON BAKER

BEST NON-FICTION

FROM HEAVEN LAKE

BY VIKRAM SETH

PHOTOS

TWO THOUSAND AND EIGHT

A summary of photographic activity with four cameras and online at flickr.com/photos/feltron.

PHOTOGRAPHS TAKEN

1,468

CANON EOS 5D (665 PHOTOS), CANON 30D70 12 (603 PHOTOS), LEICA M6 (178 PHOTOS), BLACKBIRD FLY (20 PHOTOS)

LAST PHOTO OF THE YEAR

THE GOLDEN GATE BRIDGE

DECEMBER 29, 2008

FLICKR FAVORITES

TYPE & DESIGN 33%
CARS, TRAINS & OTHER VEHICLES
ARCHITECTURE 6%
OBJECTS 4%
PEOPLE 17%
CATS, DINOSAURS & ANIMALS 8%
FOOD, ASTRONOMY & ALL ELSE 8%
OUTDOORS 16%

DIGITAL PHOTOS BY WEEK

JAN — DEC

PHOTOS POSTED TO FLICKR

9%

124 PHOTOS & 6 VIDEOS

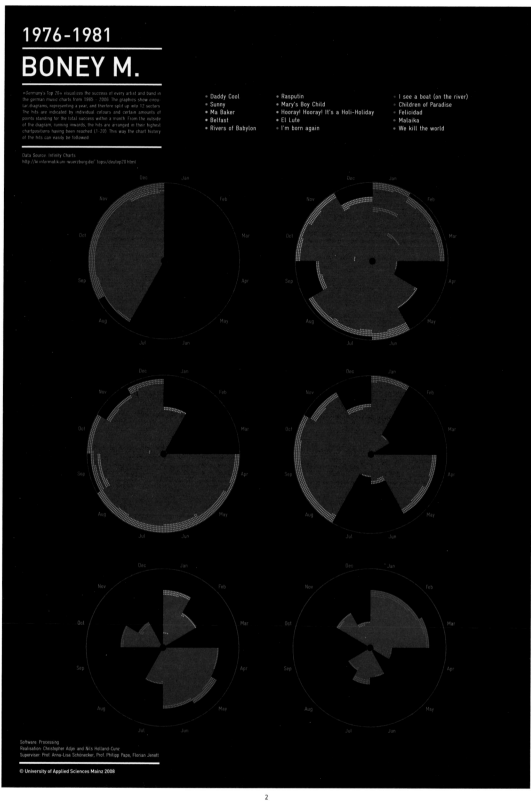

1976-1981
BONEY M.

»Germany's Top 20« visualizes the success of every artist and band in the german music charts from 1965 - 2006. The graphics show circular diagrams, representing a year, and therfore split up into 12 sectors. The hits are indicated by individual colours and certain amounts of points standing for the total success within a month. From the outside of the diagram, running inwards, the hits are arranged in their highest chartpositions having been reached (1-20). This way the chart history of the hits can easily be followed.

Data Source: Infinity Charts
http://ai.informatik.uni-wuerzburg.de/~topsi/deutop20.html

- Daddy Cool
- Sunny
- Ma Baker
- Belfast
- Rivers of Babylon
- Rasputin
- Mary's Boy Child
- Hooray! Hooray! It's a Holi-Holiday
- El Lute
- I'm born again
- I see a boat (on the river)
- Children of Paradise
- Felicidad
- Malaika
- We kill the world

Software: Processing
Realisation: Christopher Adjei and Nils Holland-Cunz
Superviser: Prof. Anna-Lisa Schönecker, Prof. Philipp Pape, Florian Jenett

© University of Applied Sciences Mainz 2008

2

FELTRON 2008 ANNUAL REPORT
Nicholas Felton

/›PP. 198, 199/ A personal tradition and annual ritual, US data maven and information graphic designer Nicholas Felton maps out his past in a series of annual reports. Akin to an intimate CV, this smart exercise in navel gazing anchors deliberately non-work related high and lowlights in a personal timeline and NYC map. A rich collection of graphs that reflect the year's travel, photography, music, food, drink and reading; his FELTRON 2008 ANNUAL REPORT juxtaposes private events and select public landmarks. The result is a rich collation of surprising, astute insights that dissect the vagaries of Felton's existence — and the world around him.

2

GERMANY'S TOP 20
Christopher Adjei and
Nils Holland-Cunz

GERMANY'S TOP 20 records the success of every artist or band that graced the German music charts between 1965—2006. Each circular diagram, or year, is split into 12 segments. Separate colours indicate hits, while points keep tab of each month's success. Hits are arranged from the outside in, according to their highest chart position. / Created at University of Applied Sciences Mainz / Mentoring: Prof. Philipp Pape, Prof. Anna-Lisa Schönecker, Florian Jenett (Processing) / Datasource by Markus Tolksdorf, Infinity Charts /

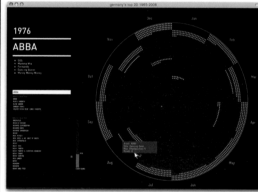

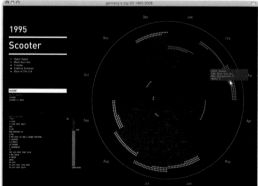

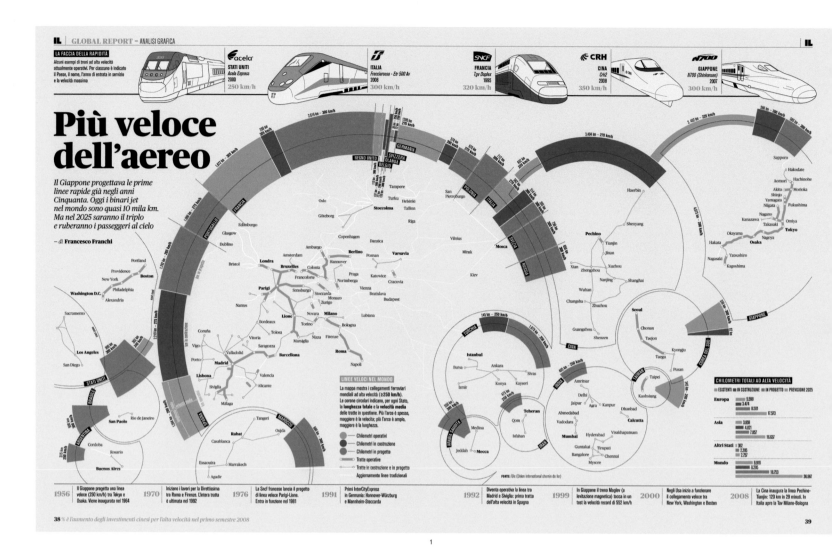

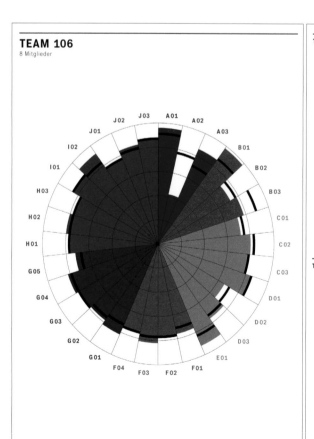

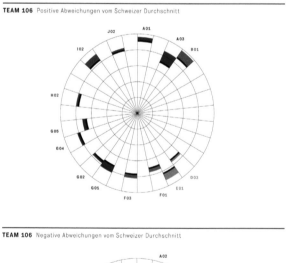

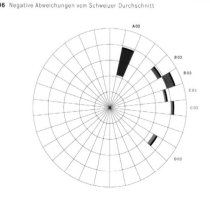

1
PIÙ VELOCE DELL'AEREO
Francesco Franchi
/›P.207/ From TGV to Shinkansen — across the globe, bullet trains reach speeds of up to 350 km/h. This image shows the rail lines in operation, under construction and being planned for each continent (including total length and average speed).

2
TEAM DIAGNOSTIC SURVEY
Hahn und Zimmermann
How do teams work and function? For this study, each team member was asked to evaluate 30 aspects of teamwork on a scale from one to five. Team averages are reflected in circular segments and may be compared to the Swiss average. The diagram also allows for analysis of positive and negative deviations from the norm.

3
WOMEN'S PHONE SOCIAL MAPS
Hahn und Zimmermann
This visualisation depicts the social network and communication habits of seven people. Coloured marks reveal their respective means of communication (face-to-face, phone, e-mail, mail, skype), while a cold-to-warm colour gradient defines the relationship with each communication partner.
/ Research project "Women's Phone" / Deutsche Telekom Laboratories / Management: Prof. Dr. Gesche Joost /

Women's Phone: **Social Maps**

Kommunikationsverhalten der Personen A–E

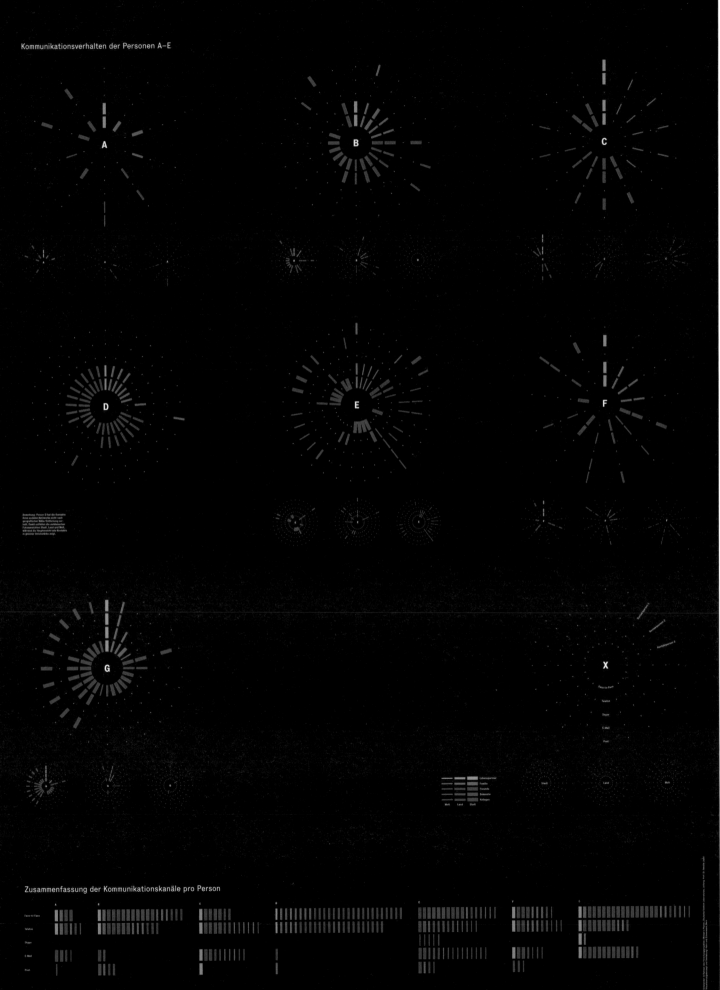

Zusammenfassung der Kommunikationskanäle pro Person

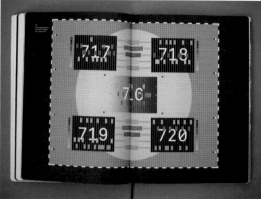

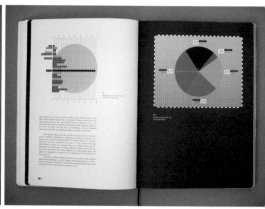

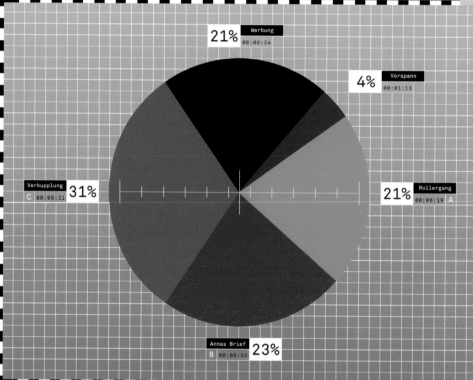

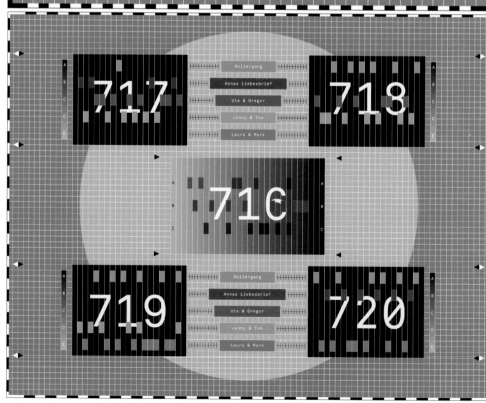

1
MONTAG — FREITAG 17:30,
ZUR ANALYSE VON SOAP OPERAS
Manuel Trüdinger
The medium is the message? "Monday —
Friday 5.30 pm, On the Analysis of Soap
Operas" employs test pattern aesthetics to
convey the (unwritten) rules of television.

2
UNSC/R
Piero Zagami
UNSC/R (United Nations Security Council
Resolutions) aims to structure and facilitate
access to decisions by the UN's executive
body. A welcome shortcut through the
dense information jungle for students and
researchers, the project applies information
design strategies to the Council's 1,700+
documents.

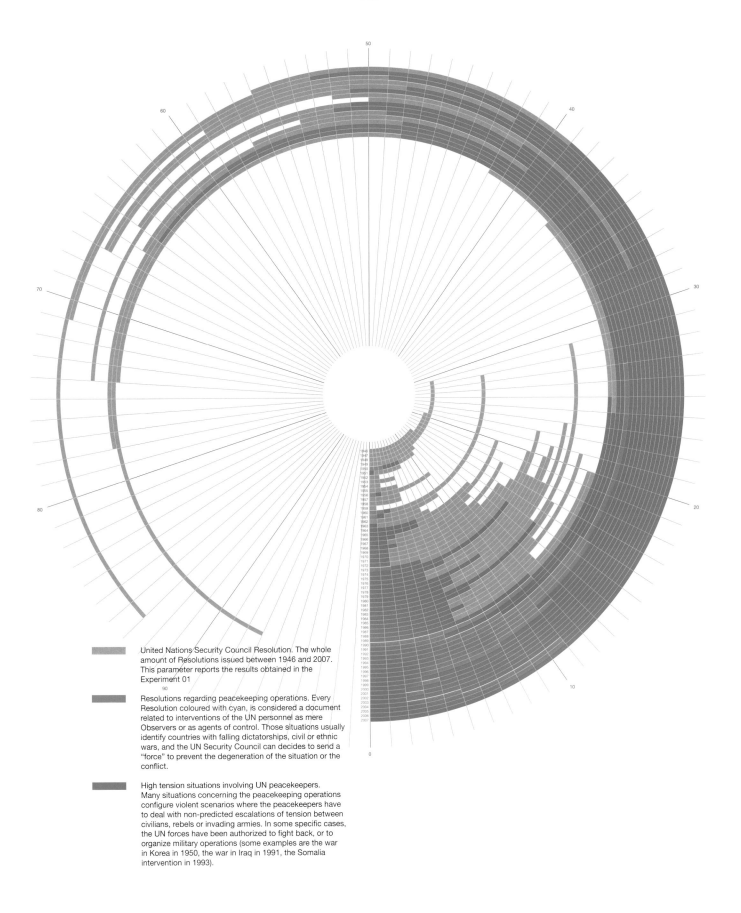

United Nations Security Council Resolution. The whole amount of Resolutions issued between 1946 and 2007. This parameter reports the results obtained in the Experiment 01

Resolutions regarding peacekeeping operations. Every Resolution coloured with cyan, is considered a document related to interventions of the UN personnel as mere Observers or as agents of control. Those situations usually identify countries with falling dictatorships, civil or ethnic wars, and the UN Security Council can decides to send a "force" to prevent the degeneration of the situation or the conflict.

High tension situations involving UN peacekeepers. Many situations concerning the peacekeeping operations configure violent scenarios where the peacekeepers have to deal with non-predicted escalations of tension between civilians, rebels or invading armies. In some specific cases, the UN forces have been authorized to fight back, or to organize military operations (some examples are the war in Korea in 1950, the war in Iraq in 1991, the Somalia intervention in 1993).

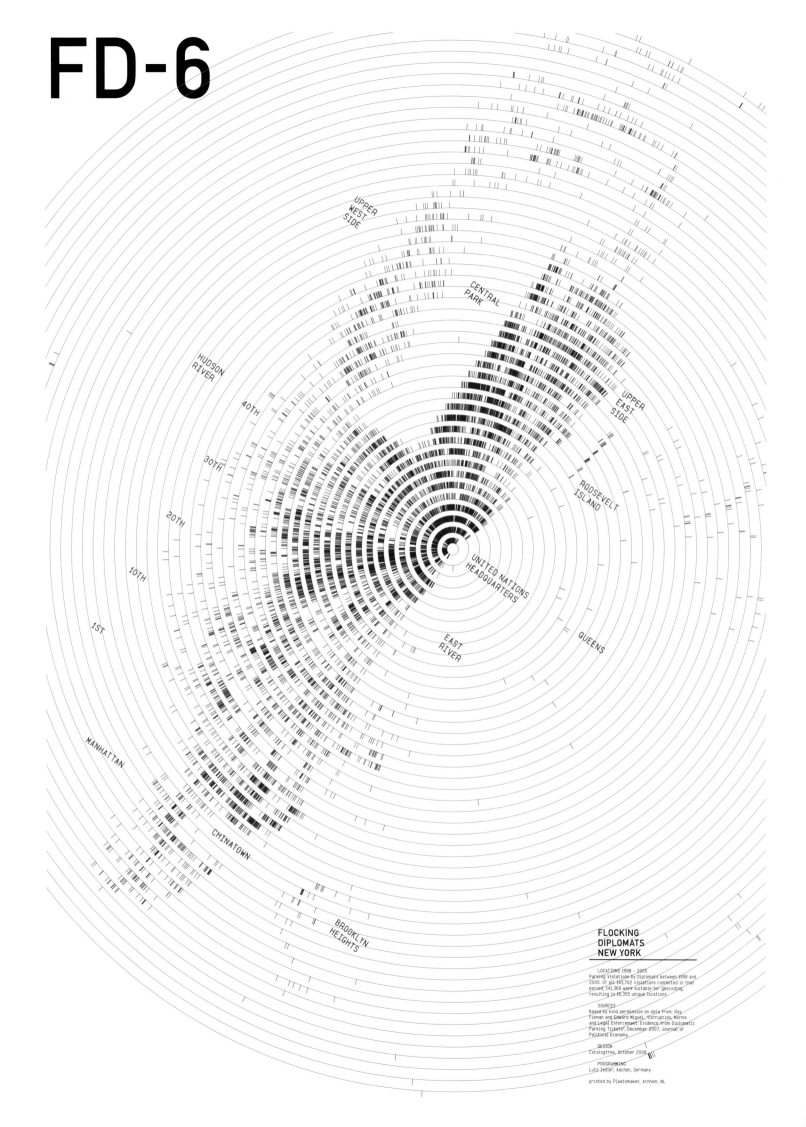

FD-6

UPPER
WEST
SIDE

CENTRAL
PARK

HUDSON
RIVER

40TH

UPPER
EAST
SIDE

30TH

20TH

ROOSEVELT
ISLAND

10TH

UNITED NATIONS
HEADQUARTERS

1ST

QUEENS

EAST
RIVER

MANHATTAN

CHINATOWN

BROOKLYN
HEIGHTS

**FLOCKING
DIPLOMATS
NEW YORK**

LOCATIONS 1998 - 2005
Parking violations by Diplomats between 1998 and
2005. Of all 143,702 violations committed in that
period, 141,369 were suitable for geocoding,
resulting in 16,355 unique locations.

SOURCES
Based by kind permission on data from: Ray
Fisman and Edward Miguel, "Corruption, Norms
and Legal Enforcement: Evidence from Diplomatic
Parking Tickets", December 2007, Journal of
Political Economy.

DESIGN
Catalogtree, October 2008

PROGRAMMING
Lutz Issler, Aachen, Germany

printed by Plaatsmaken, Arnhem, NL

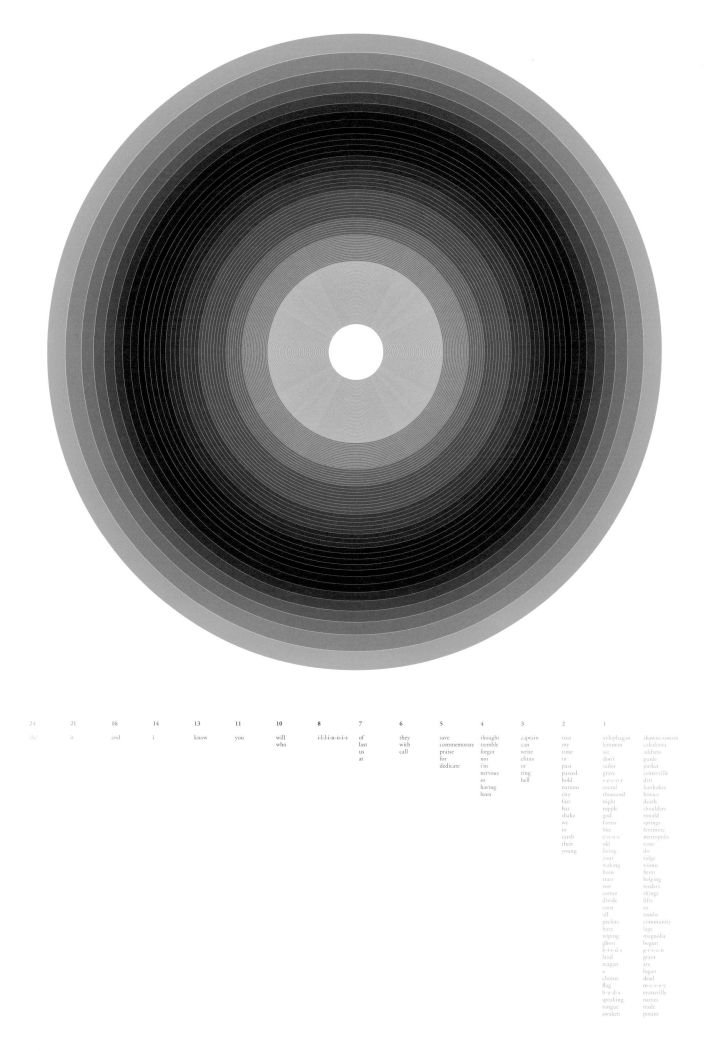

24	21	16	14	13	11	10	8	7	6	5	4	3	2	1	
the	it	and	i	know	you	will	i-l-l-i-n-o-i-s	of	they	save	thought	captain	rust	xylophagan	shawne-townn
						who		last	with	commemorate	tremble	can	my	lemmon	caledonia
								us	call	praise	forgot	write	time	see	address
								at		for	not	clitus	in	don't	guide
										dedicate	i'm	or	past	sailor	parker
											nervous	ring	passed	grave	centerville
											so	bell	hold	s-e-c-o-r	dirt
											having		nations	sound	kankakee
											been		city	thousand	horace
													fast	night	death
													has	topple	shoulders
													shake	god	ronald
													we	farms	springs
													to	bite	feminine
													earth	e-n-o-s	metropolis
													their	old	taste
													young	living	do
													sour		ridge
													waking		rooms
													horn		from
													starr		helping
													rest		reeders
													corner		things
													divide		lifts
													corn		ax
													all		tombs
													peelers		community
													have		lags
													wiping		magnolia
													ghost		begun
													b-i-r-d-s		g-r-e-e-n
													land		grant
													reagan		are
													a		logan
													chorus		dead
													flag		m-c-v-e-y
													b-u-d-a		evansville
													speaking		names
													tongue		trade
													awaken		potato

They Are Night Zombies!! They Are Neighbors!!
They Have Come Back from the Dead!! Ahhhh!

PREVIOUS PAGE (LEFT)
FLOCKING DIPLOMATS 6
Catalogtree
/›PP.168,224/

PREVIOUS PAGE (RIGHT)
ILLINOIS: VISUALIZING MUSIC
WORD USAGE CIRCLE 11
Jax de León
/›P.170/

1
WHEN WE FLY
Andrew van der Westhuyzen

Just a minute — in an age where flying has become almost a reflex, just another mode of transport, the overall numbers of flights in the air at any particular point in time has reached truly staggering proportions. According to the ACI (Airports Council International), in 2008, 4.874 billion passengers travelled by air on a total of 77 million flights.

This particular view of the aerial net that spans the earth is based on one-minute snapshots of the number of passengers and planes in the air at a given moment in time — little blips on the global radar that add up to an impressive whole. /Technical Director: Hugh Carrick-Allen, Collider/

2
NEU — WEGE ZUM FORTSCHRITT
Martin Gorka

*2008_*
global unique aircraft flights per minute

{*146*}

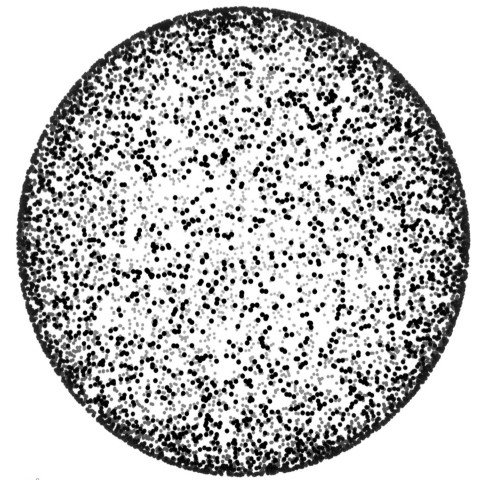

*2008_*
global passenger air traffic per minute.

{*9273*}

1

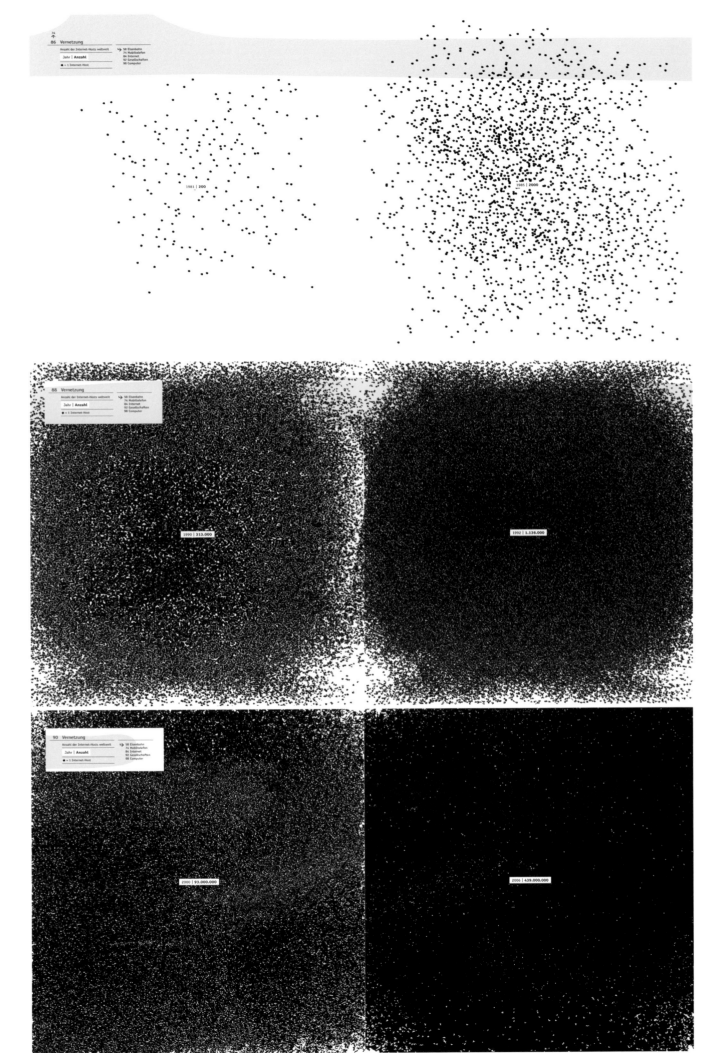

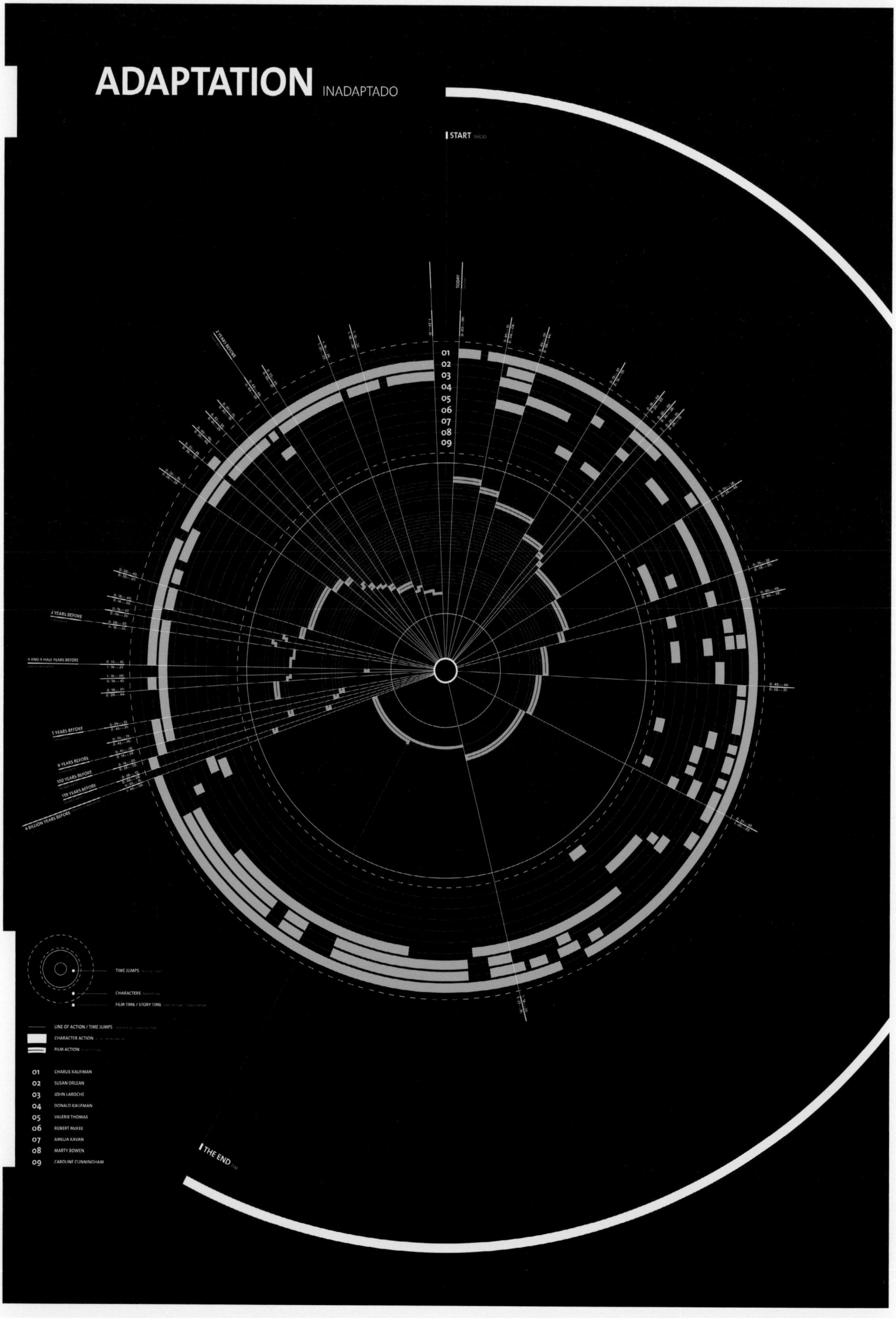

ADAPTATION INADAPTADO

START INICIO

TODAY

01
02
03
04
05
06
07
08
09

6 YEARS BEFORE

7 YEARS BEFORE

4 AND A HALF YEARS BEFORE

5 YEARS BEFORE

9 YEARS BEFORE

100 YEARS BEFORE

119 YEARS BEFORE

4 BILLION YEARS BEFORE

TIME JUMPS

CHARACTERS

FILM TIME / STORY TIME

LINE OF ACTION / TIME JUMPS

CHARACTER ACTION

FILM ACTION

01	CHARLIE KAUFMAN
02	SUSAN ORLEAN
03	JOHN LAROCHE
04	DONALD KAUFMAN
05	VALERIE THOMAS
06	ROBERT McKEE
07	AMELIA KAVAN
08	MARTY BOWEN
09	CAROLINE CUNNINGHAM

THE END FIN

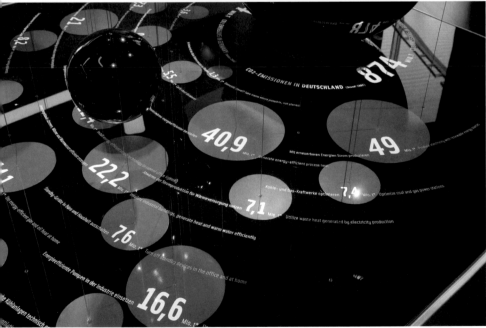

2

1
ADAPTATION — INADAPTADO
Rodrigo Machado
ADAPTATION (2002) as data: Rodrigo Machado's project transforms the film into an infographic. The resulting map shows the length of the film, the flashbacks and flash-forwards within the story, the time each character appears onscreen and the relationships between the protagonists.

2
LEVEL GREEN
ART+COM AG
Car manufacturer VW staged an exhibition on sustainability at their brand park in Wolfsburg. Deliberately hands-on, the show encourages visitors to get involved and find out more about what they can do to prevent climate change and its main culprit, the greenhouse gas carbon dioxide.   Here, a large sphere — representing Germany's combined CO_2 emissions — dissolves into a number of smaller plastic globules. Each of these bubbles indicates potential savings through for example, increased fuel efficiency or reduced meat consumption. Akin to symbolic shadows of the hovering spheres, a range of graphics at the sculpture's base put tangible numbers to these reduction measures.

ACP DONOR WHEEL
Joshua Kirsch
Commissioned by the Arts Council of Princeton, the ACP DONOR WHEEL is a permanent donor recognition sculpture for the Paul Robeson Center for the Arts in Princeton, New Jersey. The motorised disk displays approximately 2000 names, loosely grouped by alphabet. Visitors may press letters on an adjacent control panel to rotate the disk into position and highlight all corresponding names with white LED backlight. /2008/

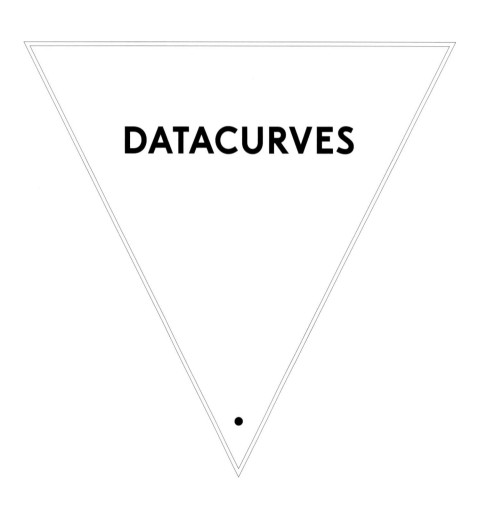

DATACURVES

When progressions over intervals of time are visualized, a line graph is often the diagram of choice. Stock market trends spring to mind when thinking about curved shapes, but the next pages show that they can be applied to various other topics. For example sound, which ultimately is a dense, chronological sequence of numerous individual data points.

•

In the wake of the worldwide financial crisis, the line chart – a classic in data visualization – experienced a revival. Representing developments of stock values and the overall economic climate, the downward-pointing curve has become an almost iconic symbol. A diagram like the one on the previous page looks threatening to us, although it is unclear what it is about. It is going down, it is alarm-red – it must be bad. Conditioned by a prevailing doctrine of growth, a simple curve like this makes us think of a crisis, although it could represent crime rates, CO_2 emissions, or HIV infections. All figures we would like to decrease.

Financial data however, does not always have to be presented in a typical line chart, as Anna Filipova shows. Because the credit crunch has hit many as surprisingly and heavily as an earthquake, she uses the Richter scale to visualize the movements of the stock markets.   /1/   The medium becomes the message. Adrien Segal's medium of choice is furniture. The young designer collected data about tidal movements as the basis for her lavish table.   /2/   Line charts were created as a blueprint for the design, the curves were then turned into steel and mounted in a walnut table frame. The resulting wavy sculpture transcends the underlying data set: without knowing what data has been used – without even knowing that any data has been used – the dynamic pattern suggests the theme.

A different kind of wave results when sound is visualized. Different volumes and frequencies form a curved shape. These can be turned into beautiful objects as well, as French design studio NOCC proves with their *Objects of Sound*.   /3/   Jorinde Voigt's *Symphonic Area Var. 4*   /4/   also deals with the visualization of sound, but the artist examines the structure of a musical piece, rather than its acoustic features. An intricate, alternative score emerges – a curved shape that resembles part of a helix. An association which might be not too far off: eventually we are looking at the DNA of the symphony.

An interesting question arises: how does a visualization change the way we perceive – or perform – music? In electronic music we can find some answers. Because it is created on computers or machines that have a graphical representation of the sound, because the musician is not only hearing the music, but also seeing it simultaneously (e.g. a beat pattern in a sequencer), it often sounds more "designed." Another example of how visualizations can deeply change behavior.

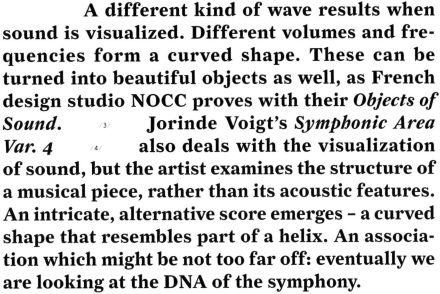

1
EXTINCT
Dongwoo Kim
/Dr George Amato, American Museum of Natural History, Sin
Kim, Sofia Kim, Bairon Garzon, Matt Muzard, Chun Wo Pat,
Alexa Nosal, Richard Reiss, Artist As Citizen, New York Times/

2
SLEEP AGONY CHART
Christoph Niemann
The suffering of those who toss and turn
at night: according to Christoph Niemann's
illustration, getting a good night's sleep is
actually a lot more complicated than one
might think.

3
STATISTICS STRIP IN THE EXHIBITION
"WORK. MEANING AND WORRY"
ART+COM AG
/Curating: Praxis für Ausstellungen und Theorie/Concept
and Design: ART+COM/

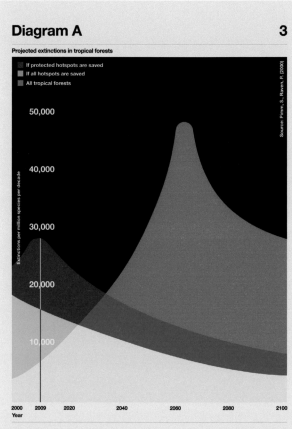

Diagram A
3

Projected extinctions in tropical forests

- If protected hotspots are saved
- If all hotspots are saved
- All tropical forests

Source: Pimm, S., Raven, P. (2000)

Extinctions per million species per decade

50,000

40,000

30,000

20,000

10,000

2000 2009 2020 2040 2060 2080 2100
Year

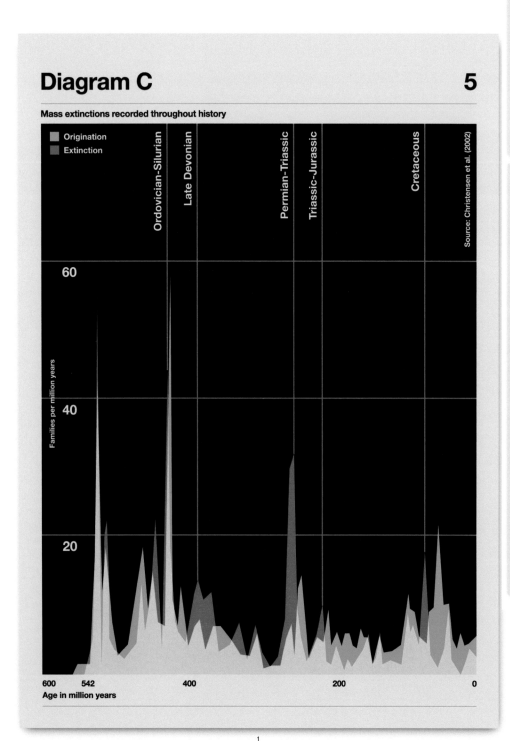

Diagram C
5

Mass extinctions recorded throughout history

- Origination
- Extinction

Ordovician-Silurian

Late Devonian

Permian-Triassic

Triassic-Jurassic

Cretaceous

Source: Christensen et al. (2002)

Families per million years

60

40

20

600 542 400 200 0
Age in million years

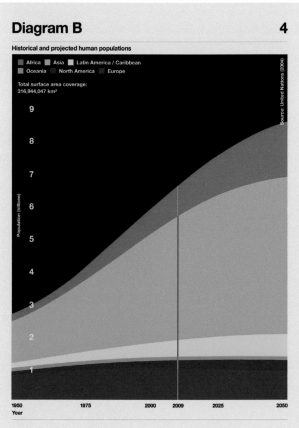

Diagram B
4

Historical and projected human populations

- Africa
- Asia
- Latin America / Caribbean
- Oceania
- North America
- Europe

Total surface area coverage:
316,944,047 km²

Source: United Nations (2004)

Population (billions)

9
8
7
6
5
4
3
2
1

1950 1975 2000 2009 2025 2050
Year

2

3

INDIA
PAKISTAN
1981-2009

1

NEW YORK YANKEES
NEW YORK METS
1984-2009

2

1
NYTIMES THREADS: INDIA & PAKISTAN
Jer Thorp
This graph charts the frequency of articles mentioning India and Pakistan in THE NEW YORK TIMES between 1981 and 2009. At the same time, the image exposes bias and weighting — darker lines denote prominent front-page placement, lighter lines indicate stories buried further back in the paper.

2
NYTIMES THREADS: YANKEES & METS
Jer Thorp
Akin to NYTIMES THREADS: INDIA & PAKI-STAN, this diagram reveals the frequency of references to the New York Yankees and New York Mets in THE NEW YORK TIMES between 1984 and 2009.

3
60 JAHRE BRD
EIN RUNDES JUBILÄUM
Golden Section Graphics
60 JAHRE BRD — EIN RUNDES JUBILÄUM celebrates the 60th anniversary of the Federal Republic of Germany with up-to-date information on economic and population data — and shows how far the country has come. /Katharina Erfurth/

Ein rundes Jubiläum

Am 23. Mai feiert die Bundesrepublik Deutschland Geburtstag.
Wir zeigen, wie sich die wichtigsten demografischen und ökonomischen Werte
seit der Gründung der Republik 1949 veränderten. Die Zahl der in Deutschland
lebenden Personen hat sich seitdem fast verdoppelt. Eines aber bleibt immer
gleich: Nur rund die Hälfte aller Deutschen erwirtschaftet unser
Bruttoinlandsprodukt, welches starken
Schwankungen unterliegt.

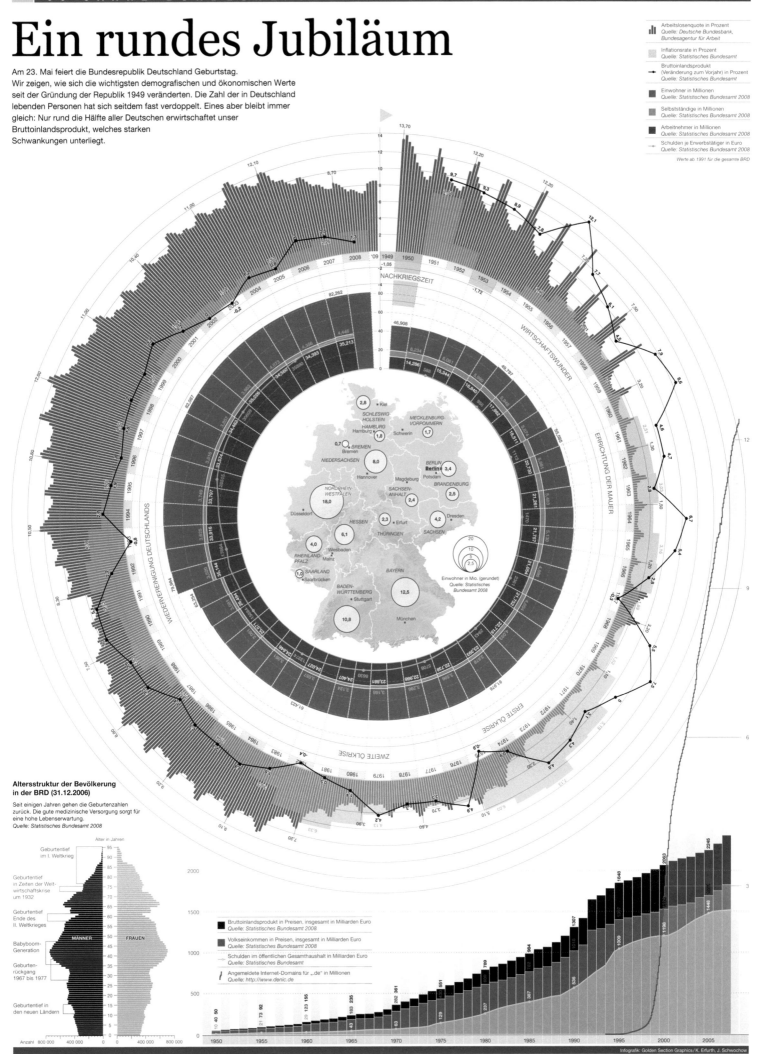

Altersstruktur der Bevölkerung
in der BRD (31.12.2006)

Seit einigen Jahren gehen die Geburtenzahlen
zurück. Die gute medizinische Versorgung sorgt für
eine hohe Lebenserwartung.
Quelle: Statistisches Bundesamt 2008

Infografik: Golden Section Graphics / K. Erfurth, J. Schwochow

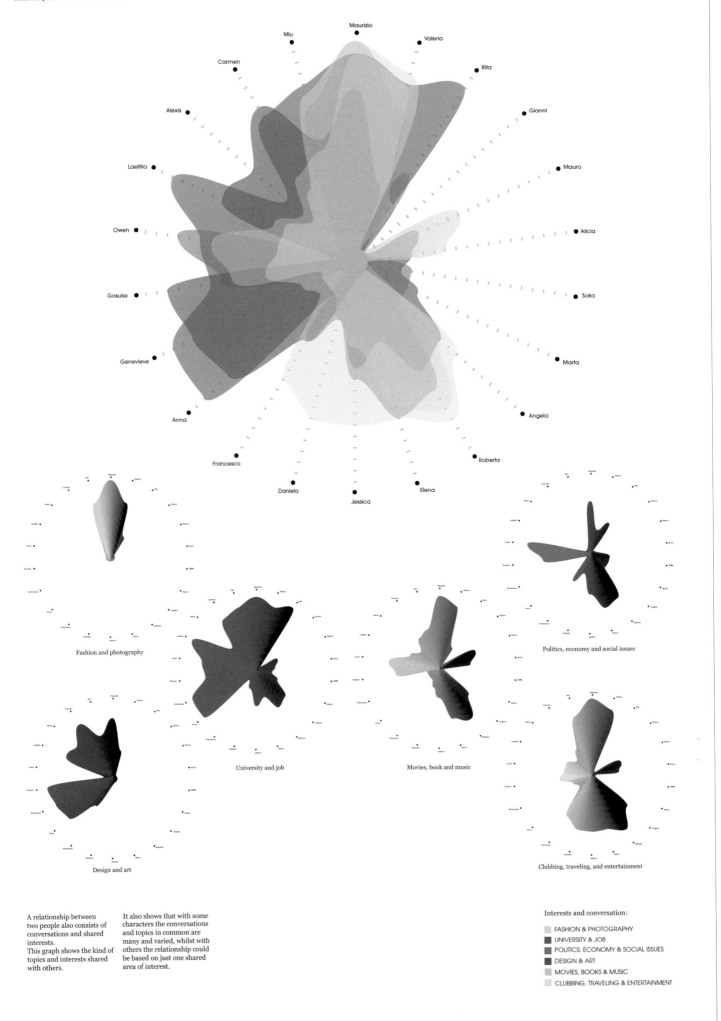

Fashion and photography

University and job

Movies, book and music

Politics, economy and social issues

Design and art

Clubbing, traveling, and entertainment

A relationship between two people also consists of conversations and shared interests.
This graph shows the kind of topics and interests shared with others.

It also shows that with some characters the conversations and topics in common are many and varied, whilst with others the relationship could be based on just one shared area of interest.

Interests and conversation:

- FASHION & PHOTOGRAPHY
- UNIVERSITY & JOB
- POLITICS, ECONOMY & SOCIAL ISSUES
- DESIGN & ART
- MOVIES, BOOKS & MUSIC
- CLUBBING, TRAVELING & ENTERTAINMENT

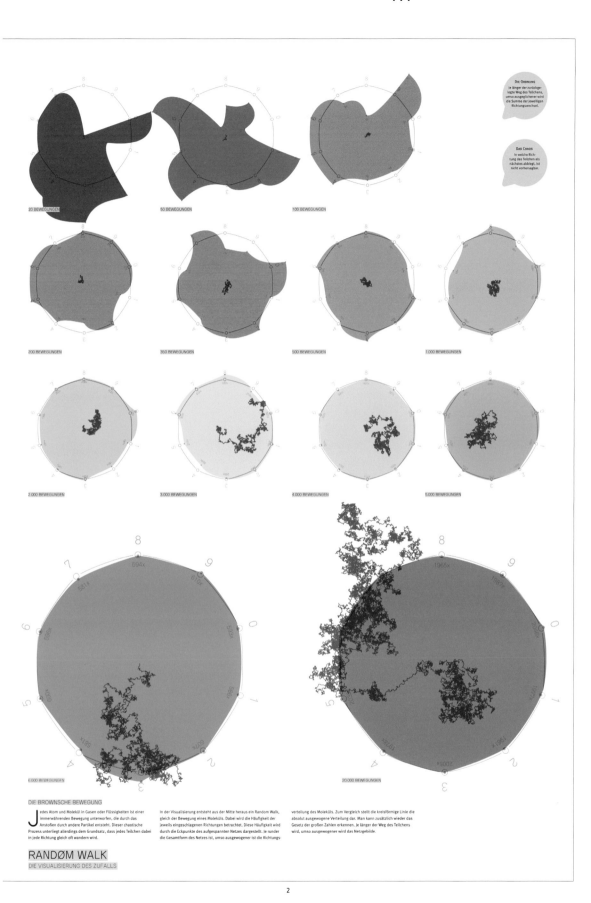

DIE BROWNSCHE BEWEGUNG

Jedes Atom und Molekül in Gasen oder Flüssigkeiten ist einer immerwährenden Bewegung unterworfen, die durch das Anstoßen durch andere Partikel entsteht. Dieser chaotische Prozess unterliegt allerdings dem Grundsatz, dass jedes Teilchen dabei in jede Richtung gleich oft wandern wird.

In der Visualisierung entsteht aus der Mitte heraus ein Random Walk, gleich der Bewegung eines Moleküls. Dabei wird die Häufigkeit der jeweils eingeschlagenen Richtungen betrachtet. Diese Häufigkeit wird durch die Eckpunkte des aufgespannten Netzes dargestellt. Je runder die Gesamtform des Netzes ist, umso ausgewogener ist die Richtungs-

verteilung des Moleküls. Zum Vergleich stellt die kreisförmige Linie die absolut ausgewogene Verteilung dar. Man kann zusätzlich wieder das Gesetz der großen Zahlen erkennen. Je länger der Weg des Teilchens wird, umso ausgewogener wird das Netzgebilde.

RANDØM WALK
DIE VISUALISIERUNG DES ZUFALLS

1
RELATIONSHIP MATTERS. A SOCIOGRAM INVESTIGATION
Valentina D'Efilippo

All too often, sociometric diagrams ignore the fact that their data reflects the lives of real people. Abstract and unemotional, they tend to lack the human factor.   RELATIONSHIP MATTERS sparks the discussion on social interactions with a simple, but vital question: is it even possible to show the relationships between people, places or things — not by oversimplification, but rather through a form that captures their intrinsic dynamics?   Five different case studies explore alternate ways of highlighting the links within the artist's own social network, focusing on various aspects of its relationships and interdependencies: time, affection, space, conversations and emotions.

2
RANDOM WALK
THE VISUALIZATION OF RANDOMNESS
Daniel Becker

RANDOM WALK — THE VISUALIZATION OF RANDOMNESS explores the principle of randomness through a variety of visualisations. In this particular case, Daniel Becker turns the "half-life" phenomenon into a no-nonsense papercraft exercise.   In chemistry, half-life denotes the predicted time span after which half the atoms of an unstable substance will have decayed. In some cases this might take mere milliseconds, in others it takes billions of years. And although the measure is remarkably correct, no one can predict which particular atoms will be affected.   Exponential by nature, the process resembles the continual folding of a sheet of paper — after each fold, it is up to chance which of the remaining halves is folded again. In its randomness, the string of folds — and atomic decay — always takes a different turn, as visualised in this particular illustration.

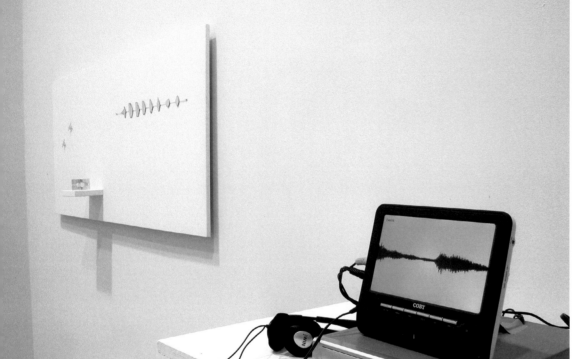

1
OBJECT OF SOUND
NOCC
NOCC's OBJECT OF SOUND collection encompasses a candleholder, a lampshade and a vase. Each item is shaped according to the sound profile of its spoken name, which is transformed into a 3D approximation of the depicted object. In this way, each creator adds a further, personal touch to the object and imbues it with new meaning.

2
"I DO" WEDDING BAND
3
CHURCH BELL (CUFF BRACELET)
4
ATCHOUM — SNEEZE (BROOCH)
5
INSTALLATION VIEW
Sakurako Shimizu
Church bells, wedding vows, a fleeting sneeze ... Sakurako Shimizu translates pertinent sounds into laser-cut waveforms, preserved for eternity in durable metal. / "I DO" WEDDING BAND / Material: Silver / Dimension 7 × 5.5 cm / CHURCH BELL (CUFF BRACELET) / Material: 18K yellow gold, palladium / Dimension 7.5 and 8.5 mm wide / ATCHOUM — SNEEZE (BROOCH) / Material: Silver / Dimension 9 × 3.5 cm / Photo: Takateru Yamada /

6
WAVEFORM NECKLACE
David Bizer
The WAVEFORM NECKLACE is a customised piece of jewellery. Potential buyers submit a digital audio sample (e.g. a voice recording or a favourite hookline) to be assembled into an individual necklace that proudly displays their recording's sound wave frequencies.

1

2

1
TRIKOTON
2
GELSOMINA
THE VOICE KNITTING MACHINE
Trikoton
Communication and fashion define our surroundings and help us to express our individuality. In an update on the knitting circle, a social event and a place to swap styles and skills, Trikoton turns user-submitted voice signals into individual knitting patterns — as personal and unique as the human voice itself. / Photo: Hanna Wiesener /

3
VISIBLE SOUND
SOUNDS.BUTTER
"A stitch in time ..." VISIBLE SOUND transforms frequency patterns into tangible stereo strips. Unlike other types of sound visualisations (equalisers, subtitles etc.), this project focuses on the physical representation of audio input generated by a sewing machine.

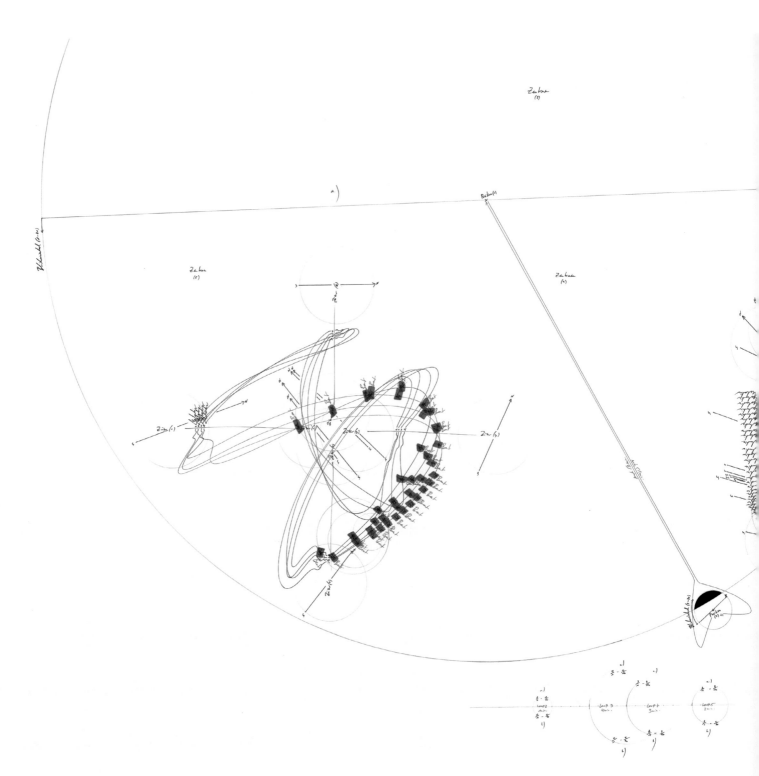

SYMPHONIC AREA VAR. 4
Jorinde Voigt
In SYMPHONIC AREA, Berlin-based artist
Jorinde Voigt interlaces up to eight different parameters in ever changing variations.
She moves easily from the musical notation
of a fictional symphonic area to physical
standpoints within the diagram, and even
positions the North and South Poles in her
drawings. The notations appear to represent
acoustic and spatial information about the
world, but in fact they represent a math-
ematically perfect declination that extends
from the first to the 27th drawing of the
series. A mental space of options and pos-
sibilities is thereby created, which has to
be filled by the viewer. / Berlin / 2009 / Ink, Pencil on
Paper / 27 Drawings / 80×180 cm each / Unique /

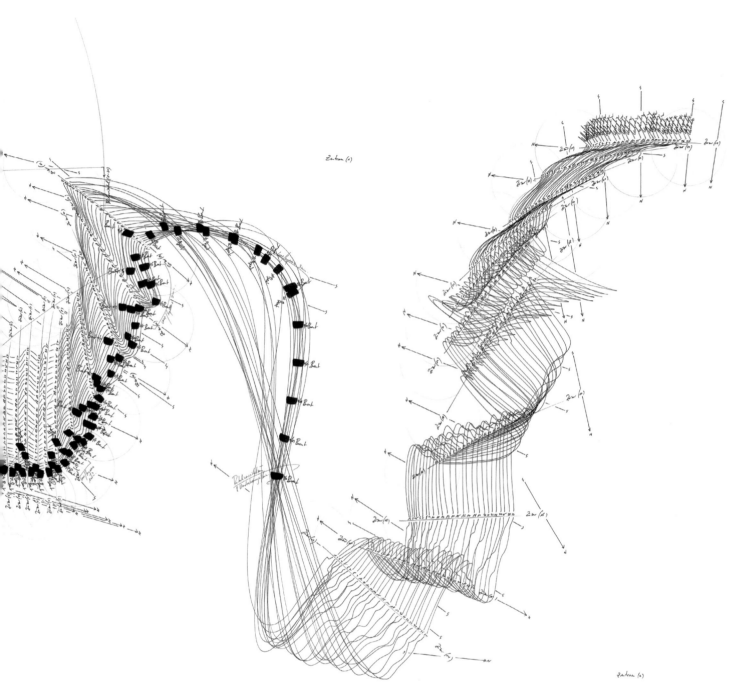

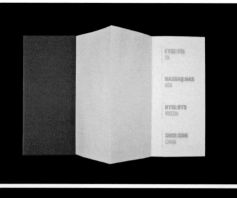

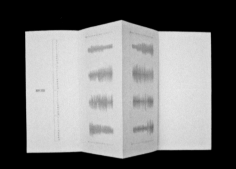

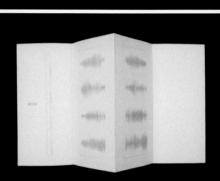

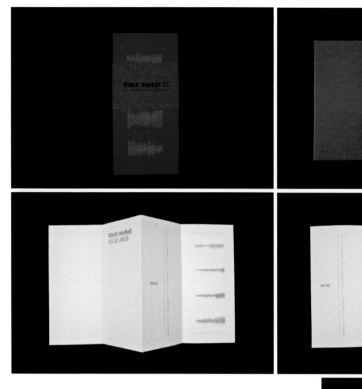

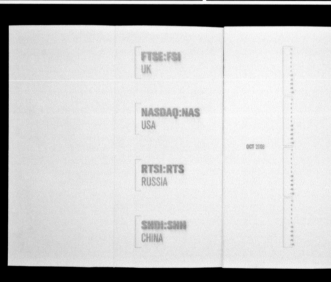

1
STOCK MARKET
Anna Filipova

In a further variant of credit crunch dissection, Anna Filipova compares the fallout from the slump to seismic waves. In their own way, earthquakes have a similar effect on the population as financial upheaval: people lose their money, houses and livelihood.

By exploring the parallels between tectonic shifts in the earth's crust and the marketplace, the resulting economic/geological hybrid graphs (Richter scale on top, Williams %R scale below) provide a more immediate narrative on how this latest crunch shook up the financial community and the human population.

2
BICYCLE BUILT FOR TWO THOUSAND
Aaron Koblin and Daniel Massey

BICYCLE BUILT FOR TWO THOUSAND blends more than 2,000 voice recordings collected via Amazon's MECHANICAL TURK web service. Although predominantly a platform for mindless micro jobs, the call for participation yielded an astonishing variety of vocal contributions.   Assignees were prompted to listen to a short sound clip, then record themselves imitating what they had heard. The resulting chorus of many, a Chinese whispers version of DAISY BELL — the first song to implement musical speech synthesis in 1962 — is reconstruction as rendered by a distributed system of human voices.

Translated into its underlying frequency patterns however, the score displays no homogeneous harmony, but reveals a wealth of discordant notes, of personal flourishes and interpretations, that stick out from the overall chorus and reveal the irrepressible individuality within the mass.

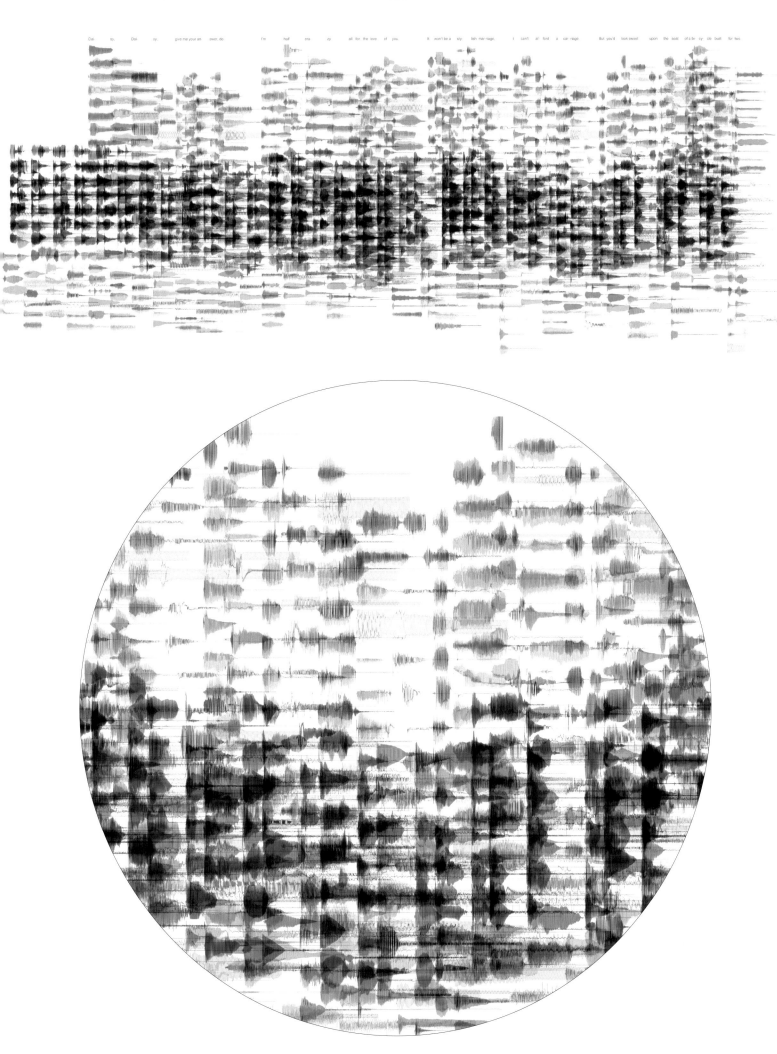

1
NARRATIVES 2.0
Matthias Dittrich

For its music visualisations, NARRATIVES 2.0 analyses the frequency channels of pieces as diverse as Beethoven's famous SYMPHONY NUMBER 5, rock anthem WE WILL ROCK YOU or the JARHEAD soundtrack. Separate channels are displayed in a fan-like arrangement and hint at the work's rhythm and pacing.

2
CINEMATIC PARTICLES
Eva Schindling

Going anywhere? Or just moving around in endless circles? From subtitles to subtext — CINEMATIC PARTICLES charts film interactions across time and space, from the dense dialogue of everyone's favourite dysfunctional family, The Royal Tenenbaums, to the ramified search for deliverance in the mythological forest of Pan's Labyrinth.

In this automated replay of verbal movie interactions, timecoded subtitles drive drawing particles: their size, speed and attraction force is determined by the letters of the processed dialogue and reveals the film's spoken rhythm, pacing and direction. While long silent pauses become long lines and curves, movies defined by a rapid succession of spoken exchanges produce mainly black ink blobs — their particles are constantly reset with new parameters.

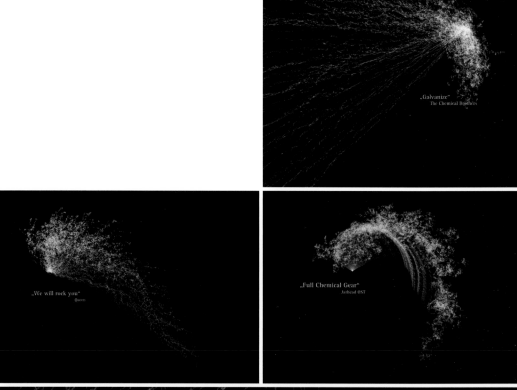

„Galvanize"
The Chemical Brothers

„We will rock you"
Queen

„Full Chemical Gear"
Jarhead OST

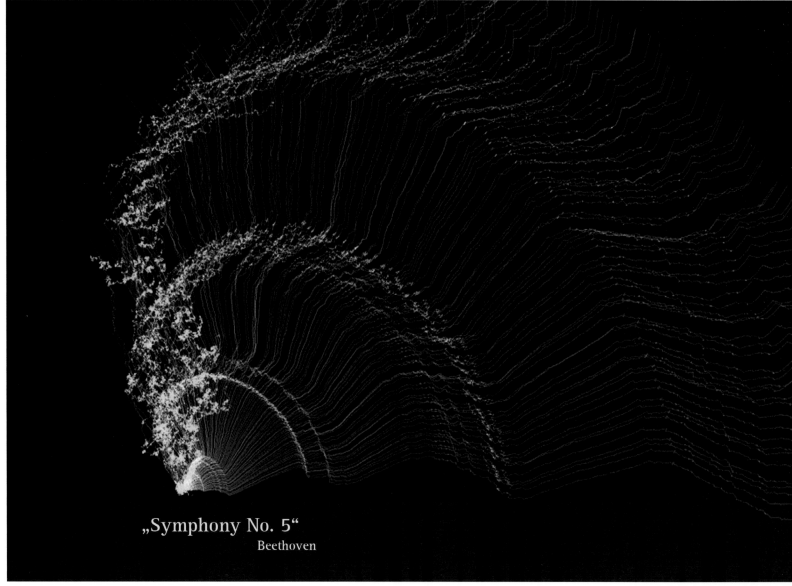

„Symphony No. 5"
Beethoven

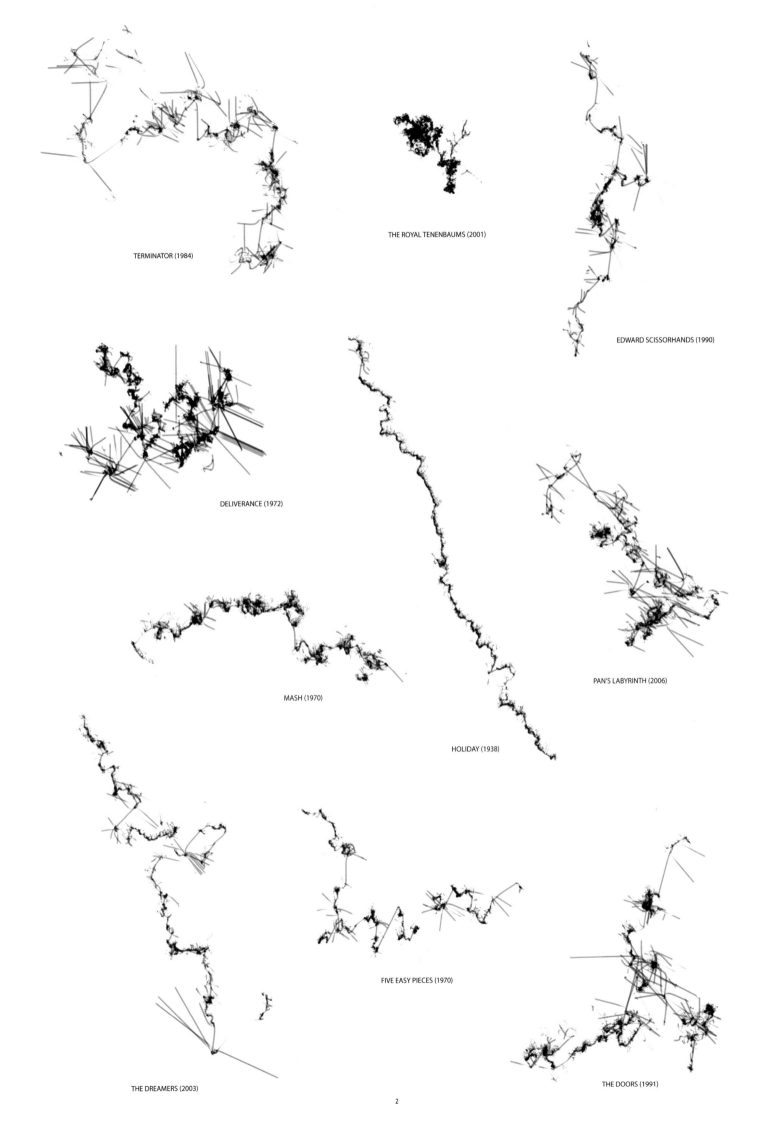

TERMINATOR (1984)

THE ROYAL TENENBAUMS (2001)

EDWARD SCISSORHANDS (1990)

DELIVERANCE (1972)

MASH (1970)

PAN'S LABYRINTH (2006)

HOLIDAY (1938)

THE DREAMERS (2003)

FIVE EASY PIECES (1970)

THE DOORS (1991)

DIE GESTALT DER DIGITALEN IDENTITAET

BACHELOR-VERTEIDIGUNG VON STEFFEN FIEDLER & JONAS LOH

DI. 14.07.09 18:00 UHR
CASINO DER FHP
Fachhochschule Potsdam, Pappelalle 8-9

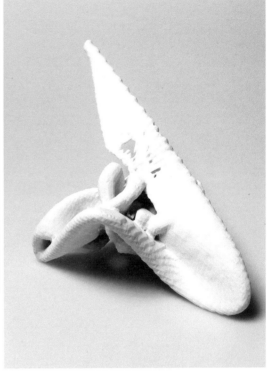

2

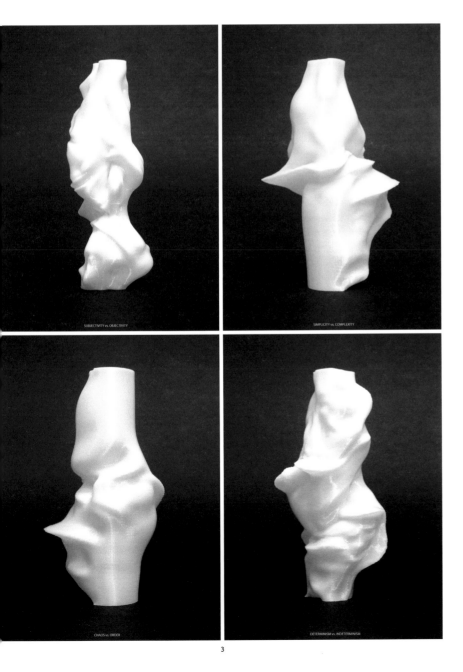

SUBJECTIVITY vs. OBJECTIVITY   SIMPLICITY vs. COMPLEXITY

CHAOS vs. ORDER   DETERMINISM vs. INDETERMINISM

1, 2
~IDENTITÄT
THE «GESTALT» OF DIGITAL IDENTITY
Jonas Loh and Steffen Fiedler
Let's begin at the beginning: before we analyse a concept or entity, we require a solid
analytical framework. ~IDENTITÄT — THE
«GESTALT» OF DIGITAL IDENTITY aims to do
just that — the study sets out to determine
how a digital identity is created to define
parameters that would enable its compa-
rable analysis.   Culled from the internet,
more than one hundred thousand personal
raw data sets served as "test subjects" for
the study. After analysis by custom computational tools, the collected data was then
reinterpreted as a physical shape — to give
each disembodied digital identity a unique
and characteristic "Gestalt" in the form of
a generated sculpture.   Like the empty
shells of undiscovered deep-sea creatures,
the resulting abstract and amorphous models might appear alien, but they nevertheless
carry the gist of their online identities within
them. /Photo: Matthias Steffen/

2
LIQUID SOUND COLLISION
Eva Schindling
Akin to misshapen vases that fell off the
wheel — all kinks and curves and skewed
alignments — Eva Schindling's LIQUID
SOUND COLLISIONS send opposing sound
waves into battle.   In each example, two
spoken audio files of dualistic views — chaos
and order, mind and body etc. — collide in
a fluid simulation. Broadcast from opposite
ends, these statements run towards each
other until they interfere with the other's
sound wave patterns. A snapshot of the resulting collision is then translated into a 3D
model.   In this contorted clash of seman-
tics, natural linguistic antagonists relinquish
their underlying meaning to become neutral
opponents in the physical quest to make
waves and spread their vibrations. /2009/open-
Frameworks, MSAFluid library, Processing, Dimensions uPrint 3D
Printer/ Produced at the Advanced Research Technology Lab at
the Banff New Media Institute/

1

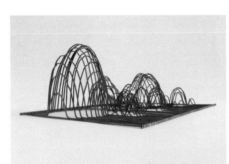

1
TIDAL DATUM TABLES
Adrien Segal

TIDAL DATUM TABLES is a record of a specific time and place. Collected over a four-week period off San Francisco Bay, the curves of the USA's National Oceanic and Atmospheric Administration (NOAA)'s historic tidal graphs are translated into flat-bar steel. Set within a solid walnut table frame, these twenty-eight days of a full lunar cycle display the changes in tidal patterns over time. /2007/Photo: Daniel Lorenze/

2
FUNDAMENT
Andreas Nicolas Fischer

FUNDAMENT offers a new, exploratory approach to the macro-economic triggers that led to the financial crisis. Based on data available from the CIA's THE WORLD FACT-BOOK and the International Monetary Fund, Andreas Nicolas Fischer carved a statistical map — a hybrid between physical and conceptual space — from a block of beech wood to visualise the global relationship between gross domestic product and financial derivatives volume.   Technological advances, combined with financial deregulation, have caused the global derivatives volume to proliferate to ten times the world's gross domestic product (GDP). The sculpture's swooping curves betray this imbalance across the globe. While the lower half of the sculpture represents the distribution of GDP across an (invisible) world map, the top layer represents the corresponding volume of derivatives by country. /2008/cnc-milled beech wood, laser-cut poplar plywood/Dimensions: 40×60×25 cm/

2

3

3
INDIZES
Andreas Nicolas Fischer
For an even simpler piece of economic critique, INDIZES charts the graphic decline of the market rate and places it centre stage. To this end, the data sculpture displays the development of the stock market indices S&P 500, Dow Jones Industrial and NASDAQ between January and November 2008. The central premise — the economy is not built to last — is reflected in the work itself. Made out of cheap, honest plywood, the same applies to this transient sculpture. / 2008 / Poplar plywood, paint / 46 × 140 × 120 cm /

4
SOUND MEMORY
(OSLO RAIN MANIFESTO)
Marius Watʒ
SOUND MEMORY invites viewers to experience the full spectrum of music (well, one song at least) in this fast Fourier transform (FFT) analysis of Alexander Rishaug's OSLO RAIN MANIFESTO. Sliced and diced into staggered disks, the basic arc form is repeated and scaled according to the song's

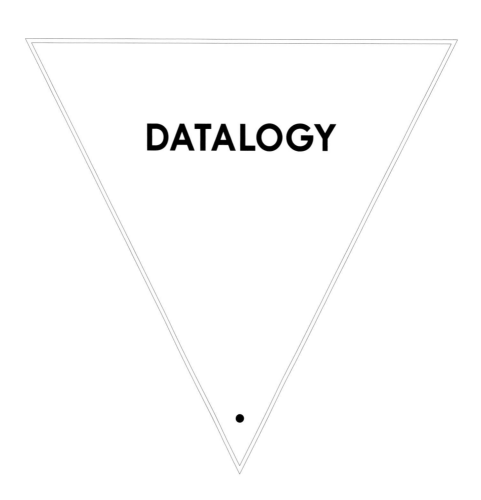

DATALOGY

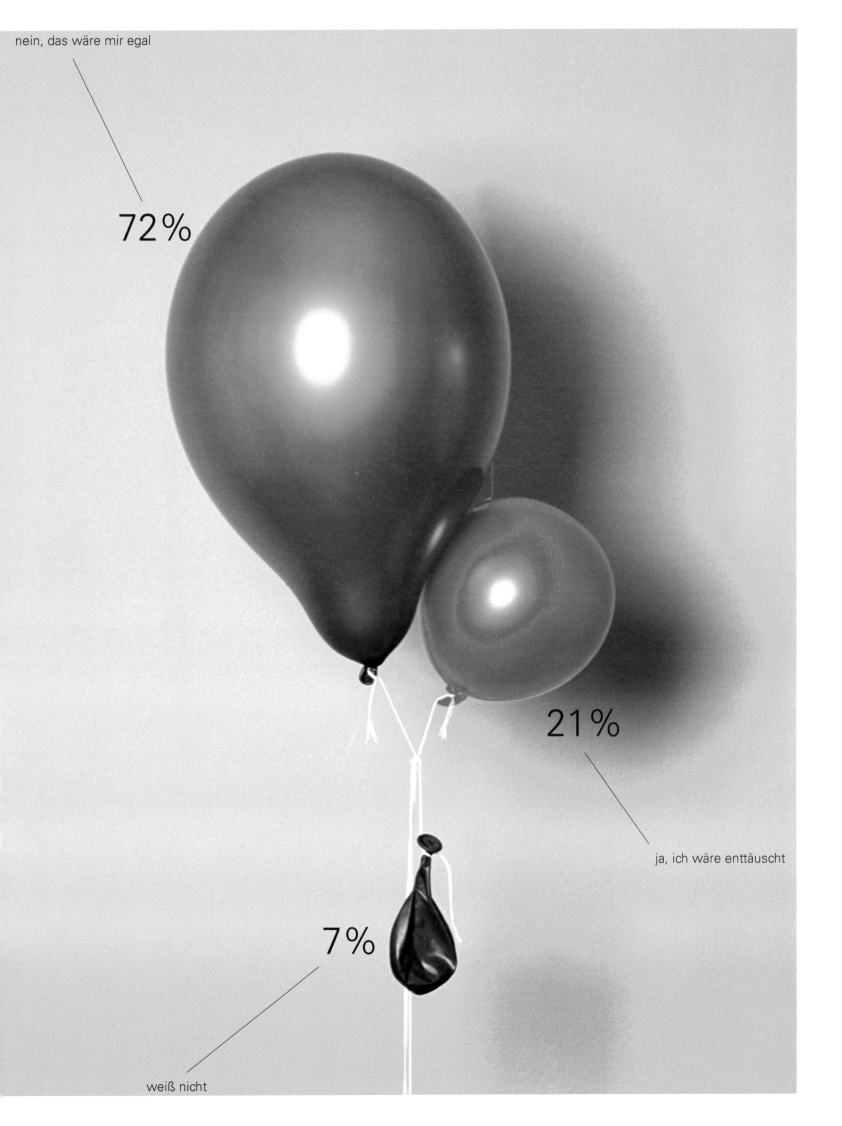

nein, das wäre mir egal

72%

21%

ja, ich wäre enttäuscht

7%

weiß nicht

The projects shown in this chapter deliver their message by trying to build a bridge between abstract data and familiar symbols, objects, spaces, or experiences. Rather than using neutral, interchangeable diagrams, the information is put in the direct context of its theme. Analogies are drawn which rely on the viewer's interpretation in order to enhance and intensify the meaning.

•

Here is something we all know: sea levels are rising due to climate change. The figures alone are alarming. If this information was turned into a graph comparing it with data from previous decades and centuries, it would be even more startling because we could see how fast the water is rising. Using a map showing which parts of the land mass will be gone in 50 years would be even more impressive. But, it is still all abstract. Now imagine walking down a street. You see the brick walls to your left and right, you can feel the texture of the sidewalk, you can smell the air and hear the sound of the area you are in. On this old, beautiful building, a straight line and a few words are projected: "Future High-Water Level."

Using the same data as the other visualization methods mentioned above, this is most likely the one that gets you thinking. You realize that your children's children will not be able to walk down this very street. That bush over there – gone. The bench in front of you – drowned. The Ground floor of this house – flooded. *Watermarks* /1/ is so effective because it is such a simple idea – you might even get chilly feet, because this visualization has got you imagining you are standing in cold water up to your waist.

1
WATERMARKS PROJECT
Chris Bodle
/›P.160/

Sugarstacks uses a similar principle. By placing sugar cubes in front of food and beverage products, /2/ we do not just learn how much of that saccharine white stuff is in there – we might even taste an unpleasant sweetness and internalize a link to the respective item. No chart could do this, let alone dry numbers. Presenting the information with a direct connection to its subject tickles more than our prefrontal cortex, it also addresses our emotions and feelings. A valuable asset, if the aim is to educate and inform about health, social, or environmental problems. *In-Formed* /3/ is another good example. The length of each prong shows the calorie consumption per capita of various countries: a bar chart turned fork. Try to pick up your tasty pasta with this unusual instrument and you will realize that more food is sticking to the longer prongs (the rich industrial nations). As a commodity this object would fail. As a visualization it shines.

2
SUGARSTACKS.COM
Sugar Stacks
/›P.133/

3
IN-FORMED
Nadeem Haidary
/›P.151/

However, caution is advised. By using analogies, the designer relies on the subjective interpretation of the viewer. Therefore, cultural context has to be taken into account, otherwise distraction, confusion, or even misinterpretation can be the result. If considered carefully however, analogy is a powerful device in the designer's tool box.

1
DIE GROSSE NEON SEX UMFRAGE
Sarah Illenberger
In her illustrations for a sex survey by German magazine NEON, Sarah Illenberger gets up close and personal with intimate facts and graphic details.

Wie würdest du deine sexuelle Orientierung beschreiben?

3%
bisexuell

1%
nichts davon

2%
homosexuell, aber mit
Heteroerfahrung (Männer: 1%,
Frauen: 2%)

7%
heterosexuell, aber mit
Homoerfahrung (Männer: 5%,
Frauen: 10%)

83%
heterosexuell
(Männer: 87%,
Frauen: 78%)

3%
homosexuell
(Männer: 4%, Frauen: 1%)

Hast du schon mal für Sex bezahlt?

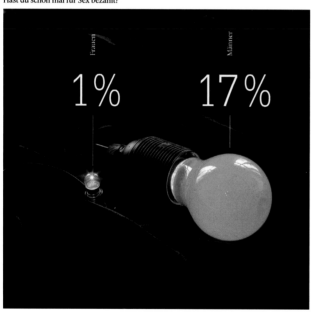

Frauen

Männer

1%

17%

Wie oft im Monat schaust du pornografische Seiten im Internet an? (49% aller Befragten tun dies, 71% der Männer und 26% der Frauen.)

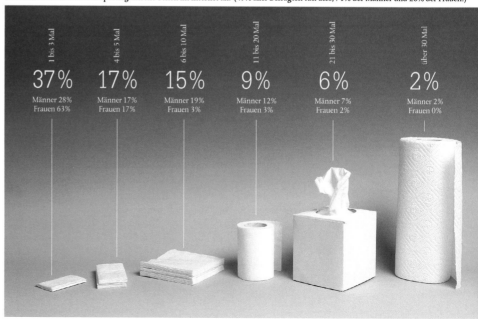

1 bis 3 Mal

4 bis 5 Mal

6 bis 10 Mal

11 bis 20 Mal

21 bis 30 Mal

über 30 Mal

37%
Männer 28%
Frauen 63%

17%
Männer 17%
Frauen 17%

15%
Männer 19%
Frauen 3%

9%
Männer 12%
Frauen 3%

6%
Männer 7%
Frauen 2%

2%
Männer 2%
Frauen 0%

If the world were a village of 100 people

LITERACY

86 can read

14 can't read

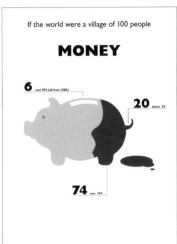

If the world were a village of 100 people

MONEY

6 own 59% (all from USA)

20 share 2%

74 own 39%

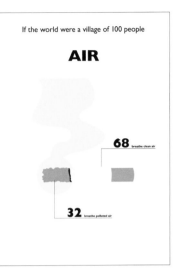

If the world were a village of 100 people

AIR

68 breathe clean air

32 breathe polluted air

If the world were a village of 100 people

WATER

17 don't have clean/safe water

83 have clean/safe water

If the world were a village of 100 people

EDUCATION

1 has college education

99 haven't

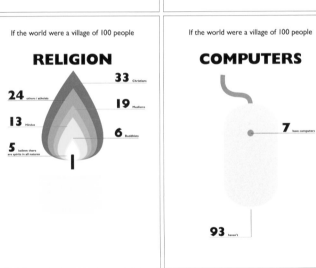

If the world were a village of 100 people

RELIGION

33 Christians

24 others / atheists

19 Muslims

13 Hindus

6 Buddhists

5 believe there are spirits in all natures

If the world were a village of 100 people

COMPUTERS

7 have computers

93 haven't

2

2
THE WORLD OF 100
Toby Ng Kwong To
Boiled down to their most basic, yet friendly and familiar signifiers, THE WORLD OF 100 explores a range of statistic binaries to convey information on the global distribution of gender, language, freedom, eating habits etc. in the most accessible way.

3
REFLEX POINTS
FEET FROM VISUAL AID
Draught Associates

Brain
Pituitary
Face
Neck/tonsils
Neck
Thyroid
Heart
Shoulder
Lungs
Diaphragm
Gallbladder
Adrenals
Stomach
Liver
Spleen
Pancreas
Kidneys
Spine
Colon
Intestine
Bladder
Appendix
Sciatic nerve

REFLEX POINTS

3

1
I LEGO N.Y.
Christoph Niemann
Stack them up! A playful homage to the Big
Apple. /From the book "I Lego NY", Abrams Image, 2010/

2
APPLE GLOBE
Kevin Van Aelst

3
LOCAL TIMES
Kevin Van Aelst
In Kevin van Aelst's foodist views of the
world, carved apples teach geography les-
sons and crackers crumble into global time
zone reminders.

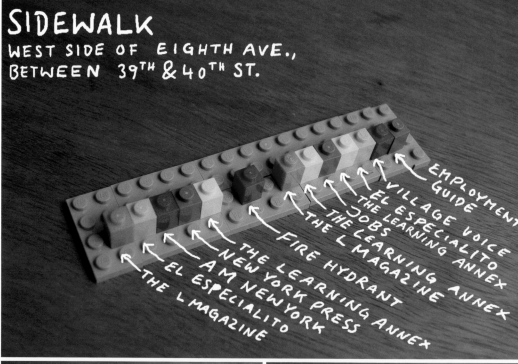

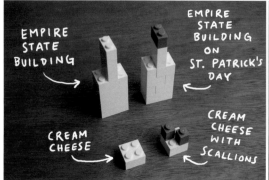

1

2

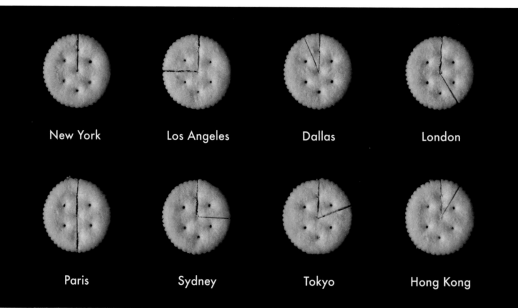

3

4

SUGARSTACKS.COM
Sugar Stacks
Stack them up! SUGARSTACKS.COM uses sugar cubes to show just how much hidden sugar our favourite snacks and staples contain.

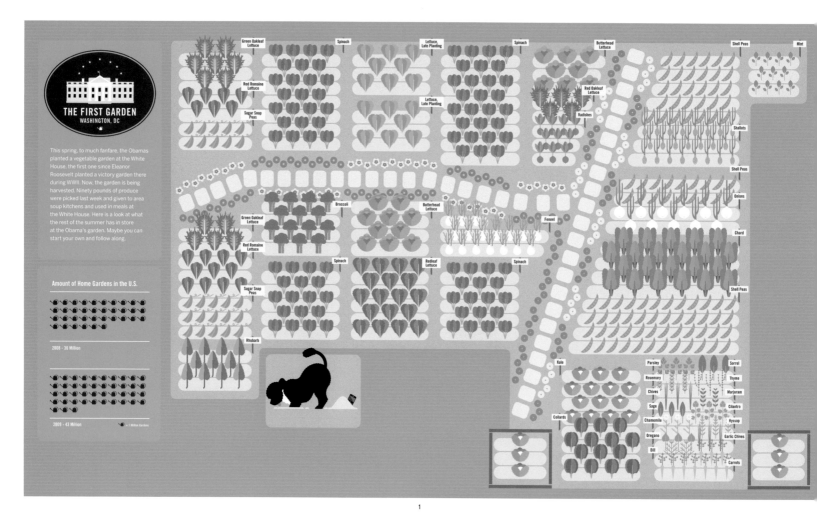

1

1
TRANSPARENCY:
OBAMA'S PRESIDENTIAL GARDEN
alwayswithhonor
A graphic exploration of the data available
on the White House garden (commissioned
by GOOD magazine)./ A collaboration between
GOOD and Always With Honor/

2
WHAT'S IN THE CUSTOMER'S
MAILSTREAM?
Jude Buffum
WHAT'S IN THE CUSTOMER'S MAILSTREAM?
opens the average American roadside
mailbox for a breakdown of US Post Office throughput./ Art directed by Grayson Cardinell
at Campbell-Ewald/

3
BALANCE YOUR MEDIA DIET
Jason Lee
Is there life beyond the screen? Between
work and play, laptop and gadgets, it can be
hard to find the right balance. WIRED's daily
media diet takes apart our digital habits
and suggests a healthier mix./ Creative Director:
Scott Dadich/ Design Director: Wyatt Mitchell/ Art Director:
Maili Holiman/

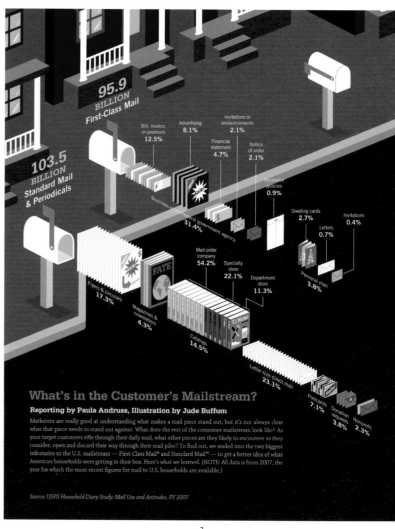

2

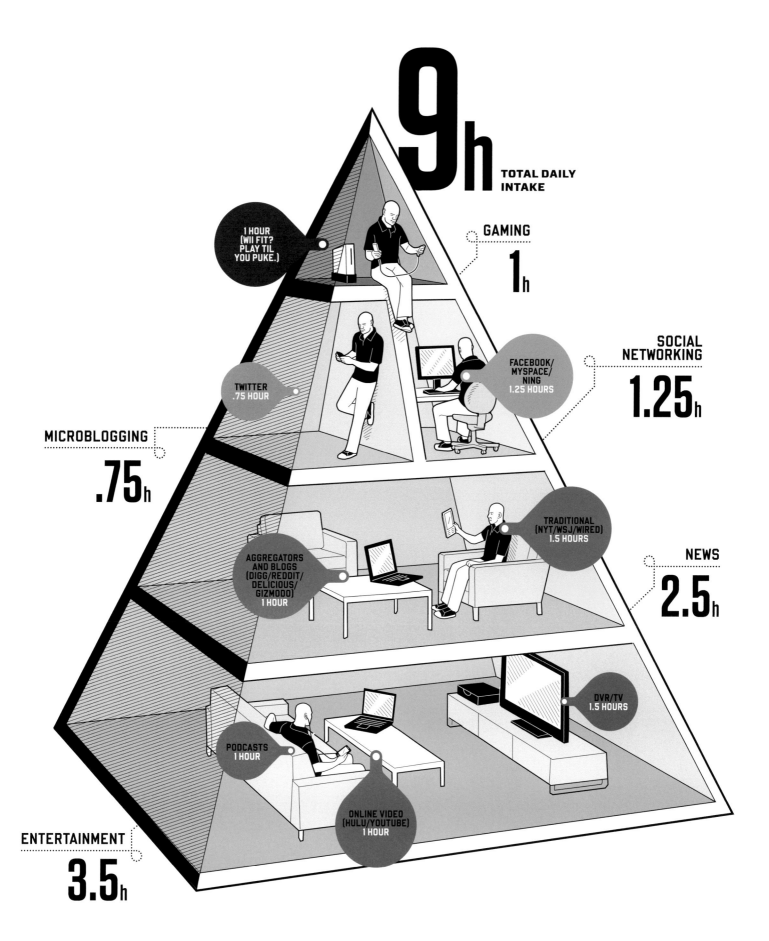

9h **TOTAL DAILY INTAKE**

1 HOUR (WII FIT? PLAY TIL YOU PUKE.)

GAMING 1h

TWITTER .75 HOUR

FACEBOOK/ MYSPACE/ NING 1.25 HOURS

SOCIAL NETWORKING 1.25h

MICROBLOGGING .75h

AGGREGATORS AND BLOGS (DIGG/REDDIT/ DELICIOUS/ GIZMODO) 1 HOUR

TRADITIONAL (NYT/WSJ/WIRED) 1.5 HOURS

NEWS 2.5h

DVR/TV 1.5 HOURS

PODCASTS 1 HOUR

ONLINE VIDEO (HULU/YOUTUBE) 1 HOUR

ENTERTAINMENT 3.5h

HELLMANN'S "FAMILY DINNER"
crush

Think global, eat local: Hellmann's two minute FAMILY DINNER animation drives the message home by lifting the lid on a typical Canadian family dinner — how much of it is actually produced within the country?
Laid out on an inviting dinner table, the short clip dissects our eating habits and navigates pertinent food facts in a familiar context for a more lifelike, close to home explanation of easily digested dinner table analogies. / Ogilvy and Mather Toronto, Canada / Director: Steve Gordon from Sons and Daughters and Crush Co / Creative Directors: Gary Thomas and Stefan Woronko of Crush / Art Director: Yoho Hang Yue of Crush / CG Supervisor: Aylwin Fernando /

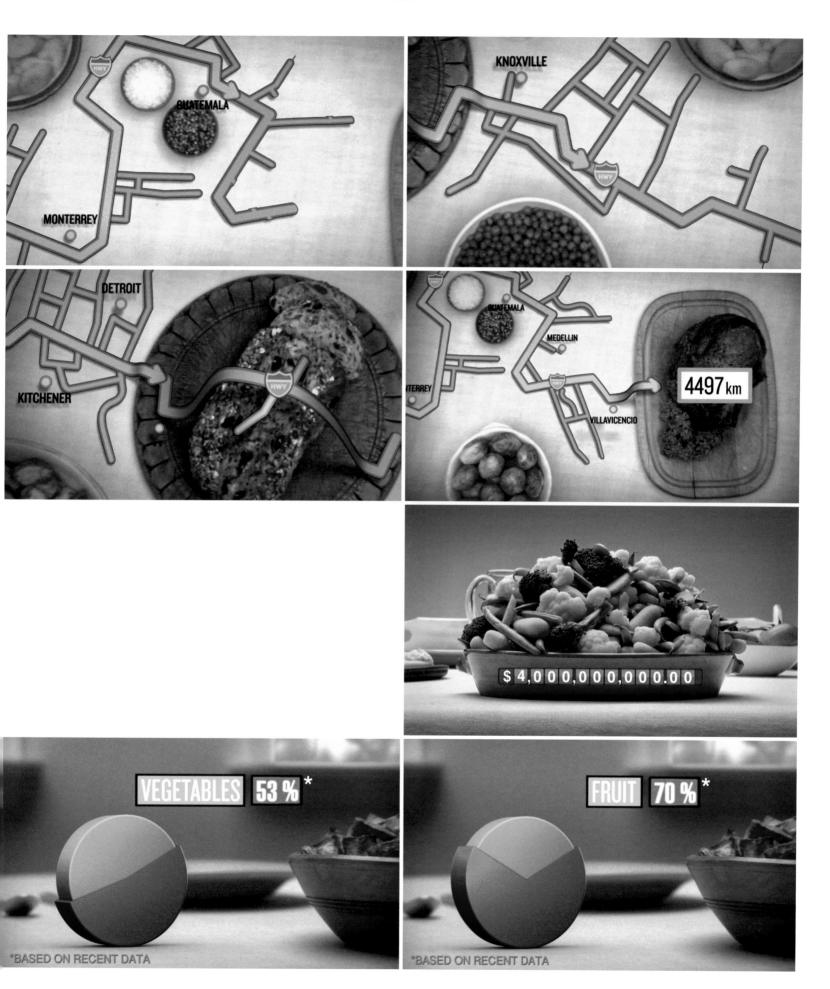

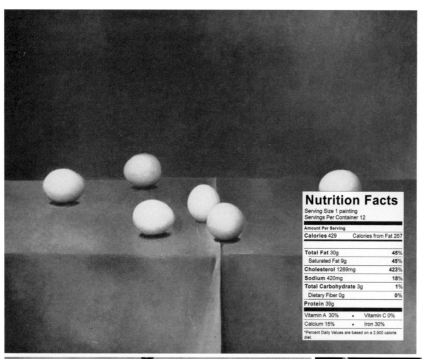

Nutrition Facts

Serving Size 1 painting
Servings Per Container 12

Amount Per Serving	
Calories 429	Calories from Fat 267

	%
Total Fat 30g	**45%**
Saturated Fat 9g	**45%**
Cholesterol 1269mg	**423%**
Sodium 420mg	**18%**
Total Carbohydrate 3g	**1%**
Dietary Fiber 0g	**0%**
Protein 39g	

Vitamin A 30%	•	Vitamin C 0%
Calcium 15%	•	Iron 30%

*Percent Daily Values are based on a 2,900 calorie diet.

Nutrition Facts

Serving Size 1 painting
Servings Per Container 12

Amount Per Serving	
Calories 9914	Calories from Fat 873

	%
Total Fat 97g	**179%**
Saturated Fat 52g	**161%**
Cholesterol 320mg	**107%**
Sodium 3300mg	**138%**
Total Carbohydrate 1007g	**289%**
Dietary Fiber 128g	**426%**
Protein 83g	

Vitamin A 128%	•	Vitamin C 1221%
Calcium 147%	•	Iron 326%

*Percent Daily Values are based on a 2,900 calorie diet.

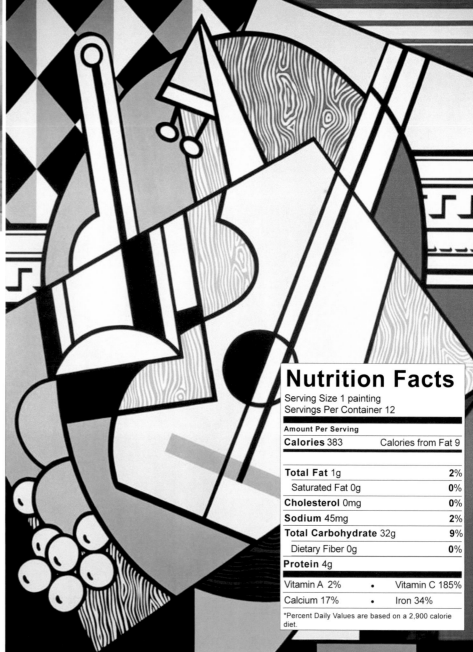

Nutrition Facts

Serving Size 1 painting
Servings Per Container 12

Amount Per Serving	
Calories 383	Calories from Fat 9

	%
Total Fat 1g	**2%**
Saturated Fat 0g	**0%**
Cholesterol 0mg	**0%**
Sodium 45mg	**2%**
Total Carbohydrate 32g	**9%**
Dietary Fiber 0g	**0%**
Protein 4g	

Vitamin A 2%	•	Vitamin C 185%
Calcium 17%	•	Iron 34%

*Percent Daily Values are based on a 2,900 calorie diet.

Nutrition Facts

Serving Size 1 painting
Servings Per Container 12

Amount Per Serving

Calories 39,851 Calories from Fat 14,076

	% Daily Value*
Total Fat 1564g	**1618%**
Saturated Fat 566g	**1756%**
Cholesterol 18,051mg	**6017%**
Sodium 12,029mg	**501%**
Total Carbohydrate 1525g	**407%**
Dietary Fiber 262g	**875%**
Protein 4786g	

Vitamin A 547%	•	Vitamin C 1352%	
Calcium 282%	•	Iron 7132%	

*Percent Daily Values are based on a 2,900 calorie diet.

Nutrition Facts

Serving Size 1 painting
Servings Per Container 12

Amount Per Serving

Calories 4832   Calories from Fat 384

	% Daily Value*
Total Fat 32g	**64%**
Saturated Fat 32g	**96%**
Cholesterol 0mg	**0%**
Sodium 44,256mg	**1856%**
Total Carbohydrate 1088g	**352%**
Dietary Fiber 96g	**384%**
Protein 128g	

Vitamin A 640%	•	Vitamin C 1728%	
Calcium 96%	•	Iron 480%	

*Percent Daily Values are based on a 2,900 calorie diet.

THE FOOD OF ART
Nadeem Haidary

THE FOOD OF ART exposes the nutritional content of famous still lifes. Although humorous in nature, the pieces can indicate the artist's own economic situation — compare the 39,851 calorie feast of court painter Frans Snyders to Paul Cezanne's relatively frugal, but healthy spread. / William Bailey, EGGS, 1966 / Paul Cézanne, STILL LIFE WITH BASKET OF APPLES, 1890–1894, Art Institute of Chicago / Roy Lichtenstein, CUBIST STILL LIFE, 1974, National Gallery of Art, Washington D.C. / Frans Snyders, STILL LIFE WITH FRUIT, VEGETABLES AND DEAD GAME, c. 1635–1637, The Detroit Institute of Arts / Andy Warhol, CAMPBELL'S SOUP CANS, 1962, The Museum of Modern Art, New York City /

STEVE DUENES

The New York Times probably has a large share in responsibility for the increase of interest in information visualization. The world's most famous newspaper has a long tradition of well-crafted info-graphics, but in recent years they seem to have shifted up a gear or two. *The New York Times's* use of functional, care-fully edited and well-executed visualizations is impres-sive, particularly on its hugely popular website. The graphics staff at *The Times* can largely take credit for this. They are a team of 25 reporters, cartographers, designers, and program-mers who produce the diagrams, charts, and maps for the newspaper and the interactive graphics for the website. Steve Duenes (director) and Mat-thew Ericson (deputy direc-tor) lead the team. Steve is interviewed here:

•

The King of Pop dies, oil prices rise, health-care issues are discussed and the Pittsburgh Steel-ers win the Super Bowl. Who decides what's going to be visualized? /SD/ Mostly, the graphics department. With breaking news stories, we're expected to react the way other news desks do, so once we hear that Michael Jackson has died or that a plane has crashed into the Hudson River, we react immediately and start gathering informa-tion to prepare for a visu-alization. We also try to respond to important continu-ing stories like the ones you've mentioned – the debate over health-care reform or the price of oil. Again, we follow these stories like journalists and develop ideas to cover them with visualizations. There are times when different news desks like the national desk or the foreign desk will approach us with a specific idea, and we turn quite a few of these concepts into visualizations. And of course, we work from the daily list of stories that each news desk produces.

How many infographics does your team pro-duce on a typical day? /SD/ We produce

> WE'RE USED TO WORKING UNDER PRESSURE. IT CAN ACTUALLY BE FUN.

between five and ten print graphics each day and three or four online graphics each week.

That's quite a few. I guess your work must be influenced a lot by tight deadlines and other con-straints, like limited space in the newspaper. How do you deal with this? /SD/ The space constraints of the newspaper are actually helpful on the web. It means we have to edit tightly, which can only benefit readers. Deadlines are another story. The experience of deal-ing with daily deadlines for many years helps a bit now that we're "on deadline" nearly all the time with the web report. We're used to wor-king under pressure. It can actually be fun.

How much of your work is actually "journalism" and how much is "design"? /SD/ It's difficult to boil this down to percentages be-cause we think about design or have a design in mind while we are doing research. And when we're designing, we're making decisions about the structure of the information, which is edit-ing. I guess I'm saying that it's not a linear pro-cess where we do one and then the other. They're somewhat intertwined. That said, it's probably half and half.

Are your team members involved in the whole process, from the journalistic work to the design part? /SD/ Yes, it is often the same people doing research, fact checking and executing the visualization.

Why are visualizations becoming more and more popular, especially among younger people? Are they used to thinking more visually? /SD/ It's hard to say just how popular visualizations are becoming, and it's difficult to know why. Your guesses are as good as any I could come up with. It is possible that younger readers are used to different kinds of computer interfaces, and they've been flooded with all kinds of imagery their entire lives. Perhaps we have some popularity among these readers because we've simply carved out some space in that environment.

That seems to have worked pretty well; your output has got a lot of attention recently. Do you think information visualizations will be a growing field in journalism? /SD/ I hope so. Obviously, a couple of our journalistic goals are to inform and clarify. Making information visual can aid in both of those pursuits. Frankly, there have been good information visualizations in newspapers for a long time, but journalism is squeezing itself onto new platforms that are clearly more visual. It's a great opportunity for people like us.

Those new platforms – e-readers, tablet PCs, phones and other mobile devices – are not just more visual, but also highly interactive. Therefore a visualization can do more than just convey information; it can be an explorative tool. You provide a framework with information, but it's ultimately the users – formerly known as readers – who will shape the layout in a way that answers their questions. That seems to be a pretty major shift in journalism, doesn't it? /SD/ Well, yes and no. There has always been a substantial service aspect to real journalism, which in many cases meant supplying a lot of information and allowing the reader to navigate to something he or she wanted.

Obviously, the internet can be highly interactive, and we have made the most of that with a number of our data visualizations, including some of the interactive graphics covering the 2008 US elections and some of the graphics we created to cover the financial crisis. Those graphics supplied readers with an enormous amount of data, and the visualizations organized it and made it easy to navigate. But those visualizations – the successful ones – did something else. On top of all that data, they told a story. We didn't just create a nifty interface and then say to readers, "Here you go, you figure it out." We tried to make sense of it, and we brought our explanation alongside the nifty interface that let readers explore and draw their own conclusions. In our department, I sit behind Amanda Cox, an extremely talented journalist and designer. She always cautions against creating visualizations that don't make a point. She thinks we shouldn't simply say to readers, "Here is some data." I agree completely. Readers who are interested in serious journalism expect journalists to uncover things for them. They expect us to do the legwork and to tell them things. As journalists create explorative tools, they shouldn't shift away from conveying information. Explorative tools should augment your notion of traditional journalism, not replace it.

EXPLORATIVE TOOLS SHOULD AUGMENT YOUR NOTION OF TRADITIONAL JOURNALISM, NOT REPLACE IT.

INFORMATION VISUALIZATIONS HAVE THE MOST IMPACT ON THEIR OWN WHEN THEY CLARIFY A SUBJECT IN WAYS THAT WORDS CANNOT.

Once in a while there are certain articles in newspapers which are so powerful that they shake people up, change their minds and spur them into action. Have you experienced an information visualization doing the same? /SD/ I wish I had a bunch of stories about charts that have changed the world. Honestly, it's hard to know what impact our graphics have because so many of them accompany written articles like the ones you've mentioned. Obviously, if the charts are good, they can only augment the impact of the article. Information visualizations have the most impact on their own when they clarify a subject in ways that words cannot. Thinking back, the department did this pretty effectively immediately after September 11, when New Yorkers really wanted concrete information about the status of Lower Manhattan. We also got a lot of feedback telling us that our maps were really important.

We see a lot of creative and interesting projects in information visualization these days. Do you keep an eye on current trends and developments in this field? Or do you get more inspired by the "classics," like Edward Tufte? /SD/ We don't get a chance to see everything, but we try to consume as much as we can. There are plenty of interesting visualizations out there and a lot to draw inspiration from. Of course, the classics endure. Younger designers could learn a lot from old, printed information graphics. Many of the design problems they struggle with have been solved in many ways by designers in the past.

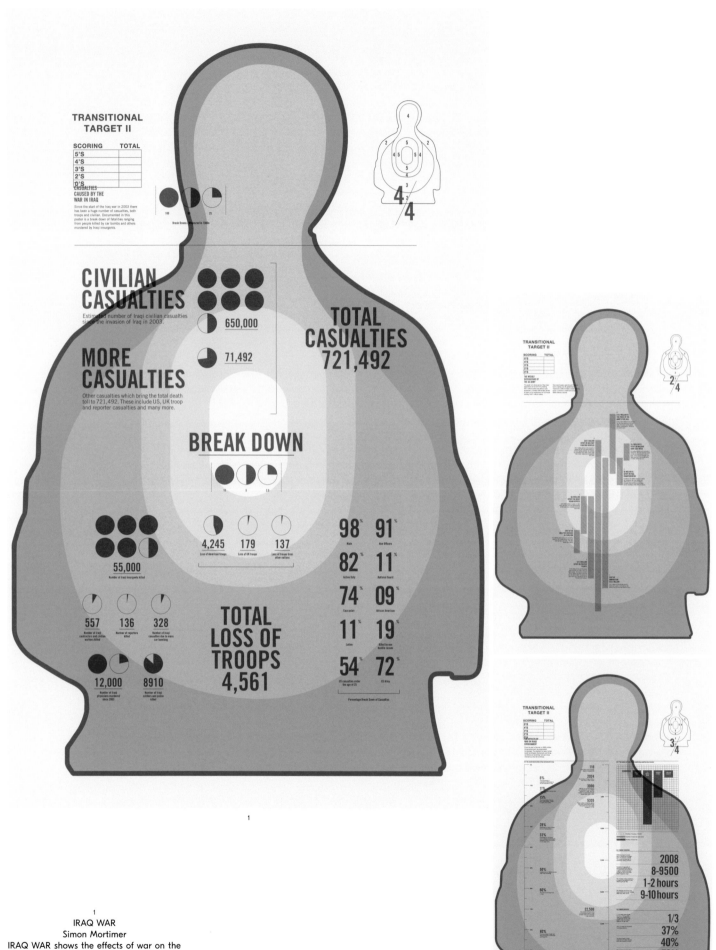

1
IRAQ WAR
Simon Mortimer
IRAQ WAR shows the effects of war on the country and its civilian population. The four posters highlight casualty data, environmental deterioration and US war expenditure on troops and missiles. Screen-printed range targets create a direct link between the graphics and their subject matter.

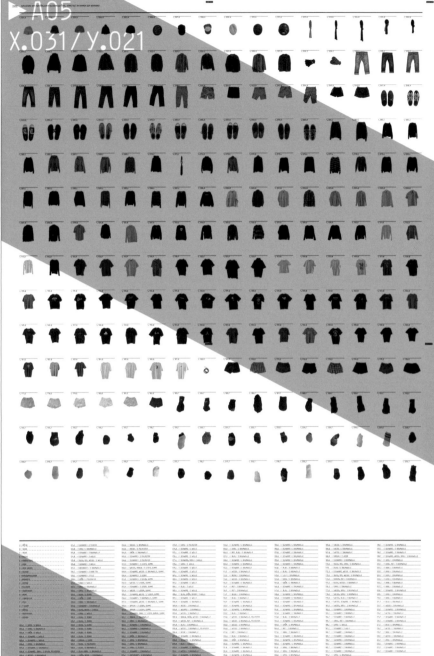

2

HERR F. UND ICH
Lars Thorben Fischer

Lars Thorben Fischer strips off for his thesis
and lays himself bare; from hat to boxers,
codified according to colour and material,
HERR F. UND ICH (Mr. F. and I) exposes the
200+ items hiding in the artist's wardrobe.
A graphic analysis of the designer himself,
this rather personal and fragmented tale is
based on a hexagonal grid, which also serves
as a section reference. First wall installation, now a book, each segment consists of
16 double pages, structured from the inside
out. In order to recreate the poster view,
owners may take the tome apart again and
restage the original in its fragmented glory.
      Nevertheless, once split into the various
sections, readers face a peculiar challenge —
in its disassembled state, disjointed pages
face each other and put our perception to
the test.

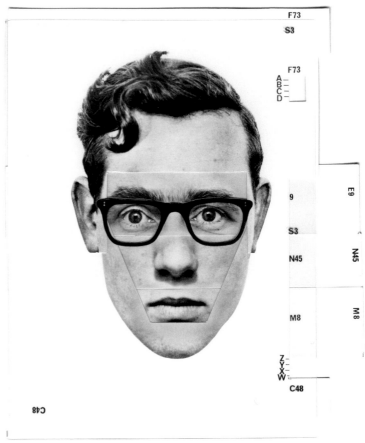

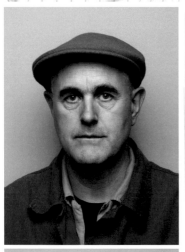

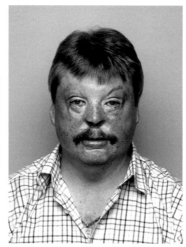

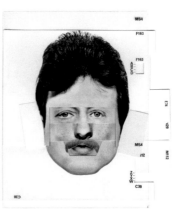

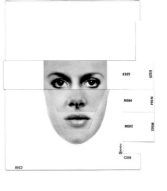

1
PHOTOFIT: SELF-PORTRAITS
Giles Revell and Matt Willey
Using the old and now outdated Penry Facial photofit kits from the 1970s, test subjects were asked to compose their own identikit image. Without the aid of mirrors or other immediate frames of reference, the results were a string of distorted self-images that reveal a lot more about the subject's personality than a straightforward photograph.

2
DIALOGUE OF EMOTIONS
Guðmundur Ingi Úlfarsson
Take your pick and choose your mood — cut-up and reassembled, Guðmundur Ingi Úlfarsson comes face to face with himself in this dialogue between pleasant and unpleasant emotions.

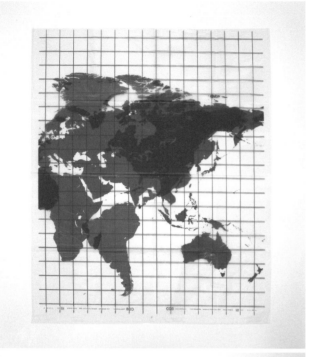

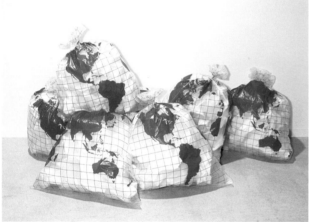

1

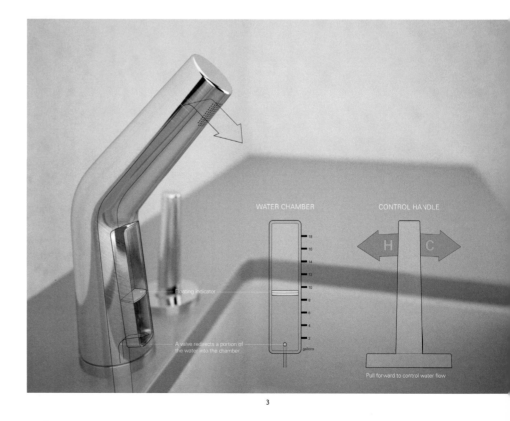

1
CGB
Kenjiro Sano
An eco-friendly and design-conscious waste bag, Sano's CGB reflects the habits of a throwaway society. Once filled with refuse, it adopts the ball-shape of our own planet — as a last-minute reminder of a fragile environment and finite resources.

2
EAU PROPRE = BONNE SANTÉ
Slang
Clean water equals good health: EAU PROPRE = BONNE SANTÉ takes this message to Africa with an informational poster about the correct uses of water. Distributed in Bafilo, Togo. /With Jaana Davidjants/Wiyumi/

3
IN-FORMED
Nadeem Haidary
/›P.151/ In WATER USAGE, the faucet displays the amount dispensed each time the water is switched on. To encourage awareness, a fraction of the water is redirected into the faucet's glass chamber, showing current water consumption and allowing users to track their usage habits over time.

RONDOUT RESERVOIR 85 MILES

ASHOKAN RESERVOIR 163 MILES

CROTON RIVER 41 MILES

A River Runs Near It:
Where America's largest cities get their water

ONE JUG HOLDS 400 BILLION GALLONS

RIVER | LAKE | RESERVOIR | LOCAL WATER (GROUND, RECYCLED and SURFACE WATER) | AQUIFER

New York City

396 BILLION GALLONS/YEAR

146 BILLION GALLONS/YEAR

Houston

Phoenix

100 BILLION GALLONS/YEAR

76 BILLION GALLONS/YEAR

San Diego

Los Angeles

207 BILLION GALLONS/YEAR

118 BILLION GALLONS/YEAR

Chicago

Philadelphia

93 BILLION GALLONS/YEAR

55 BILLION GALLONS/YEAR

San Antonio

4

396 BILLION GALLONS/YEAR

146 BILLION GALLONS/YEAR

10% CROTON RIVER 39.6 BILLION GAL.
40% ASHOKAN RESERVOIR 158 BILLION GAL.
50% RONDOUT RESERVOIR 198 BILLION GAL.

5% EVANGELINE AQUIFER 7 BILLION GAL.
5% TRINITY RIVER 7 BILLION GAL.
5% CHICOT AQUIFER 7 BILLION GAL.
25% LAKE CONROE 36.5 BILLION GAL.
25% LAKE LIVINGSTON 36.5 BILLION GAL.
25% LAKE HOUSTON 36.5 BILLION GAL.

4
A RIVER RUNS NEAR IT
Fogelson-Lubliner
A RIVER RUNS NEAR IT shows the distance between major US cities and their respective water sources.   Created as a commission for GOOD MAGAZINE, purveyor of handy information on leading a responsible, sustainable life without relinquishing joy and aesthetics, the diagram opts for unusual, yet familiar reference points, from the common gallon jug to actual human beings. Colour-coded and divided into natural and engineered sources — river, aquifer, lake, reservoir or local water — the precious spring of life is embodied by real people, spread out over the reference beach to indicate distance to the respective city.

Stuhl
Vegetarier
Boot

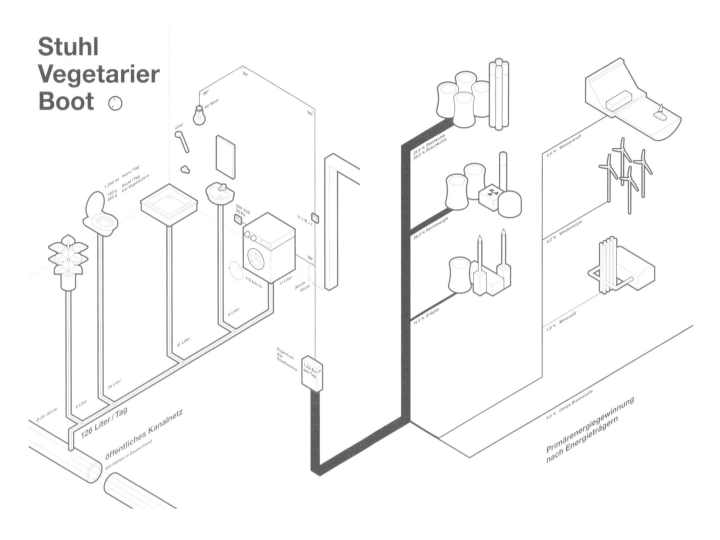

90°
90°
60 Watt
90°
4 bar

1.250 ml Harn/Tag
150 g Stuhl/Tag
350 g bei Vegetariern

220 Volt
50 Hz

U = R · I

21,6 % Steinkohle
25,0 % Braunkohle

26,3 % Kernenergie

11,3 % Erdgas

113 km/h   17 Liter
30 cm
15 cm

90°

4,5 % Wasserkraft

4,2 % Windenergie

1,8 % Mineralöl

0,25–60 cm   6 Liter

6 Liter

Eigentum
der
Stadtwerke

1,23 Eu/d
am Tag

34 Liter

41 Liter

126 Liter/Tag

öffentliches Kanalnetz
486.000 km in Deutschland

5,0 % übrige Brennstoffe

Primärenergiegewinnung
nach Energieträgern

Farbstoff
Bass
Grundhaltung

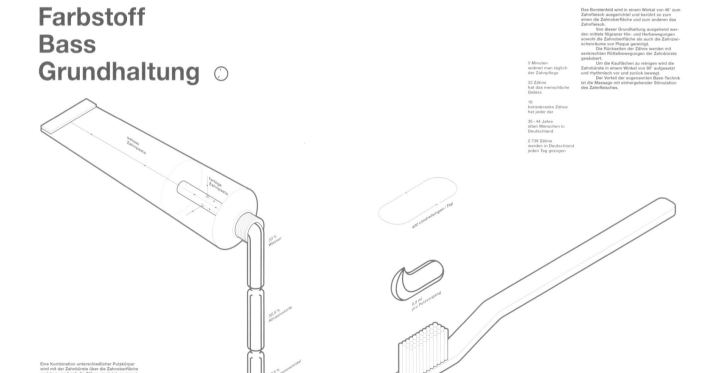

weiße
Zahnpasta

farbige
Zahnpasta

33 %
Wasser

32,5 %
Abrasivstoffe

27,8 %
Suspensionsmittel

2 %
Detergentien
1,5 %
Aromatika
1,5 %
Süßmittel
1 %
Konservierungsmittel
0,2 %
Farbstoffe
0,5 % spezifische Wirkstoffe

Eine Kombination unterschiedlicher Putzkörper
wird mit der Zahnbürste über die Zahnoberfläche
gerieben, wodurch die Zähne gereinigt, angeraut
und poliert werden.
    Dabei setzen die Detergenzien die Ober-
flächenspannung der Paste herab, wodurch
der Putzeffekt und die Schaumbildung verstärkt
werden.
    Durch die Zugabe spezifischer Wirkstoffe
entsteht die prophylaktische Eigenschaft der
Zahnpaste.

5 Minuten
widmet man täglich
der Zahnpflege

32 Zähne
hat das menschliche
Gebiss

16
karieskranke Zähne
hat jeder der

35–44 Jahre
alten Menschen in
Deutschland

2.739 Zähne
werden in Deutschland
jeden Tag gezogen

400 Umdrehungen/Tag

0,8 ml
pro Putzvorgang

1.100 Borsten

Das Borstenfeld wird in einem Winkel von 45° zum
Zahnfleisch ausgerichtet und berührt so zum
einen die Zahnoberfläche und zum anderen das
Zahnfleisch.
    Von dieser Grundhaltung ausgehend wer-
den mittels filigraner Hin- und Herbewegungen
sowohl die Zahnoberfläche als auch die Zahnzwi-
schenräume von Plaque gereinigt.
    Die Rückseiten der Zähne werden mit
senkrechten Rüttelbewegungen der Zahnbürste
gesäubert.
    Um die Kauflächen zu reinigen wird die
Zahnbürste in einem Winkel von 90° aufgesetzt
und rhythmisch vor und zurück bewegt.
    Der Vorteil der sogenannten Bass-Technik
ist die Massage mit einhergehender Stimulation
des Zahnfleisches.

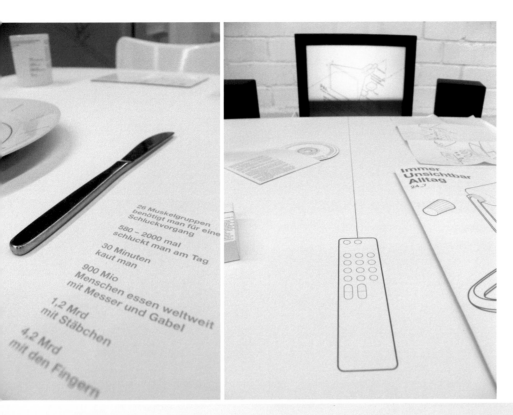

24_7
Benjamin Schulte
24_7 exposes the automated — and thus invisible — aspects of our life, the omnipresent routines and motions that have become our second nature.   Superimposed on the austere and pragmatic setting of a "standard life", these objects, procedures and functionalities find themselves in the spotlight and become exhibits in their own right.   An exercise in everyday statistics, the results can be a little unsettling. Where pie becomes pie chart and our lives an assemblage of knifes or chopsticks, water use and breakfast habits. Statistics and averages start to threaten our subjectivity, that vital illusion of being one of a kind.

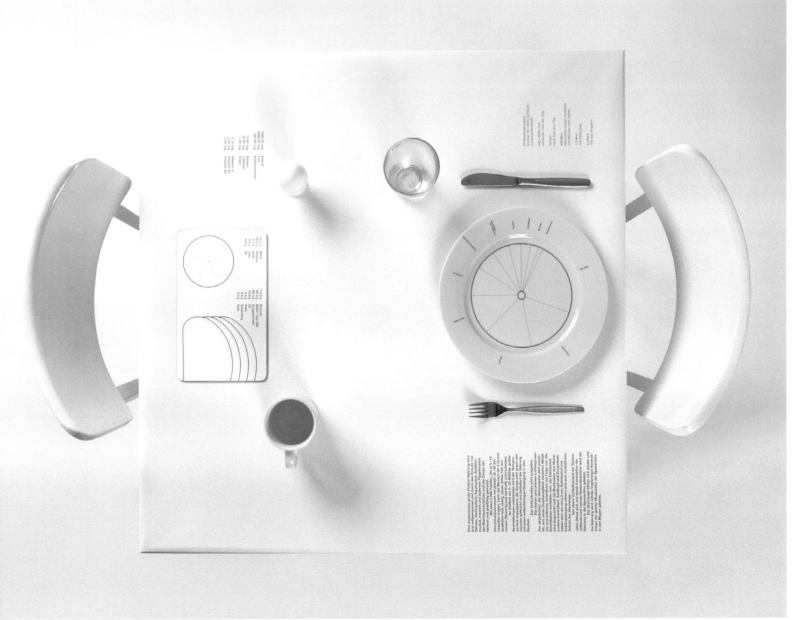

1
FORM FOLLOWS DATA
Iohanna Pani
In FORM FOLLOWS DATA Iohanna Pani tracks and quantifies her own everyday habits in the guise of familiar objects. Here, a bar chart of glasses — or topographical lines inside a coffee cup — might chart her daily caffeine consumption while pie charts on plates disclose the results of a recent blood test.

2
ONE, TWO, TREE...
studio veríssimo

3
HELP
studio veríssimo
Studio Veríssimo add a twist to those everyday helpers with instructions on perfect rice preparation and how to add just the right amount of sweetness to your life. / Photo: Ricardo Faria /

1

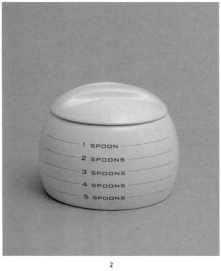

2

3

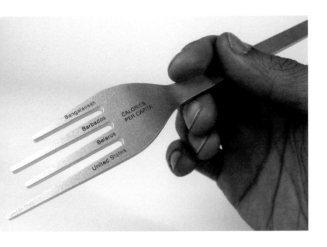

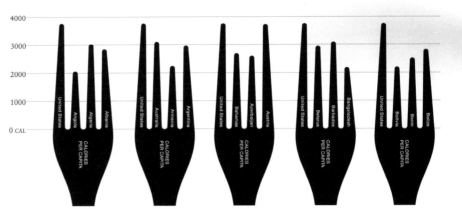

4

4
IN-FORMED
Nadeem Haidary
What's on your plate? A starter dish for Africa, a full meal for Europe: in CALORIC CONSUMPTION, the represented data — calories per capita around the world — is visualised by the length of each prong and the size of each plate. Benchmarked against the undisputed champion of consumption, the United States, the resulting dinner and silverware serves up an alphabet of (mal)nutrition — from Algeria to Australia, from Bolivia to Belize — to visualise the unequal availability of nutrition on our collective forks and plates.

5
DREAMING MILANO
Salottobuono
DREAMING MILANO, a series of ceramic decal plates, dares us to peek over the rim of our own sheltered existence. As part of an urban planning proposal, it explores city boundaries as philosophically and psychologically charged regions, where metropolis and natural environment state their distinction and coexistence becomes ever more vital. / Project by Salottobuono and YellowOffice / Collaborators: Giorgio Bologna, Gabriele Malvolti, Gian Paolo Morelli, Wei Jia Tian, Jean-Benoit Vetillard /

1
FINGERBOWL
Judith Seng

Inverted identity: A graphic reminder of to-day's transparent public profiles, of privacy issues and data protection, Seng's FINGER-BOWL turns this particular political issue into an aesthetic gesture. /Photo: Ilvio Gallo /

2
HOLLEY PORTRAIT / JARED GREENE
3
HOLLEY PORTRAITS / NICCOLÒ MAZZONI
4
HOLLEY PORTRAIT / AURORA BIANCARDI
5
HOLLEY PORTRAITS / TOMMASO SPERETTA
6
HOLLEY PORTRAIT / BRITTANY SUBERS
Daniel Eatock

Inspired by a typographic self-portrait of his friend Richard Holley, London-based de-signer Daniel Eatock devised a simple set-up to tease out the cornerstones of our identity.

The basic rules: Leave your thumbprint on the centre of a white page. Enlarge the print to the size of your face. Overlay it with a thin sheet of copy paper and secure it in place with tape or paperclips. Starting anywhere you like, compose a text about yourself in your natural handwriting, retrac-ing the lines of your own fingerprint. The final result is a pertinent self-portrait, a distillate of what makes you unique: your story, your handwriting and the whorls and lines of your fingerprint.   In his expanding col-lection of "identities", Eatock presents a set of self-portraits that are formally consistent, yet on closer study, a celebration of their author's individuality.

1

2

3

4

5

6

7
FAST FAUST
Boris Müller
Akin to an optometrist's eyesight chart, where each consecutive line gets increasingly smaller, FAST FAUST crams the entire text of Goethe's FAUST into a single poster display. Here, the play becomes a sizing chart: each word's frequency determines its placement and prominence on the poster.

8
3 MINUTES
Charlie de Grussa
The brief: an investigation of 3 Minutes on a single A1 sheet. Charlie de Grussa's newsprint solution compares two jobs that share the same principles of handling calls, yet differ in public perception: an emergency call handler and a cold-call telemarketer.

Although one is considered a vital helper and the other almost universally reviled, de Grussa's analysis reveals a number of surprising similarities as well as predictable differences in communication techniques. Broken down into aspects like percentage of time on the phone, number of words spoken or wages earned, the study not only exposes prevalent rhetoric strategies — straight to the point or faux-personal — but also conveys the true cost of any 3-minute call (emotional, financial and in terms of time) to both the caller and recipient.

Civil War

Grandfather started learning textile practice 19291102-1931722

Chinese Soviet Republic 1931117-1934106

Encirclement Campaign against Northern Jiangxi Soviet 1930126-1931115

Chang River Floods 193173-1931025

Civil War 1927181-19361212

Makden Incident 1931918

Pacification of Manchukuo Incident 1931114

January 28 Battle 1932128

Grandfathers Marriage Chinese Soviet Republic 1934106

Marco Polo Bridge Incident Dis- 193777 established 1934106

Long March 19341016-19341022

Yellow River floods 1933810-19331018

The state of Manchuria 1932218-194568

Zhou Pengfei (1st Aunt's Husband) 1932316

January 28 Battle 1932128-1932

New life movement 1934217

Yellow River Floods II 19354

Encirclement Campaign against Hebei-Shanxi-Henan Soviet 1935131-1935525

Grandfather started his textile business 19361213-1937812

Sino-Japanese War II

December 9th movement 19351129

Huang Zhenwen (Uncle) 193510 3

Chen Fa Yun (Uncle's wife) 193521

Xi'an Incident 19361212

The 2nd Yellow River floods 193869-1938815

United front 1937922

Nanking Massacre 19371213-1938212

Chongqing Bombing 1938 218

War II 193777-194599

PingXingGuan Battle 1937924

Nanking Battle 19371109-19371126

Huang Zhen Yi (1st Aunt) 1939827

Taierzhuang Battle 1938329

Changsha Battle 1939913-1939108

the state of Mengjiang 1936512

Shang Hai Battle 19378139

Pan Yu Yang (3rd Aunt's Husband) 19391028

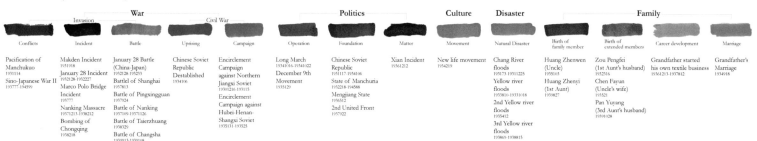

The Cell Phone Revolution

In the developed world, we're tethered to our mobile devices. In the developing world, the phones are essentially primary computing devices, as well as communication tools. Mobile phone usage has skyrocketed in recent years in several parts of the world. It begs the question: Is increased connectivity making us more productive?

Sources: International Telecommunication Union, United Nations Statistics Division

PERCENTAGE OF POPULATION WITH MOBILE CELLULAR SUBSCRIPTIONS

0%　25%　50%　75%　100%

$ GDP PER CAPITA (2002-2007)

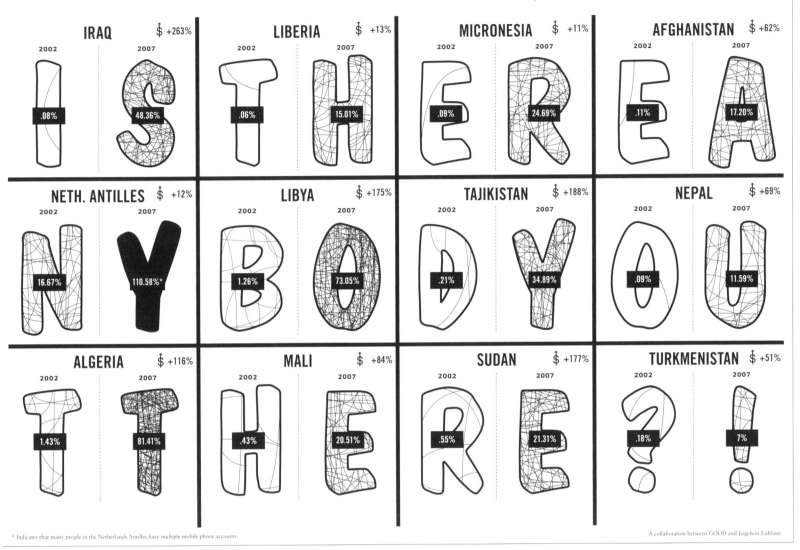

	IRAQ	LIBERIA	MICRONESIA	AFGHANISTAN
$	+263%	+13%	+11%	+62%
2002	.08%	.06%	.09%	.11%
2007	48.36%	15.01%	24.69%	17.20%

I S T H E R E A

	NETH. ANTILLES	LIBYA	TAJIKISTAN	NEPAL
$	+12%	+175%	+188%	+69%
2002	16.67%	1.26%	.21%	.09%
2007	110.58%*	73.05%	34.89%	11.59%

N Y B O D Y O U

	ALGERIA	MALI	SUDAN	TURKMENISTAN
$	+116%	+84%	+177%	+51%
2002	1.43%	.43%	.55%	.18%
2007	81.41%	20.51%	21.31%	7%

T T H E R E ? !

* Indicates that many people in the Netherlands Antilles have multiple mobile phone accounts.

A collaboration between GOOD and Fogelson-Lubliner

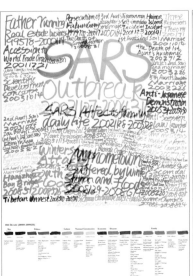

2

1
MAPPING TIME BASED ON GENEALOGY
AND HISTORICAL STUDY – POSTERS
Haohao Huang

2
THE CELL PHONE REVOLUTION
Fogelson-Lubliner
This illustration for GOOD magazine shows
the increase of connectivity in the developing world (measured in mobile phone
subscriptions).

NEXT PAGE (LEFT)
VISUELLE PROGRAMME 2.0
projekttriangle
Cedric Kiefers
Hochschule für Gestaltung Karlsruhe
/ Lecturer: Martin Grothmaak / Course Title: Visuelle Pro-
gramme 2.0 / Visual Codes 2.0 / www.visuelle-programme.de /

NEXT PAGE (RIGHT)
BLACK LOCUST
Bryan Nash Gill
In a classic case of art imitating nature (or
is it the other way around?) BLACK LOCUST
pays homage to a natural precursor of data
visualisation: in tree rings, good years and
bad are recorded for posterity in the trunk's
striated cross section. / 2009 / wood engraving on
Okawara paper, 39" × 31" /

SMS_Plant

Received Short Messages
Send to: 0179/7386329

FROM:
01. January 2007
TO:
31. December 2007

Total Number received:
1120

Quarter 2

Part 02/04 April-June

Visuelle Programme / Visual Codes
Gruppenseminar Martin Grothmaak
Student: Cedric Kiefer
Sommersemester 2008 Studienbereich Kommunikationsdesign
Staatliche Hochschule für Gestaltung Karlsruhe
www.visuelle-programme.de

FROM/ phone number

String: smsFromNumber

Different People sending Messages: 69
Average SMS received per Person: 16,2

Most received Messages from:

01.	0169/631883xx	422
02.	0172/235532xx	162
03.	0181/884733xx	98
04.	0177/023742xx	44
05.	0172/435077xx	43
06.	0169/631883xx	35
07.	0172/235532xx	31
08.	0181/884733xx	30
09.	0157/023742xx	23
10.	0152/435077xx	22

FROM/ Carrier

String: smsFromCarrier

Most received Messages from:

D1	51
D2	185
E+	135
O2	749

D1	4,55%
0151	0
0160	1
0170	20
0171	0
0175	30

D2	16,52%
0152	1
0162	5
0172	184
0173	11
0174	4

Eplus	12,05%
0157	2
0163	63
0177	33
0178	37

O2	66,88%
0159	0
0176	704
0179	45

D1   D2   E+   O2

DATE/ dd/mm/yyyy

String: smsSendDate

Average SMS received
by Day: 3,06
by Month: 93,31

Messages received per Month:

2007

Jan	138
Feb	87
Mar	80
Apr	95
Mai	130
Jun	59
Jul	94
Aug	75
Sep	80
Okt	108
Nov	77
Dec	95

Messages received per Day:

Mon	117
Tue	119
Wed	132
Thu	134
Fri	189
Sat	228
Sun	224

TIME/ hh/mm/ss

String: smsSendTime

00:00-06:00	10,36%
leafs closed	

06:00-12:00	27,32%
leafs opening	

12:00-18:00	39,91%
leafs open	

18:00-00:00	22,41%
leafs closing	

SIZE/ bytes

String: smsSize

Largest SMS in Chars/Byte 653/1342
Smallest SMS in Chars/Byte 2/22

Average Message Size in bytes 235,35
Total bytes received 263595

0-800byte > 0-15Segments
leaf Size

Design by Cedric Kiefer

Created for Visuelle Programme / Visual Codes
With Martin Grothmaak / FB Kommunikationdesign
Summer semester 2008 at HfG Karlsruhe

May-July 2008

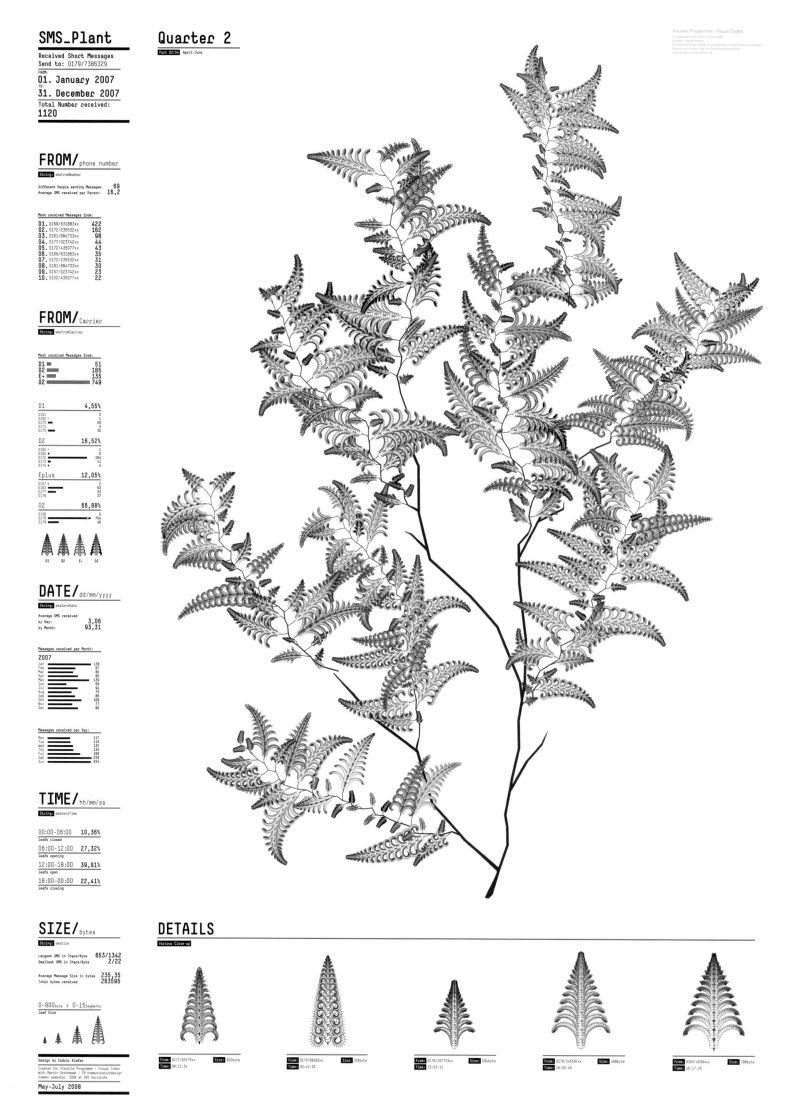

DETAILS

Various Close-up

From: 0172/63175xx	Size: 302byte
Time: 09:11:34	

From: 0176/58183xx	Size: 325byte
Time: 03:42:18	

From: 0178/207723xx	Size: 294byte
Time: 13:03:13	

From: 0178/245181xx	Size: 488byte
Time: 15:02:45	

From: 0163/45394xx	Size: 798byte
Time: 15:17:25	

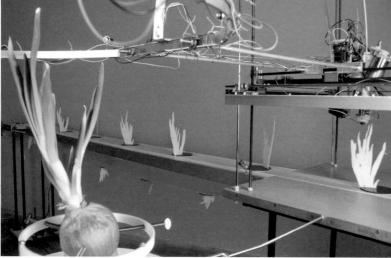

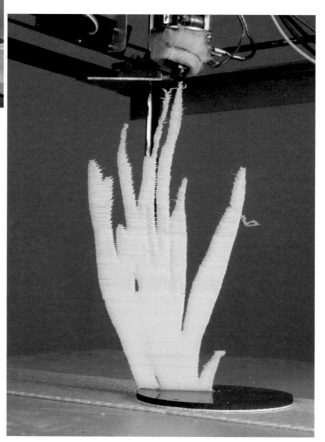

1

GROWTH MODELING DEVICE
David Bowen

David Bowen's GROWTH MODELLING DE-VICE charts the linear progression of natural growth in a series of plastic models. Reminiscent of school science projects, the basic set-up uses lasers to scan an onion plant — the staple of high school biology classes — from one of three angles. While the bulb and growth are being scanned, a fuse deposition modeller uses this information to create an equivalent plastic copy. The experiment is repeated every 24 hours, scanning from a different angle. Akin to the frames of an analogue film, removed from the projector and exposed for all to see, the result is a series of 2D models that chart the plant's 3D growth over time. /2009/

2
ROSE OF JERICHO
MOOD DATA SCULPTURE
Martin Kim Luge

The rose of Jericho is a strange flower: dried and shrivelled, it appears withered and lifeless. But treat the desert plant to a drop or two and watch it unfurl at a moment's notice. Also known as a "resurrection plant", this process is reversible many times, making it ideal for experimentation.   In his attempt to reflect the tenuous bonds fostered by online social networks — their constant, peripheral awareness of our extended social circle — Martin Kim Luge focused on the mood tags associated with status updates — how they keep us up to date on our friends' mental states without any need for direct communication.   In order to preserve the ambivalence and complexity of our emotions, never quite encapsulated in a single keyword, Luge decided to opt for a less defined, more organic translation of mood and mind. To this end, he partnered rose of Jericho plants with online friends and assigned a numerical value to each available emotional state on the platform MYSPACE. COM, from happy to sad. A microcontroller would then dispense a controlled amount of water to each of his experimental plants according to their human partner's particular mood — the happier the friend, the more the plant itself would thrive.   Based on this premise, his ROSE OF JERICHO data sculptures are never "bored", "angry" or "upbeat", but convey a more general idea of their human equivalent's state of wellbeing; and just like long-term friendships, this hardy plant is quite resilient and can survive a long drought or extended dry spell. /2008 / Rose of Jericho, Arduino, Processing /

3
WEEPING WILLOW
A TREE FULL OF FRIENDS
Martin Kim Luge

Can't see the wood for the trees? In a more ambitious take on his ROSE OF JERICHO project, Martin Kim Luge branches out to explore further ramifications of friendships and moods.   While every branch of his weeping willow symbolises an online friend, its slope reflects their overall mood — the happier the friend, the higher the branch. Strengthening virtual bonds by tangible means, Luge mails these lasercut branches to their human counterparts once a week where they can be assembled into an ever-growing sculpture and approximation of their own online psyche — a nice, tangible touch in an increasingly noncommittal world and a regular reality check on the way we portray ourselves in the virtual realm. /2008 / lasercutter /

2

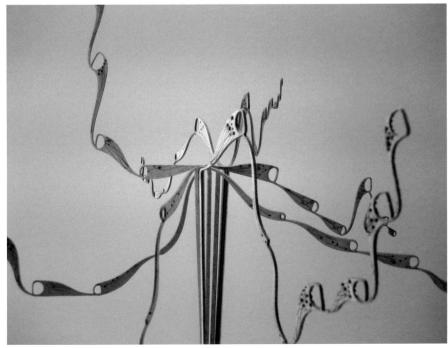

3

1
WATERMARKS PROJECT
Chris Bodle

Rise and shine? Those living near estuaries or the seaside might be used to spring tides and flooding, but climate change-induced sea level surges add an ominous new dimension to the mix.　In order to make this factor more tangible, WATERMARKS allows residents to experience the depth and extent of future flooding against the background of a familiar environment. Here, a series of flood level projections sees Bristol's bustling harbour and low-lying city centre submerged under up to two stories of water — a shocking projection based on current UK government predictions as well as other more extreme scenarios to account for the amount of variation, uncertainty and scientific dissent.

Positioned on the watershed between art and landscape architecture — between public perception and the pragmatic issues of flooding itself — WATERMARKS takes this vital topic out of the scientific context to encourage debate and creative participation among those potentially affected. / 2009 /
Digital projection / Thanks to Arnolfini (Gallery) and Bordeaux Quay (Restaurant) /

1

43-47 knots

13-17 knots

1-2 knots

2

2
WINDBARBS
Tim Knowles

Flying the flag for a new measure of wind speed and elemental forces, Tim Knowles' WINDBARBS bridge the gap between art installation and meteorological device. Gauging wind strength and direction, his ten white flags indicate how the wind blows.

Knowles' simple but ingenious trick: each banner is weighted to unfold only at wind speeds equal to or greater than the depicted symbol, and the key to decrypt them is just that — a key. Based on the decimal system, Knowles adds a new tooth for every ten knots. / 2009 / 10 Flags constructed from a range of fabrics & weighting materials / Copyright: the artist /

3
PRAYERS
Germaine Koh

Germaine Koh loves to explore the unexpected relationships between everyday actions, familiar objects, old and new technologies and common places. In this particular example, dating back to the almost prehistoric age of the digital office (1999) she captures all activities of a networked computer and broadcasts them to the building's exterior in a series of Morse coded signals. Translated into little puffs of smoke — here today, gone in a flash — the building's cerebral activities burst into the outside world like ephemeral ideas, ready to expand and dissipate at a moment's notice. / 1999 / Computer, existing office computer network, fog machine / Photo: Germaine Koh / Copyright: the artist /

4
FAIR-WEATHER FORCES (WATER LEVEL)
Germaine Koh

In her efforts to visualise natural — and decidedly non-natural — phenomena, Germaine Koh creates tangible connections that turn our world inside out. Her FAIR-WEATHER FORCES for example, transplants the power of tides — their divisive nature and forceful inevitability — to the controlled confines of a gallery. Here, the manmade waves of velvet ropes move up and down in accordance with the level of a nearby body of water. The result: an unpredictable, yet incorruptible bouncer that permits or blocks our passage according to the vagaries of nature. / 2008 / Velvet ropes attached to mechanisms housed in custom stainless steel posts, driven by microprocessors receiving data over Internet from remote ultrasonic sensor / Photo: Germaine Koh /

3

4

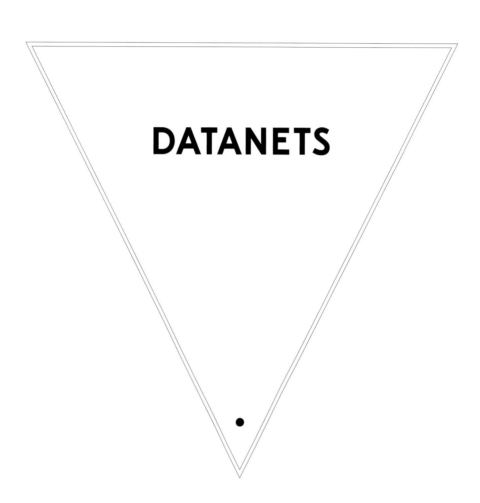

DATANETS

Sometimes information is not to be found in the single data record itself, but in its connection and relation to others. By connecting these data points, a network structure emerges where the links tell us more than the nodes. The following diagrams visualize these hierarchies, associations, relationships, interconnections and links with many diverse approaches.

•

Visualizations are not just about making complicated issues simple. Sometimes complexity can even be the message. A growing visually literate audience asks for access to intricate systems, while expecting a simple, easy-to-understand interface at the same time. This complementary relationship between simplicity and complexity – the synthesis of the two – creates an interesting challenge for visualizations.

There are enough domains where designers can apply the principles of "simplexity." Complicated networks, reticulated structures and complex organizations are all around us in almost

PREVIOUS PAGE
SPAMGHETTO
JUNK-MAIL WALLCOVERING
ToDo
/ ›P.175 /

1
MURMUR STUDY
Christopher P. Baker
/ › P. 176 /

any field we can think of – smart power grids, transportation networks, biological organisms, financial markets, organized crime, and social networks.

The latter is the subject of *Murmur Study*. The installation monitors *Twitter* messages and *Facebook* status updates /1/ for emotional utterances containing words like "argh," "grrrr," "ohhh," and "ewww" in various variations. *30* wall-mounted thermal printers spit out these personal messages continuously, creating a tangled mass on the floor. But what looks like a chaotic structure is actually archived, indexed and referenced by corporations. A matter that should make us ponder.

A simple tree diagram is the only illustration in Charles Darwin's seminal *The Origin of the Species*. /2/ Greg McInerny and Stefanie Posavec use the same visualization technique to dissect the text of this very book: a chapter divides into subchapters, which split into paragraphs, and finally sentences. The result is a flower-like formation that presents an overview of the "literary organism."

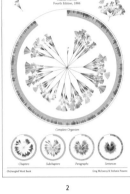

2
(EN)TANGLED WORD BANK:
THE ORIGIN OF THE SPECIES
Stefanie Posavec
/ › P. 187 /

An even more intricate network emerges in *This was 2008*. /3/ By extracting the names of people, corporations, and other organizations from the *New York Times* articles and indicating links between them, Jer Thorp creates a dense mesh of connectivity. It not only shows who was mentioned more often than others, it also reveals which names were mentioned together. Call it a hyper-tagcloud.

As visually striking as this last example is, it shows that static renderings have their limits. Intricate structure visualizations like this might give a proper overview and a good sense of the nature of the network, but they make it hard to decipher the details. Here is where interactivity can flex its muscles. By zooming in, isolating, or highlighting certain interconnections, complexity is dissolved and simplicity takes over.

3
THIS WAS 2008
Jer Thorp
/ › P. 185 /

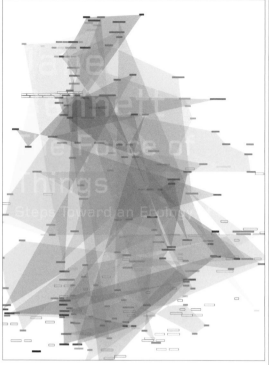

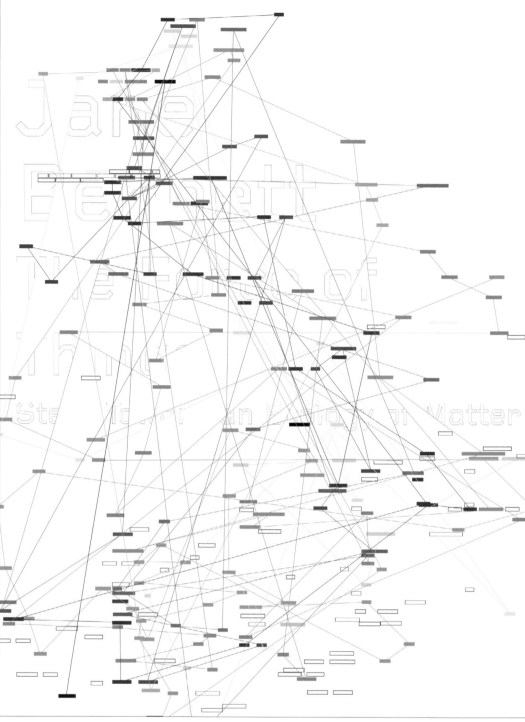

THE FORCE OF THINGS
Ian Dapot

THE FORCE OF THINGS is a series of posters mapping the relationships between cited
authors and referenced ideas in Jane Bennett's essay THE FORCE OF THINGS: STEPS
TOWARD AN ECOLOGY OF MATTER.
Bennett's work, a daring examination of the
vitality and wilfulness of nonhuman entities
and forces, quotes a wide range of thinkers —
from Spinoza to Deleuze — and creates new,
unexpected connections between different
schools of thought. In his exploration of these
intellectual leaps of faith, Dapot codes and
connects individual references to visualise the
conceptual territory they occupy within the
essay.   "I began by creating an Adobe
PDF of Bennett's essay and spreading each
page over the surface of the poster. I high-
lighted the name of every cited author and
connected each reference through line and/
or colour. I tried to demarcate the territory of
each author or work to show how Bennett's
thinking and arguments were constructed."
      In its density, the resulting image almost
obliterates the subject matter. Then again,
Dapot's interpretation creates new, vital and
vibrant tension between different views and
interpretations — thus enlivening the discussion on inanimate things.

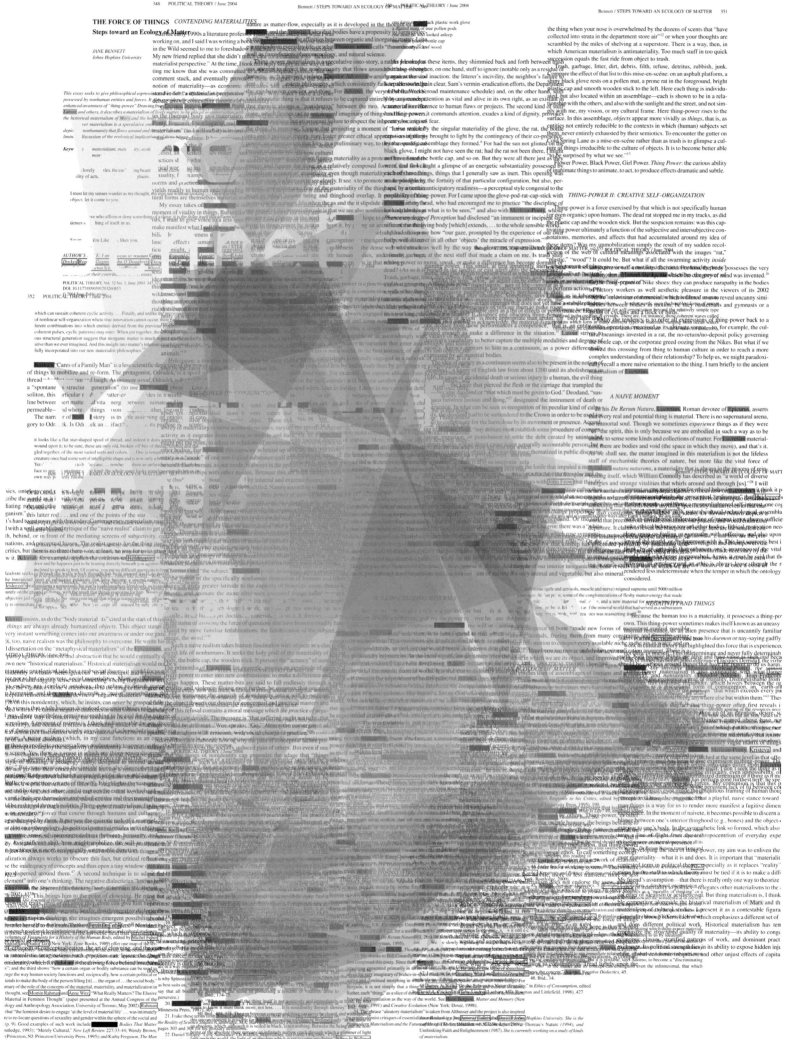

1
FLOCKING DIPLOMATS 2
Catalogtree

/›P.224 / Those roving delinquents just won't let up. Protected by immunity, diplomatic staff around the world are famous for abusing their privileges when it comes to minor infractions such as parking violations.

A further visual variation of the FLOCKING DIPLOMATS theme, this particular image reveals the most (un)usual suspects and persistent perpetrators by following in the footsteps, or car tracks, of the top 20 diplomatic offenders in 1999 and their weekly violations.

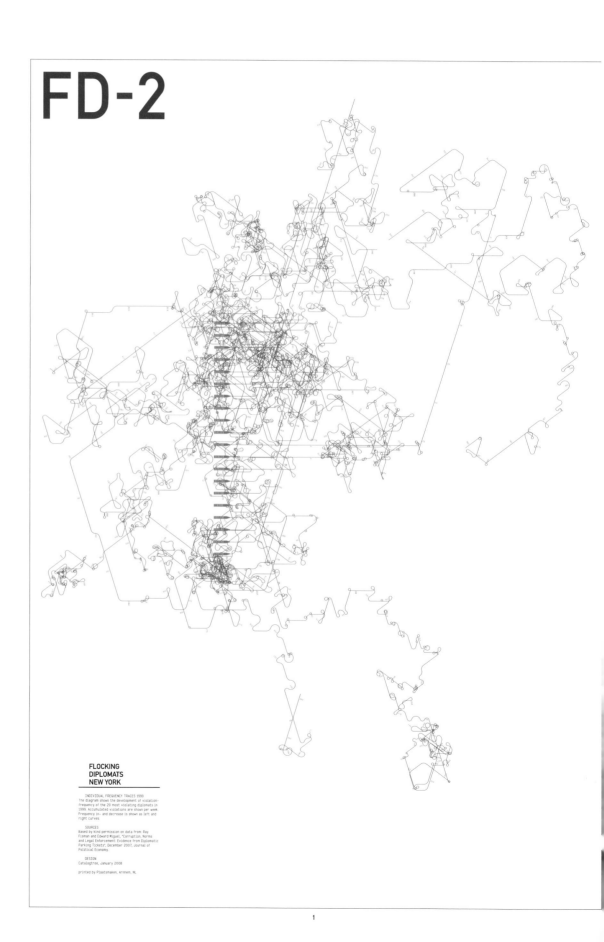

FD-2

FLOCKING
DIPLOMATS
NEW YORK

INDIVIDUAL FREQUENCY TRACES 1999
The diagram shows the development of violation-frequency of the 20 most violating diplomats in 1999. Accumulated violations are shown per week. Frequency in- and decrease is shown as left and right curves.

SOURCES
Based by kind permission on data from Ray Fisman and Edward Miguel, "Corruption, Norms and Legal Enforcement: Evidence from Diplomatic Parking Tickets", December 2007, Journal of Political Economy.

DESIGN
Catalogtree, January 2008

printed by Plaatsmaken, Arnhem, NL.

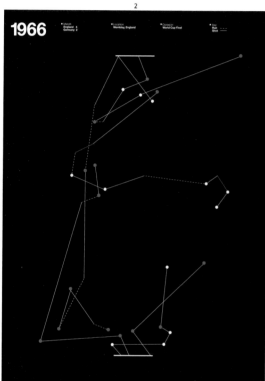

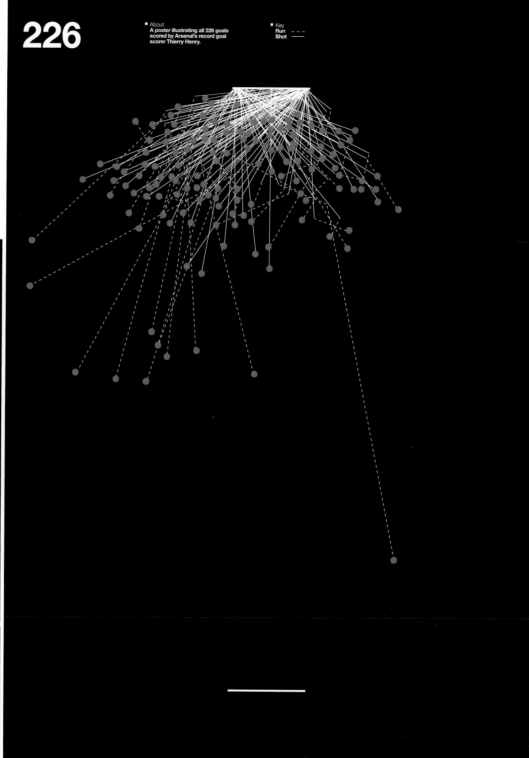

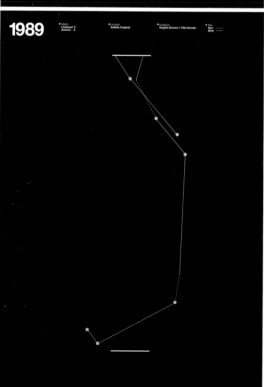

2

3

4

2
GOALS POSTER — 1966
Adrian Newell
Putting football on the map: Adrian Newell's
1966 GOALS POSTER celebrates all six goals
scored in England's victory over West Germany in the 1966 World Cup final.

3
GOALS POSTER — 1989
Adrian Newell
A poster mapping the two goals scored at
Anfield in the decisive title match of the 1989
English League 1 Championship.

4
GOALS POSTER — THIERRY HENRY
Adrian Newell
A true homage: all 226 goals scored by Thierry
Henry during his time with Arsenal FC.

1
UCF APPLY
Sean Clarke

Pick up a pen to pick your own future! In order to encourage prospective graphic design students, Sean Clarke invites them to determine their own direction of study. By connecting action and subject, they create new prospective paths.

2
ILLINOIS: VISUALIZING MUSIC
Jax de León

Jax de León's project ILLINOIS: VISUALIZING MUSIC puts the US state on the map. In his homage to prolific American songwriter Sufjan Stevens — and his landmark album "Illinoise" — León meticulously charts all locations mentioned on the sweeping pop masterpiece.   A concept album of sorts, Stevens scatters plenty of local references into the mix, from actual song titles (Chicago, Jacksonville) to fleeting mentions of lesser-known pit stops like Great Godrey Maze or Nichols Park.   With his low-tech recreation of this musical road trip, visiting all locations in the order of mention, León offers an alternative approach to the album's inherent complexity — not as a complement, but as a visual enrichment. After all, no amount of analysis could replace the emotional immediacy or visceral response of the actual music itself.

3
LIST OF SOMETHING
Jin Jung

Jin Jung spins a web of words across the wall: shuffling through examples of personal poetry, the communication designer decided to gauge and seek the public's reaction to his work by visual means. In this spirit, he asked close friends to pick their favourite words and phrases and record those at the top of the list.   The second stage of the project, the public exhibition, puts these expressions up for debate and invites visitors to make their own threaded connections. Each phrase comes with its very own pushpin and may be connected to related statements by a real and proverbial red thread.   The resulting LIST OF SOMETHING tells a new story: one that binds author and audience closer together.

1

2

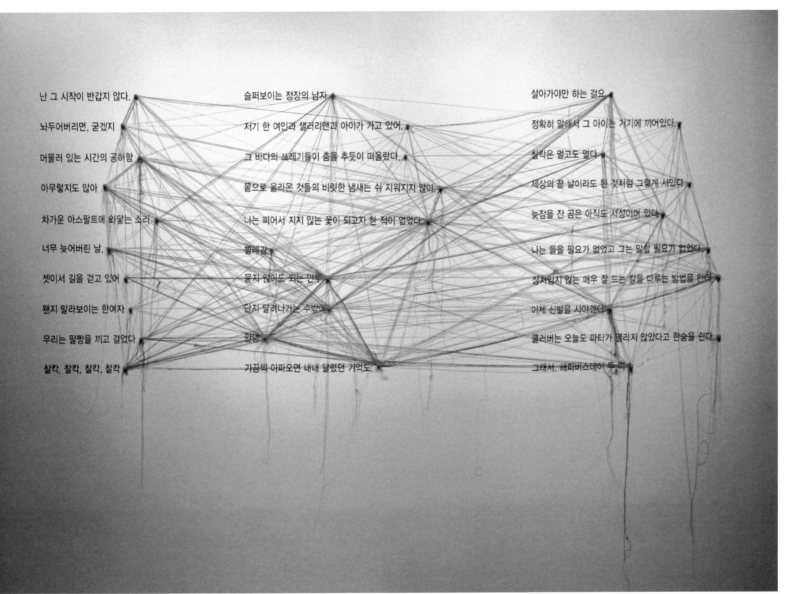

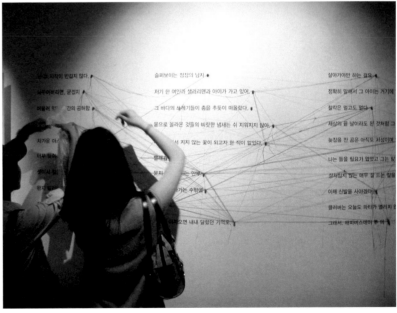

1
TEMPLATE 2.0
WEALTH VERSUS HAPPINESS GRAPHITI
TOKO
/ Template 2.0 Exhibition is part of ISEA — International
Symposium on Electronic Art /

2
DRM
DensityDesign
The Design Research Map (DRM) initia-
tive aims to build a visual record of design
research in Italy through annotated infographics and interpretive, comparative and
indexed maps. / Creative Direction: Donato Ricci / Info-
graphic: Daniele Guido, Luca Masud, Mauro Napoli, Donato
Ricci, Gaia Scagnetti / Politecnico di Milano, Dipartimento In-
daco, Agenzia SDI / The DRM book is edited by Paola Bertola
and Stefano Maffei /

1

I codici del design
(ISTAT-ATECO/NACE CODE):
una visione frammentata

50 | 50   DESIGN CODES (ISTAT/ATECO – NACE CODE): A FRAGMENTED VISION

Comunicazione e Interazione
Communication and Interaction

Comunicazione e Interazione + Strategie, Servizi e Sistemi
Communication and Interaction + Strategies, Services and Systems

Ambienti
Environments

Ambienti + Strategie, Servizi e Sistemi
Environments + Strategies, Services and Systems

Materiali
Materials

Materiali + Interni
Materials + Environments

Materiali + Prodotti
Materials + Products

Moda
Fashion

Prodotti
Products

Prodotti + Materiali
Products + Materials

Prodotti + Interni
Product + Environments

Prodotti + Comunicazione e Interazione
Products + Communication and Interaction

Strategie, Servizi e Sistemi
Strategies, Services and Systems

Strategie, Servizi e Sistemi + Prodotti
Strategies, Services and Systems + Products

Strategie, Servizi e Sistemi + Prodotti + Materiali
Strategies, Services and systems + Products + Materials

BASE = 382 RICERCHE/RESEARCHES (FONTE/SOURCE: DRM RESEARCH©SDIAGENCY_2008)   DRM

58   58 + 70   58 + 72   58 + 74   59   59 + 72   62   72 + 62   62 e 73 + 74   70 + 72   70 + 74   72 + 74   71.11.00   71.11 e 72 + 74   71.11 + 70   71.11 + 72   71.11 + 74   72   72 + 74   74

2

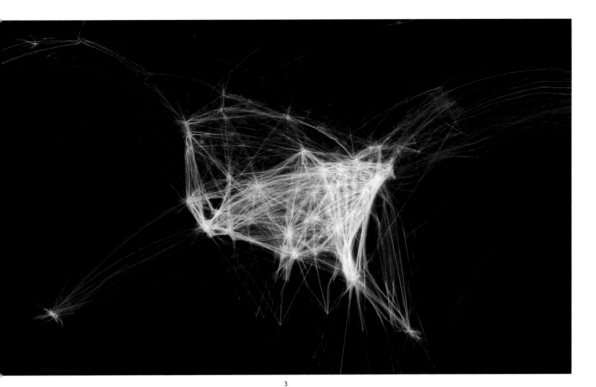

3

3
FLIGHT PATTERNS
Aaron Koblin

Just like most products of human ingenuity — and humanity itself — aircraft come in all shapes and sizes. In this particular version of connect-the-dots, Aaron Koblin draws vapour trails of light across North America and beyond, towards the outlying US territories, to chart the intensity of air travel above the continent, coded by aircraft makes and models.   Originally part of a series of experiments on "Celestial Mechanics" with Gabriel Dunne and Scott Hessels at UCLA, FLIGHT PATTERNS examines these emerging travel trends by plotting Federal Aviation Administration (FAA) data in the Processing programming environment.

4
BARCODE PLANTAGE
Daniel Becker

On Daniel Becker's "barcode plantage", the humble 2D product identifier becomes a unique tree in the garden of globalisation.

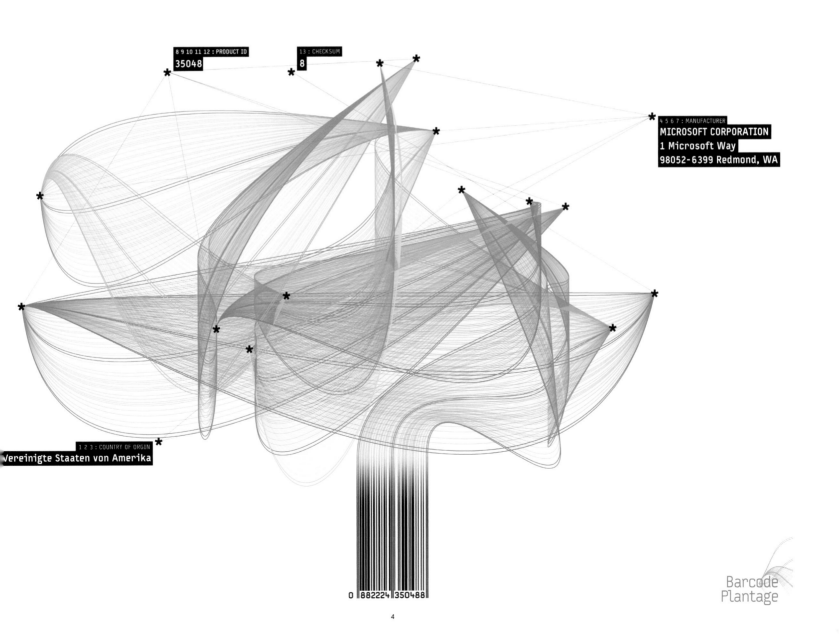

8 9 10 11 12 : PRODUCT ID
35048

13 : CHECKSUM
8

4 5 6 7 : MANUFACTURER
MICROSOFT CORPORATION
1 Microsoft Way
98052-6399 Redmond, WA

1 2 3 : COUNTRY OF ORGIN
Vereinigte Staaten von Amerika

0 882224 350488

Barcode
Plantage

4

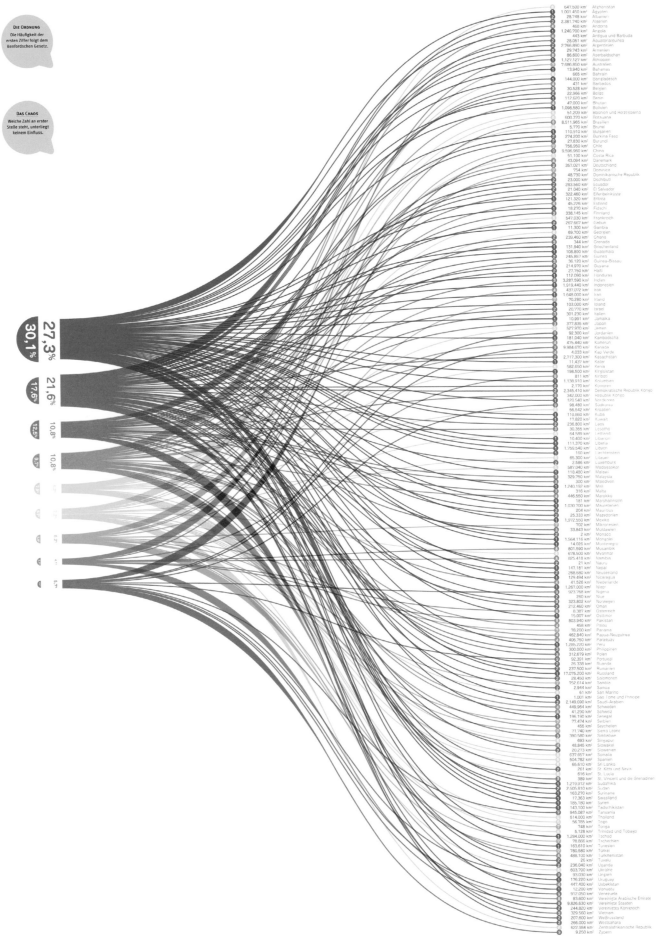

RANDØM WALK
DIE VISUALISIERUNG DES ZUFALLS

DAS BENFORDSCHE GESETZ

Bestimmte Datensätze, deren Werte nicht durch bewusste Manipulation bestimmt wurden, wie beispielsweise die Flächengrößen der Länder der Erde, haben eine interessante Eigenschaft. Betrachtet man nur die erste Ziffer der Flächengrößen, stellt man fest, dass die Häufigkeiten der Ziffern von 1 bis 9 in einem Verhältnis zueinander stehen, die auch bei völlig anderen Datensätzen wie beispielsweise DAX-Werten anzutreffen ist. Dieses Phänomen wird das „Benfordsche Gesetz", bzw. das „Gesetz der ersten Ziffer" genannt. Obwohl die Daten im einzelnen nicht bewusst beeinflusst wurden, unterliegen sie dennoch dieser Regelmäßigkeit. Sind sie hingegen manipuliert worden, kann man dies anhand des Gesetzes in einem gewissen Rahmen erkennen.

Alphabetisch sind hier alle Länder der Erde mit ihren Flächengrößen aufgelistet. Von diesen wird dabei nur die erste Ziffer berücksichtigt. Diese Ziffern sind mit Linien verbunden, die zu ihren Gruppen laufen.

Die Gruppen wachsen mit der Anzahl ihrer Ziffern. Darüber hinaus wird der prozentuale Anteil einer Ziffer an der Gesamtmenge der Ziffern gezeigt. Daneben stehen in den Halbkreisen die erwarteten prozentualen Anteile nach dem Benfordschen Gesetz. Man sieht, wie gut dieses Gesetz schon bei diesem relativ kleinen Datensatz zum Tragen kommt.

2

1
RANDOM WALK
THE VISUALIZATION OF RANDOMNESS
Daniel Becker

2
SPAMGHETTO
JUNK-MAIL WALLCOVERING
ToDo

Every day, our e-mail inboxes are flooded with unsolicited offers. Annoying to some, entertaining to others, Todo decided it was high time to stop sweeping this metaphorical junk under the carpet and instead recycle it for the greater good.   Turning (prospective) vice into virtue — or rubbish to riches — the SPAMGHETTO wallpaper gives the questionable missives a second chance and a new lease of life; when generative software transforms the guilty pleasures of gaga poetry and bizarre solicitations into well-groomed branches and fertile fronds, the result is a lesson in faux-Art Nouveau artistry and pretty Victorian flourishes. Chopped up into tiny strings of words and captured in the constraints of this domesticated SPAMGHETTO, even aggressive sales or phishing pitches become a thing of unfettered beauty.

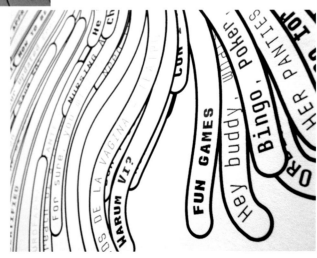

1
MURMUR STUDY
Christopher P. Baker

Christopher P. Baker's MURMUR STUDY examines the rise of micro-messaging technologies such as TWITTER or FACEBOOK status updates — today's "digital small talk". Unlike water-cooler conversations however, these fleeting thoughts are accumulated, archived and digitally indexed by corporations. While the future of these archives remains to be seen, the sheer volume of this publicly accessible — and often emotional — data should give us pause. Whether vented anger, spontaneous delight or just random thoughts to pass the time, these one-sided ephemeral outbursts are here to stay — and could come back to haunt us.   Baker's installation consists of 30 thermal printers that continuously monitor TWITTER for new messages containing variations of common emotional utterances such as "argh", "meh", "grrrr", "oooo", "ewww" and "hmph". The resulting verbal onslaught prints out as an endless waterfall of text that accumulates in tangled piles below, to be forgotten and discarded or — in this case — recycled for further projects. / 2009 / A live Twitter feed and thermal receipt printers controlled by custom hardware and software / Project Collaborator: Márton András Juhász / Photo: Márton András Juhász /

2
RELATIONSHIP MATTERS.
A SOCIOGRAM INVESTIGATION
Valentina D'Efilippo

2

1

NEXT PAGE (LEFT)
INNOVATE, PARTICIPATE! POSTER LUST

Don't fret: this is no close-up of a Death Star clone, but a visual representation of the Culture Council's exhaustive research on Arts, Culture and Media.   To illustrate one of their reports, a poster highlights the various links between the covered subjects and departments. The result is a stupendously dense, multi-dimensional, textual and textured surface that frizzes out towards the edges — and thus an impressive document of the breadth, depth and interdisciplinarity of the Council's work in arts, media and communication.

NEXT PAGE (RIGHT)
JERRY GARCIA
Marian Bantjes

A riot of colour and imagination, this musical "genealogy" of Jerry Garcia, founder of hippy icons The Greatful Dead, adds a touch of psychedelic flourishes to the visualisation of the seminal band leader's influences, contemporaries and immediate acolytes. Suffused with the era's most prominent aesthetics and colour schemes, the free-flowing pedigree gives plenty of space to those who provided him with inspiration — musical and otherwise — and those who drew on his prolific genius. / Art Director: Phil Bicker /

raad voor cultuur
raad voor cultuur
raad voor cultuur

Innoveren, participeren!

Advies
Agenda Cultuurbeleid en
Culturele Basisinfrastructuur

Maart 2007

agenderende thema's

e-cultuur

Democratisch en cultureel burgerschap staat of valt met goed geïnformeerde burgers, en in het verlengde daarvan met instellingen die onbelemmerd en bemiddelend toegang bieden tot bronnen van cultuur en informatie. Dat betekent dat ook alles wat in een gedigitaliseerde omgeving met publieke middelen tot stand komt, in de breedst mogelijke zin beschikbaar en toegankelijk moet zijn en blijven.

cultuur-verdracht

Het aanwakkeren van culturele interesse en activiteiten is dan ook niet gebaseerd op de traditionele verheffingsgedachte, maar op een maatschappelijke noodzaak. In een steeds ingewikkeldere samenleving groeit de behoefte aan betekenisgeving en verdieping. En ook de behoefte aan schoonheid, fun en verstrooiing. Kunst, erfgoed en de media spelen daarbij een vooraanstaande rol.

talent-ontwikkeling

De krachtigste bron voor de kwaliteit van de kunst- en cultuurbeoefening in Nederland en voor de toekomst van de verschillende disciplines is talent en de manier waarop dat wordt gekoesterd en geslepen tot goede kunstenaars en interessante cultuurdragers, die ook buiten de grenzen worden gewaardeerd. Zeker in de wereld van kunst, erfgoed en media is het niet de bedoeling een leven lang veelbelovend te blijven.

innovatie

Een nieuw innovatieprogramma moet door verschillende ministeries, andere overheden en uiteraard ook het bedrijfsleven worden gefinancierd. Het programma is niet bedoeld voor individuele instellingen. Alleen consortia van samenwerkende partijen, waaronder onderwijsinstellingen, culturele en wetenschappelijke instellingen, alsmede het bedrijfsleven en wellicht ook overheden kunnen er gezamenlijk op inschrijven.

continuïteit

In alles wat we vandaag doen, klinkt gisteren door. In vrijwel alle onderdelen van de cultuur is sprake van een continu proces in de tijd. Er zijn geen schotten die eerder in aanmerking komen om onder invloed van, en tegelijk met gebruikmaking van, de nieuwste technologieën te verdwijnen, dan die tussen verleden, heden en toekomst van de cultuur.

instrumenten

Juist in de cultuursector is in de loop van de tijd een goede betrokkenheid-op-afstand ontstaan – niet in de laatste plaats door een rijksoverheid die zich verantwoordelijk voelde voor vaak kwetsbare kunst- en cultuurinstellingen en tegelijkertijd besefte dat inhoudelijke bemoeienis uit den boze was. Die betrokkenheid mag door een stelselgeoriënteerd beleid niet verloren gaan.

sectoren

amateurkunst en cultuureducatie

archieven

architectuur stedenbouw monumenten archeologie landschap

beeldende kunst

bibliotheken

film

internationaal cultuurbeleid

letteren

media

musea

dans

muziek en muziektheater

theater

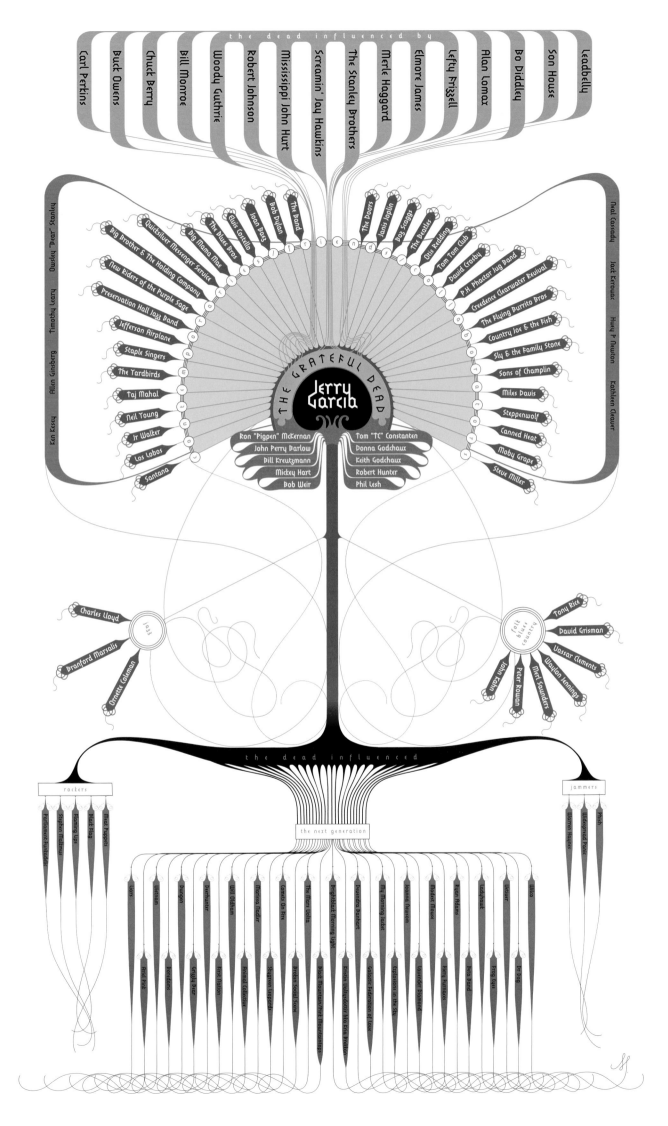

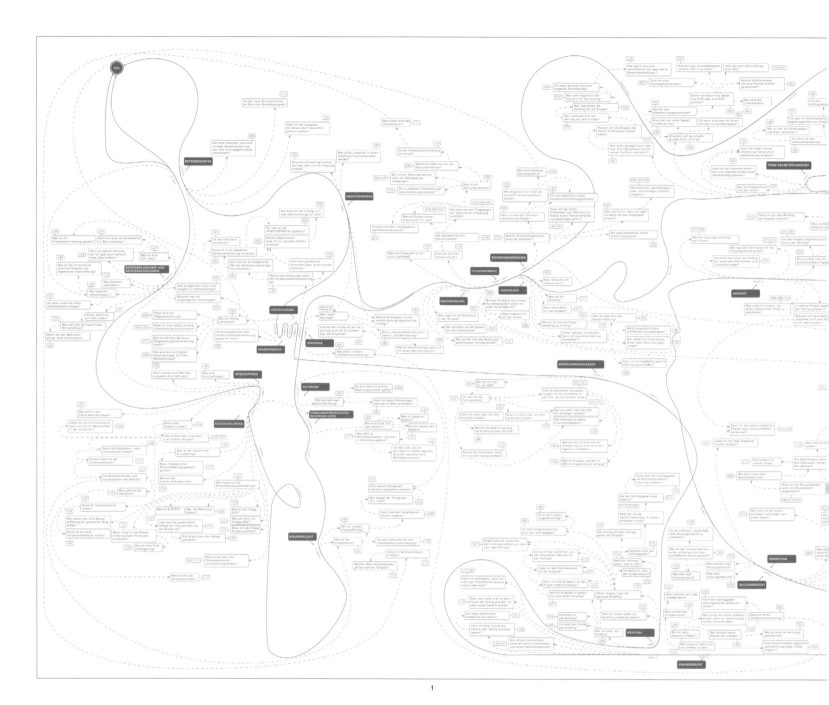

1

PARCOURS

Katrin Schacke

Katrin Schacke's PARCOURS GUIDE TO SELF-EMPLOYMENT — a how-to for aspiring artists and designers — gives bright young hopefuls a leg-up in the harsh climate of freelance employment. Divided into a poster and book, it covers questions from business practices to taxation.   Taking the classic flowchart to organic extremes — and thus exemplifying the ramified and non-hierarchical nature prevalent in this realm — the poster focuses on barriers to entry, on topical hurdles to be overcome, broken down into their individual components.   Formulated as a set of questions, it provides a handy checklist for "freelance fitness", from reduced-rate artist insurance to contracts, cost sharing and copyright.

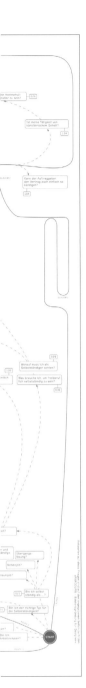

2

HOW WE ONCE BECAME ALMOST
RICH AND FAMOUS
Yvonne Feller und Florian Flechsig
Yvonne Feller and Florian Flechsig's diploma
thesis explores a life in the subjunctive, of
wishful thinking — and possible paths that
might lead us there.   HOW WE ONCE
BECAME ALMOST RICH AND FAMOUS sees
the two students aiming high. Their ambitious goal: to become millionaires within half
a year and to treat this task as a good-
natured — and well-documented — compe-
tition.   According to the maxim "every
dollar counts", they developed a variety of
money-making strategies, from a few cents
here and there on bottle deposits, to eBay
sales, risky bets and survey participations. As
part of a social crowd-sourcing experiment,
they also turned to the public for donations
and ideas via a project blog and website.
       The visual documentation of their finan-
cial experiment encompassed a book review
(including mission statement, money-making
schemes and a selection of readers' and media reactions), weekly data reports with a
detailed list of all relevant actions, e-mails,
blog posts, comments and revenues as well
as an experimental, cube-shaped stage for
alternative presentation formats, e.g. the
number of eyeballs, encouraging remarks
or pessimistic detractors.

STANLEY
THE OPEN QUESTION MAGAZINE
Katrin Schacke

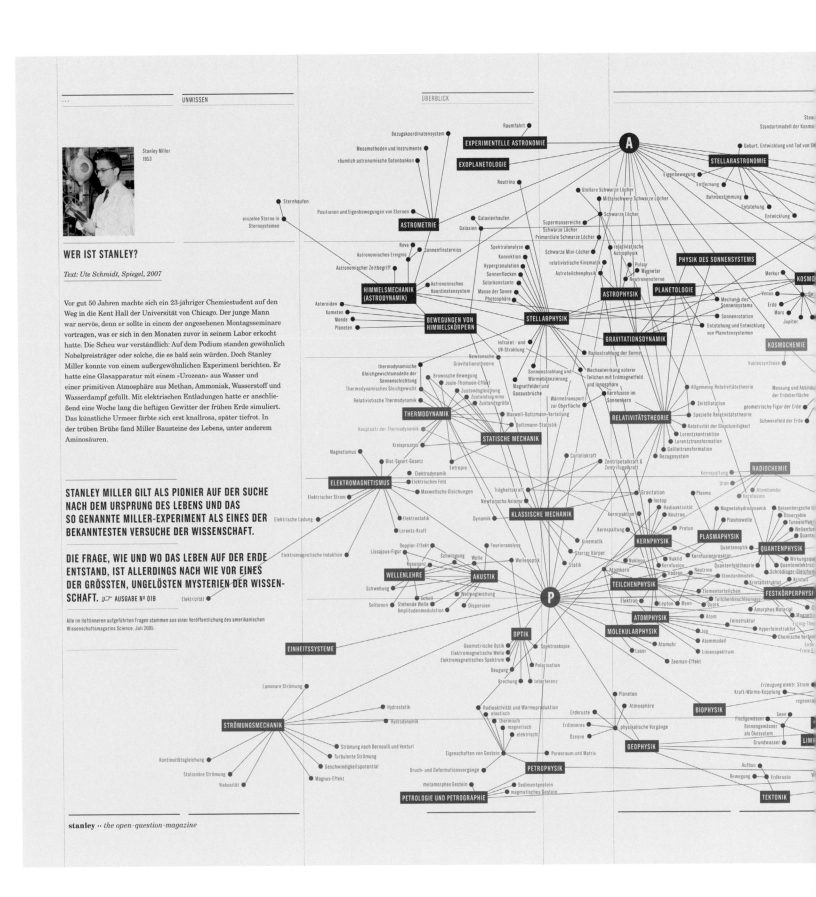

Stanley Miller
1953

WER IST STANLEY?

Text: Ute Schmidt, Spiegel, 2007

Vor gut 50 Jahren machte sich ein 23-jähriger Chemiestudent auf den
Weg in die Kent Hall der Universität von Chicago. Der junge Mann
war nervös, denn er sollte in einem der angesehenen Montagsseminare
vortragen, was er sich in den Monaten zuvor in seinem Labor erkocht
hatte. Die Scheu war verständlich: Auf dem Podium standen gewöhnlich
Nobelpreisträger oder solche, die es bald sein würden. Doch Stanley
Miller konnte von einem außergewöhnlichen Experiment berichten. Er
hatte eine Glasapparatur mit einem »Urozean« aus Wasser und
einer primitiven Atmosphäre aus Methan, Ammoniak, Wasserstoff und
Wasserdampf gefüllt. Mit elektrischen Entladungen hatte er anschlie-
ßend eine Woche lang die heftigen Gewitter der frühen Erde simuliert.
Das künstliche Urmeer färbte sich erst knallrosa, später tiefrot. In
der trüben Brühe fand Miller Bausteine des Lebens, unter anderem
Aminosäuren.

**STANLEY MILLER GILT ALS PIONIER AUF DER SUCHE
NACH DEM URSPRUNG DES LEBENS UND DAS
SO GENANNTE MILLER-EXPERIMENT ALS EINES DER
BEKANNTESTEN VERSUCHE DER WISSENSCHAFT.**

**DIE FRAGE, WIE UND WO DAS LEBEN AUF DER ERDE
ENTSTAND, IST ALLERDINGS NACH WIE VOR EINES
DER GRÖSSTEN, UNGELÖSTEN MYSTERIEN DER WISSEN-
SCHAFT.** ☞ AUSGABE № 019

Alle im Heftinneren aufgeführten Fragen stammen aus einer Veröffentlichung des amerikanischen
Wissenschaftsmagazins Science, Juli 2005.

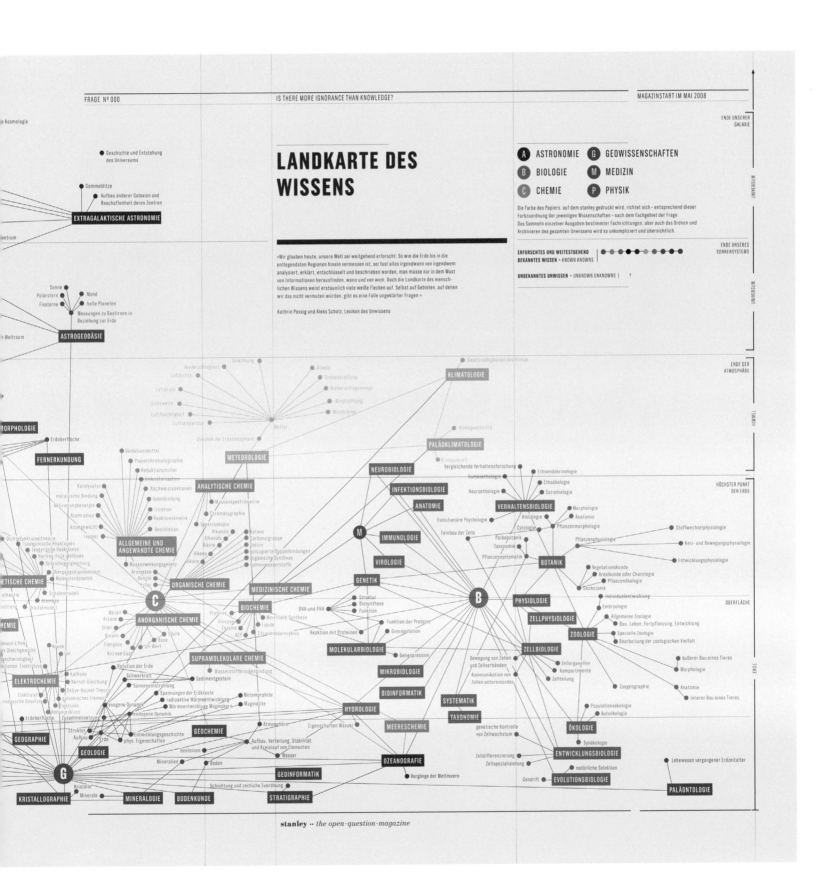

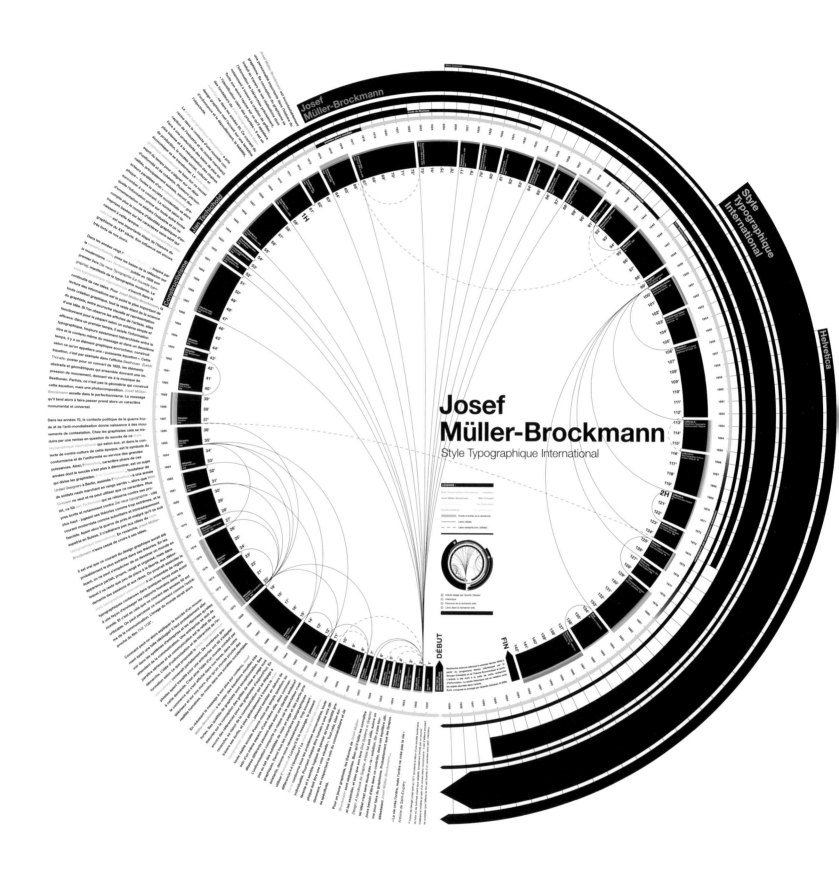

2008

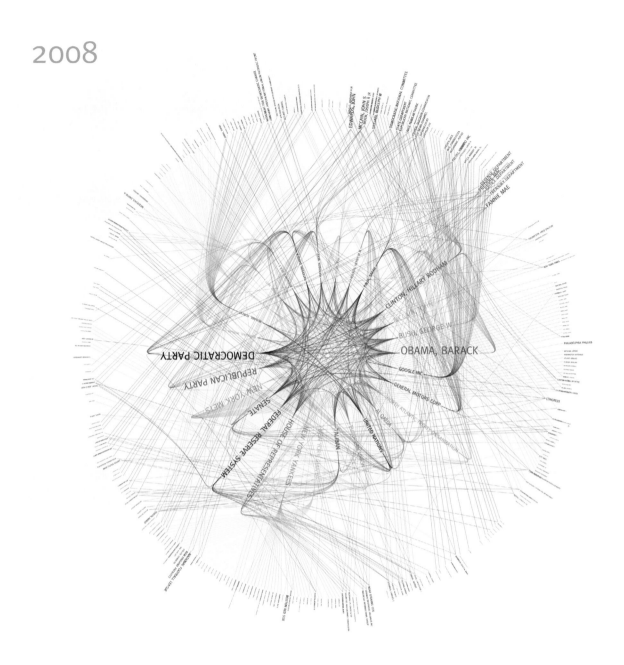

3

1984

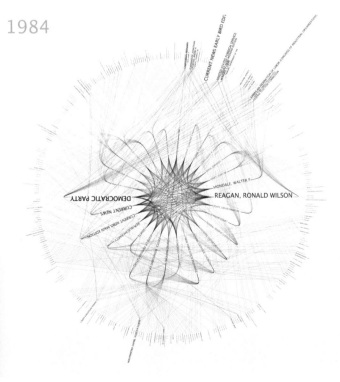

2

1
JOSEF MÜLLER-BROCKMANN &
THE INTERNATIONAL TYPOGRAPHIC STYLE
Quentin Delobel
Swiss graphic designer Josef Müller-Brockmann
is famous for his simple designs and clean
use of typography. Based on personal web
research, this diagram explores three key
factors: the research process, a chronicle of
Müller-Brockmann's life and personal reflections on the assembled insights.

2
THIS WAS 1984
3
THIS WAS 2008
Jer Thorp
A comparative study of the top organisations and personalities in 1984 and 2008
according to mentions in THE NEW YORK
TIMES articles during those years. Lines visualise connections between listed people
and organisations.

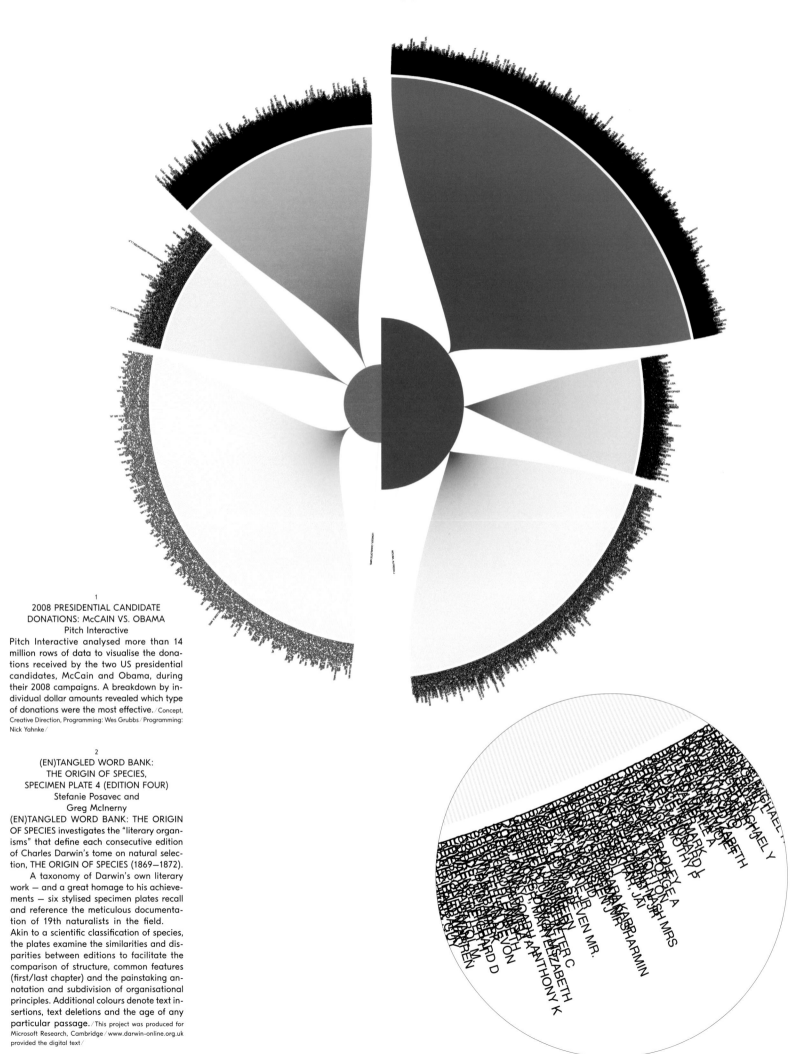

1
2008 PRESIDENTIAL CANDIDATE
DONATIONS: McCAIN VS. OBAMA
Pitch Interactive
Pitch Interactive analysed more than 14
million rows of data to visualise the donations received by the two US presidential
candidates, McCain and Obama, during
their 2008 campaigns. A breakdown by individual dollar amounts revealed which type
of donations were the most effective. / Concept,
Creative Direction, Programming: Wes Grubbs / Programming:
Nick Yahnke /

2
(EN)TANGLED WORD BANK:
THE ORIGIN OF SPECIES,
SPECIMEN PLATE 4 (EDITION FOUR)
Stefanie Posavec and
Greg McInerny
(EN)TANGLED WORD BANK: THE ORIGIN
OF SPECIES investigates the "literary organisms" that define each consecutive edition
of Charles Darwin's tome on natural selection, THE ORIGIN OF SPECIES (1869—1872).
    A taxonomy of Darwin's own literary
work — and a great homage to his achievements — six stylised specimen plates recall
and reference the meticulous documentation of 19th naturalists in the field.
Akin to a scientific classification of species,
the plates examine the similarities and dis-
parities between editions to facilitate the
comparison of structure, common features
(first/last chapter) and the painstaking an-
notation and subdivision of organisational
principles. Additional colours denote text in-
sertions, text deletions and the age of any
particular passage. / This project was produced for
Microsoft Research, Cambridge / www.darwin-online.org.uk
provided the digital text /

PLATE 4

First Chapter

The Origin of Species
Charles Darwin
Fourth Edition, 1866

Last Chapter

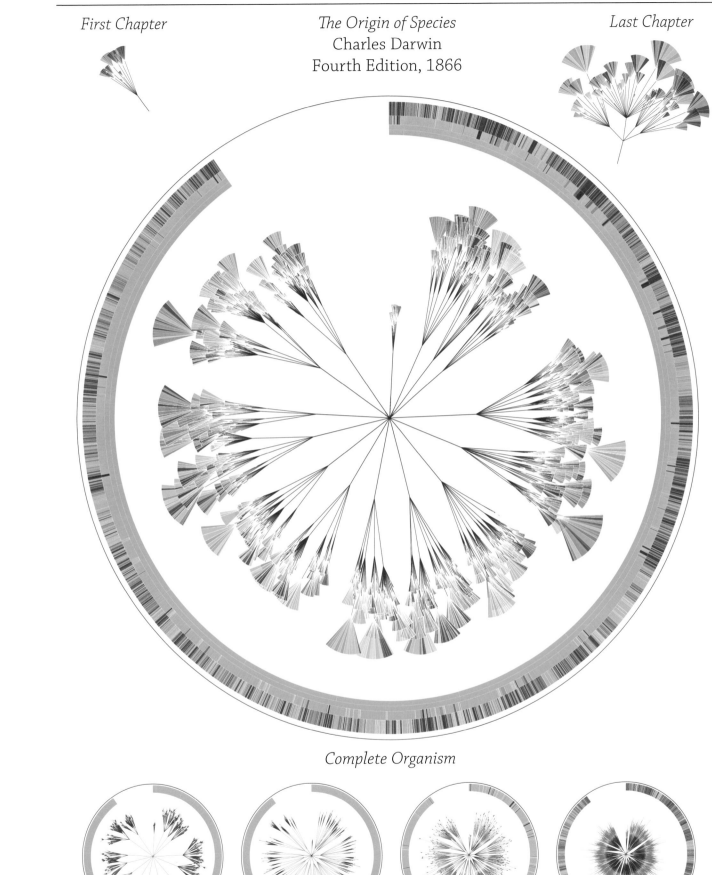

Complete Organism

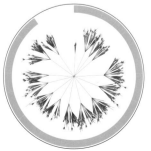

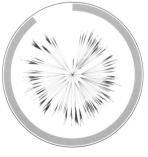

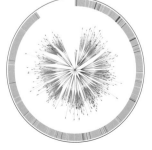

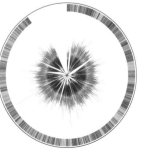

Chapters

Subchapters

Paragraphs

Sentences

(En)tangled Word Bank

Greg McInerny & Stefanie Posavec

DATAMAPS

The lion's share of the digital data currently collected includes some sort of geospatial reference. Geographical associations can be made using GPS devices – which precisely determine location by co-ordinates – but also using postal codes, names, or other notions of place. No wonder maps are so omnipresent these days. This chapter features diverse approaches to map design, from carving to processing, from minimalist to opulent.

●

Maps are fascinating. They fuel our dreams about foreign places and imaginative travel routes. They give us an overview of our huge planet and thus might make us feel more in control. They help us to understand the world by telling us about history, nature, politics, and society, and if we get lost in a strange town, they are pretty handy too. Many designers however, are drawn to maps for other reasons. With their intricate outlines, manifold color-schemes and abstract symbols, maps are to designers what an unsupervised toy store is to five-year-olds.

MAPS OF SECRET FISHING LOCATIONS
(NO 5)
Torgeir Husevaag
/ › P. 210 /

3
WALK ON RED EX1
why not smile
Hoon Kim
/ › PP. 196, 197 /

They go wild. Sometimes a bit too wild, thinks Dutch cartographer Menno-Jan Kraak. / see interview › PP. 214, 215 / But the professional map-maker also acknowledges that the often unorthodox ideas of artists and designers – their creative ways of problem solving and their sense for aesthetics – are a very much appreciated inspiration among cartographers.

This chapter is jam-packed with those inspirations. Take Torgeir Husevaag's hand-drawn map of secret fishing spots, / 1 / for example. By deliberately omitting information on exact location, but creating a sense of enchantment with his beautiful illustrations, he piques curiosity in the depicted locations and encourages the viewer to explore the area. Perhaps it is a reaction to the ubiquity of Google Maps and the like that we see lots of artfully crafted maps today. For example, Mark Webber's mix of topography and typography which could not be farther away from the many "map-mashups" we see on the internet. His *City Maps* / 2 / are carved from linoleum – something you might remember from your craft classes at school – and then printed on large, thick sheets of paper. Designer Hoon Kim pitches in a domain that has yet to be fully researched in scientific cartography: the geospatial visualization of acoustic events. / 3 / Combining the diverse and transient attributes of sound with spatial data is a very difficult challenge. But with the increasing noise that we are exposed to in urban areas, causing mental and physical damage, this information is becoming more and more important.

While the above-mentioned examples all have spatial references, not everything in this chapter does. Abi Huynh's positioning of places / 4 / is not based on latitude and longitude, but on his very own associations. A sort of mind map. The question begs to be asked: is this a map at all? (A cartographer would probably answer with a resolute *NO*.)

2
WHERE IN THE WORLD
CITY MAP SERIES
Mark Webber
/ › P. 200 /

4
EARTH MAP (EXCERPT)
abiabiabi
/ › P. 225 /

1
SEOUL RAILWAY SYSTEM
2
NEW YORK CITY RAILWAY SYSTEM
3
HOKKAIDO RAILWAY SYSTEM
ZERO PER ZERO
Captured in a snowflake's symmetry,
Zeroperzero's railway map transforms the en-
tire island of Hokkaido — famous for its fine,
powdery snow — into a single snow crystal.

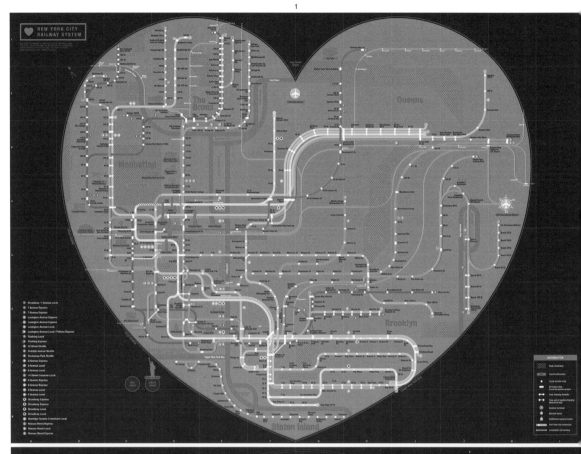

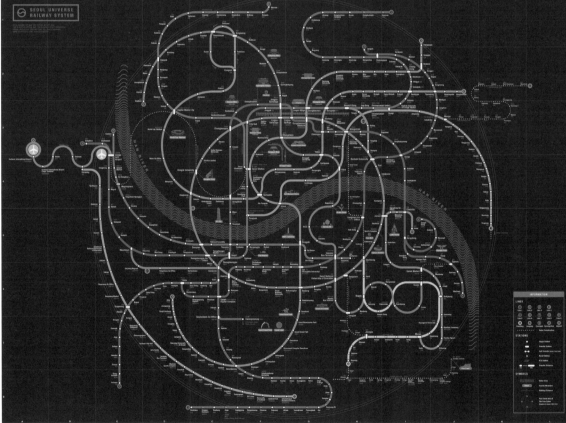

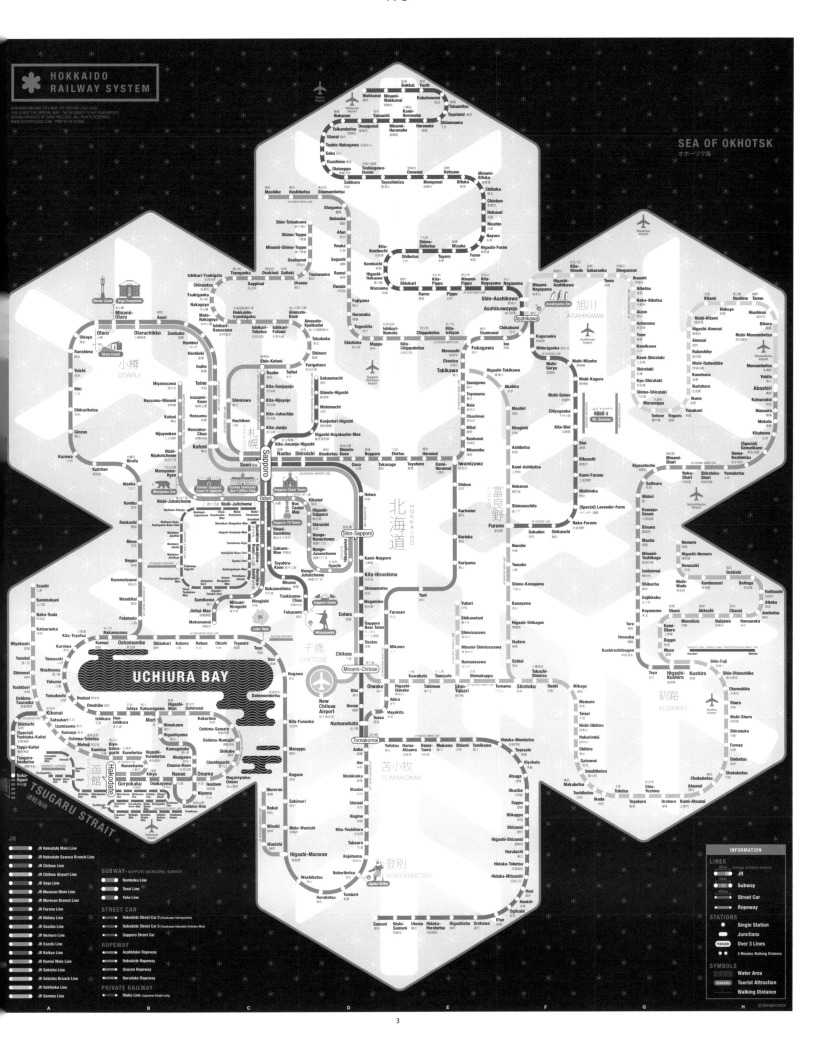

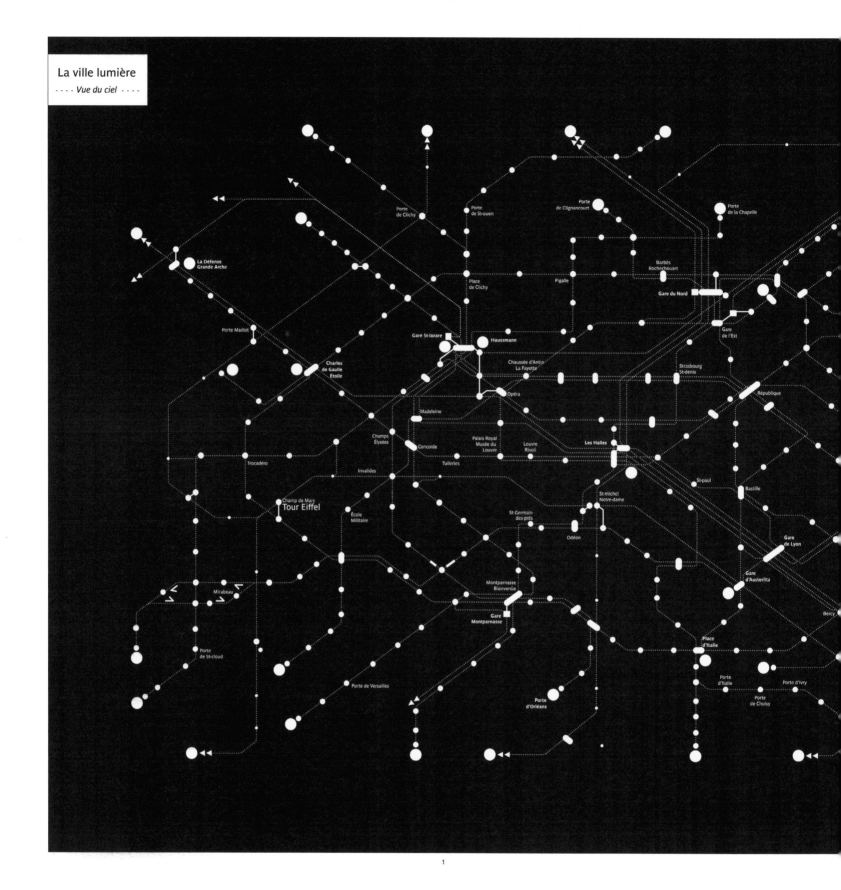

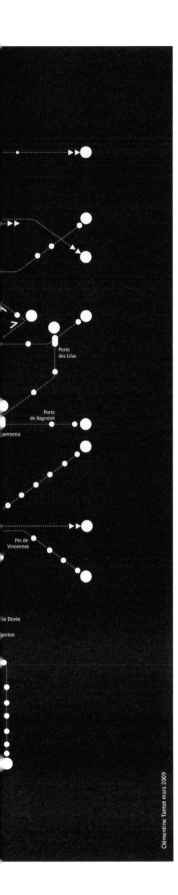

Clémentine Tantet mars 2009

⊕ **CHURCHGATE**

◎ **MARINE LINES**

⊗ **CHARNI RD**

◎ **GRANT RD**

◉ **MUMBAI CENTRAL**

⊓ **MAHALAKSHMI**

⊔ **LOWER PAREL**

⊗ **ELPHINSTONE**

⊕ **DADAR**

÷ **MATUNGA**

÷ **MAHIM**

卐 **BANDRA**

⊖ **KHAR RD**

⊜ **SANTACRUZ**

▣ **VILE PARLE**

◎ **ANDHERI**

2

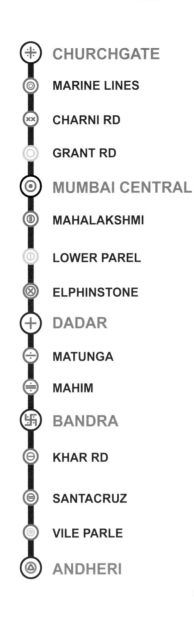

3

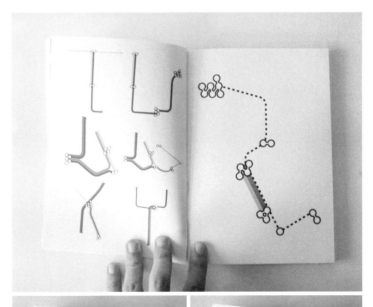

1
THE LIGHT CITY
Clémentine Tantet
Like the glistening stars and seductive constellations on the firmament, Clémentine Tantet's THE LIGHT CITY illuminates LA VILLE-LUMIÈRE with a nocturnal remake of Paris' subway map.

2
DABBAWALLA'S
GMI Grandmother India Design
Commuters in Mumbai love their home cooking. Every day, the city's 5000 Dabbawallas — or food couriers — collect nearly 200,000 meals from commuter's homes and deliver them to their workplace for lunch. In its efforts to record and catalogue Mumbai's rich typographic palette, the Typocity project proposes to digitise some of the more familiar Dabbawalla icons and incorporate them into the signage, tickets and timetables of public transport to enrich Mumbai's visual language. /Concept, Research, Reinterpretation: Kurnal Rawat / Photography, Research assistant: Danesh Anita/

3
SUBWAY OF PARIS
Mehdi Sedira
Mehdi Sedira's graphic experiments explore the aesthetic and practical differences between international subway maps. Often the backbone of a metropolis, each public transport network has its own signage system. Broken down into basic icons and pertinent elements, its particular flair, feel and aesthetics become even more apparent.

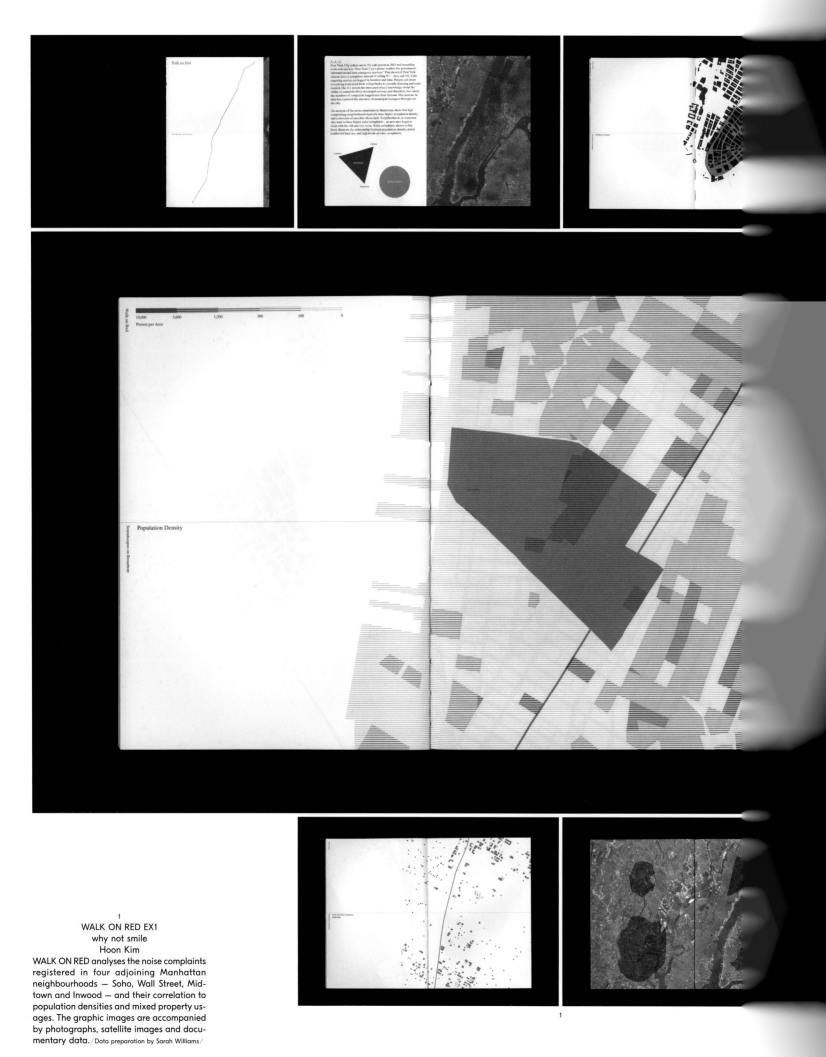

1
WALK ON RED EX1
why not smile
Hoon Kim
WALK ON RED analyses the noise complaints
registered in four adjoining Manhattan
neighbourhoods — Soho, Wall Street, Midtown and Inwood — and their correlation to
population densities and mixed property us-
ages. The graphic images are accompanied
by photographs, satellite images and docu-
mentary data. /Data preparation by Sarah Williams /

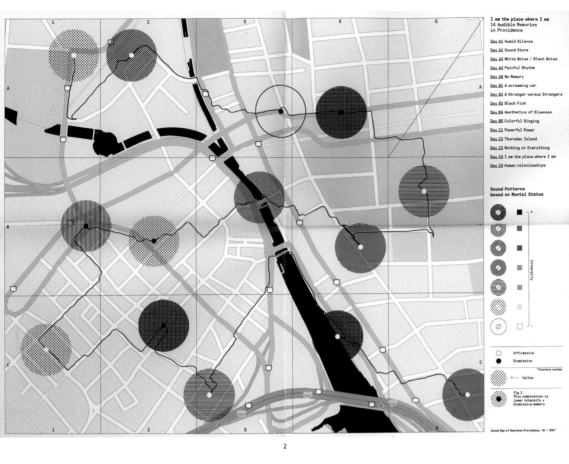

I am the place where I am
14 Audible Memories
in Providence

Day A1 Humid Silence
Day A2 Sound Storm
Day A3 White Noise / Black Noise
Day A4 Painful Rhythm
Day A5 No Memory
Day B1 A screaming car
Day B2 A Stranger versus Strangers
Day B3 Black Fish
Day B4 Aesthetics of Slowness
Day B5 Colorful Singing
Day C1 Powerful Power
Day C2 Thursday Island
Day C3 Nothing or Everything
Day C4 I am the place where I am
Day C5 Human relationships

Sound Patterns
based on Mental Status

Intensity

Affirmative
Dismissive

*Tincture system
Yellow

fig 1.
This combination is
lower intensity +
dismissive memory.

Sound Map of Downtown Providence, RI / 2007

2

2
I AM THE PLACE WHERE I AM 16
why not smile
Hoon Kim
In a slightly different take on a map, I AM THE PLACE WHERE I AM is filled with subjective representations of the artist's personal (aural) memories. The resulting work is installed at the actual site of the memory.

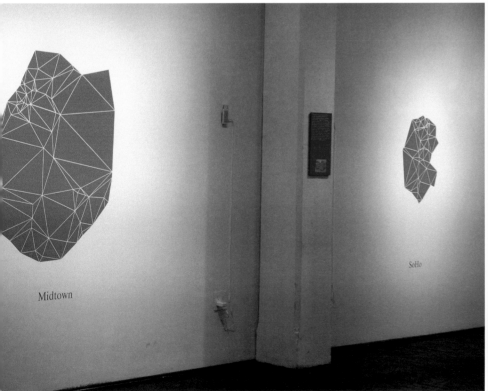

Midtown

SoHo

SoHo

I am the place where I am
Day A1 Humid Silence
Day A2 Sound Storm
Day A3 White Noise / Black Noise
Day A4 Painful Rhythm
Day A5 No Memory
Day B1 A screaming car
Day B2 A Stranger versus Strangers
Day B3 Black Fish
Day B4 Aesthetics of Slowness
Day B5 Colorful Singing

Walk on Red
Soundscapes on
Broadway

Hoon Kim &
Sarah Williams

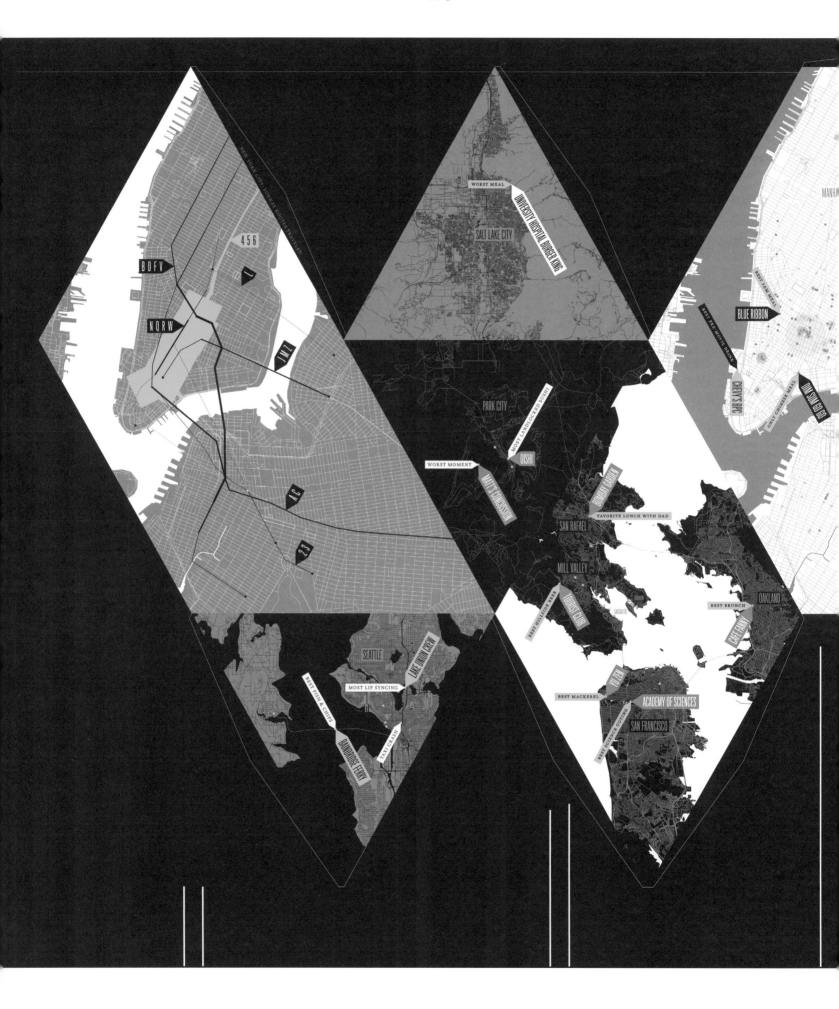

THE FELTRON
2008 ATLAS

FELTRON 2008 ANNUAL REPORT
Nicholas Felton

WHERE IN THE WORLD
CITY MAP SERIES
Mark Webber
It's all in the name: Webber's WHERE IN
THE WORLD series of city maps takes us
on a typographical excursion to Amsterdam,
London, Paris and New York. While carving
the descriptions of districts and landmarks
for his outsized lino prints, the artist himself
has to stay on track — one misplaced cut
and all would be in vain.

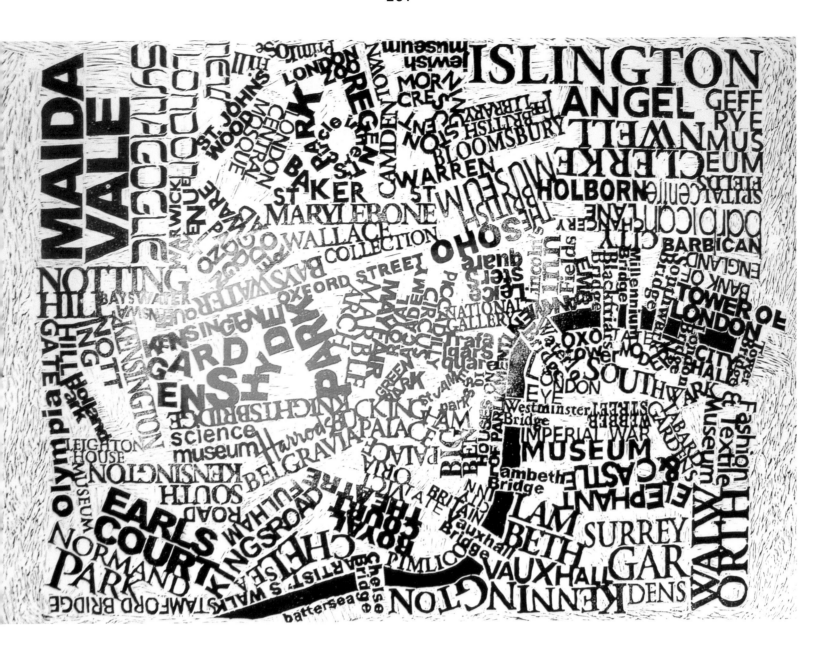

WANDERWORT
Golden Section Graphics
Craving a bratwurst? Or wishing to explore your inner hausfrau? Look no further than this map to retrace the sneaking spread of Teutonic tongue twisters. Colour-coded by topic, the WANDERWORT project tracks the surprisingly rich seepage and migration of German expressions into other languages. A treasure trove for linguists, the poster — commissioned by the German Goethe Institut — not only serves up verbal stumbling blocks for a healthy sprinkling of umlaut-laced idiosyncrasies, but also reflects emigration patterns, trade routes and cross-fertilisation with other idioms. /Jan Schwochow, Katharina Erfurth, Sebastian Piesker/

Legend:
- Gegenständliches
- Geografisches
- Geschichtliches
- Musisches
- Kulinarisches
- Medizinisches
- Pflanzliches
- Sportliches
- Technisches
- Tierisches
- Wissenschaftliches
- Sonstiges

Ausgewanderte Wörter

WANDERWORT

Diese Weltkarte enthält „ausgewanderte Wörter" aus dem Deutschen. Die meisten von ihnen stammen aus dem internationalen Wettbewerb mit dem Titel „Ausgewanderte Wörter", den der Deutsche Sprachrat gemeinsam mit dem Goethe-Institut und der Gesellschaft für deutsche Sprache im Jahre 2006 durchführte. Ziel des Wettbewerbs war es, rund um die Welt Wörter deutscher Herkunft aufzuspüren.

Goethe-Institute und private Einsender haben sich daran beteiligt, so dass viele deutsche ausgewanderte Wörter zusammen getragen und in einem Buch (Ausgewanderte Wörter. Hrsg. von Prof. Dr. Jutta Limbach. Hueber Verlag 2006) veröffentlicht wurden. Jetzt nutzen wir diese Sammlung für eine Weltkarte besonderer Art. Auch die freie Enzyklopädie

„Wikipedia" lieferte eine große Anzahl von Wortbeispielen für diese Übersicht.
Die ausgewählten Wörter stammen aus den Bereichen Handwerk, Handel, Kunst, Philosophie, Medizin, Sport und dem alltäglichen Leben. Sie sind mit den Menschen und deren Geschichten um die ganze Welt gewandert und finden sich heute in den verschiedenen Ländern und Sprachen wieder, beeinflussen und erweitern den alltäglichen Sprachgebrauch. So verändern sich Sprachen, nehmen auf und geben ab.

Diese Weltkarte soll dazu beitragen, die Wanderung deutscher Wörter nachzuvollziehen, ihre weltweite Verbreitung zu zeigen und über Veränderungen in ihrer Struktur zu informieren, die sie auf ihrer Reise erfahren haben.

 GOETHE-INSTITUT

1
FRANCE
Clio Chaffardon

Wordless yet evocative, FRANCE is just what it says on the cover. Based on drawings by a variety of people who live in this European country, Clio Chaffardon's monochrome cut-outs highlight how individual perception can change the basic appearance and character of your (native or adopted) soil and psychogeography. An exercise in symbolism and simplification, the book underscores notions of territory and identification: while the country's five main appendages around the bulky torso tend to remain recognisable, individual memories and interpretation engender marked shifts in the nation's size, shape and expanse.

2
FORTRESS EUROPE MAPS
LUST

Every year, thousands of refugees head for Europe in hope of a better life. Those who make it however, tend to end up in prison-like camps. FORTRESS EUROPE puts these rarely reported holding camps on the map and documents their continued spread: the current toll is 13,000 and counting. /In cooperation with JuangJuang Long/

Raja - Mère au foyer

André - Retraité

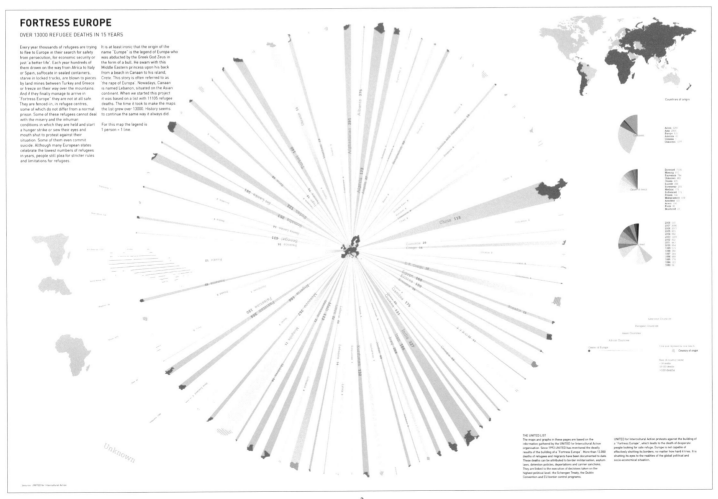

FORTRESS EUROPE

OVER 13000 REFUGEE DEATHS IN 15 YEARS

Attenti a questo dragone

Hanno attraversato il mondo aprendo rotte migratorie destinate a durare nel tempo. Ora sono i nuovi protagonisti degli scambi internazionali. E le loro "chinatown" diventano sempre più grandi. Un trend che appare inarrestabile

A CURA DI – *Francesco Franchi* e *Alessandro Giberti*
MUSICA – *The Move · Chinatown*

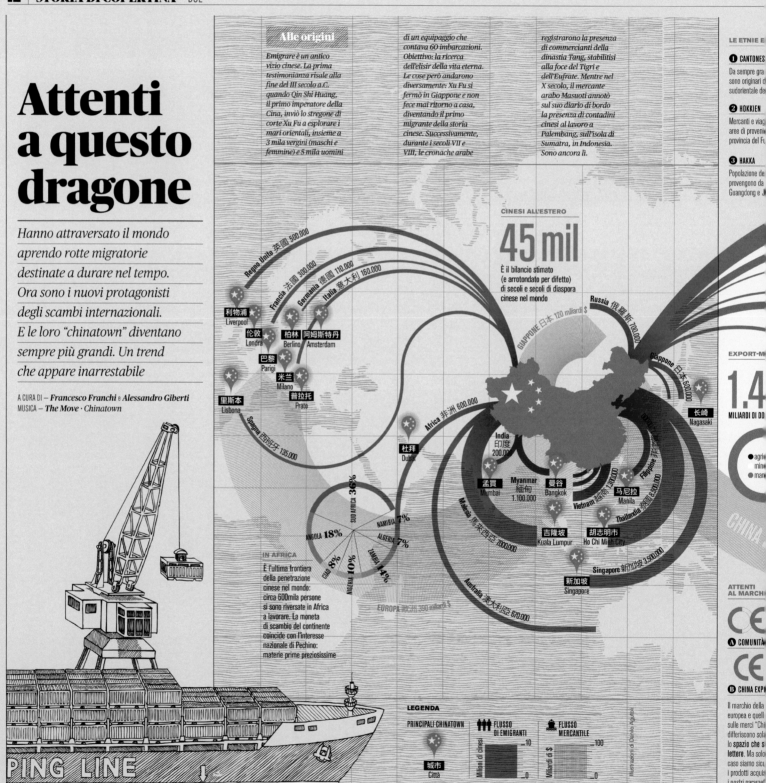

Alle origini

Emigrare è un antico vizio cinese. La prima testimonianza risale alla fine del III secolo a.C. quando Qin Shi Huang, il primo imperatore della Cina, inviò lo stregone di corte Xu Fu a esplorare i mari orientali, insieme a 3 mila vergini (maschi e femmine) e 5 mila uomini

di un equipaggio che contava 60 imbarcazioni. Obiettivo: la ricerca dell'elisir della vita eterna. Le cose però andarono diversamente: Xu Fu si fermò in Giappone e non fece mai ritorno a casa, diventando il primo migrante della storia cinese. Successivamente, durante i secoli VII e VIII, le cronache arabe

registrarono la presenza di commercianti della dinastia Tang, stabilitisi alla foce del Tigri e dell'Eufrate. Mentre nel X secolo, il mercante arabo Masuoti annotò sul suo diario di bordo la presenza di contadini cinesi al lavoro a Palembang, sull'isola di Sumatra, in Indonesia. Sono ancora lì.

LE ETNIE E

❶ CANTONES
Da sempre gra
sono originari di
sudorientale de

❷ HOKKIEN
Mercanti e viag
aree di provenie
provincia del Fu

❸ HAKKA
Popolazione de
provengono da
Guangdong e JL

CINESI ALL'ESTERO

45 mil

È il bilancio stimato (e arrotondato per difetto) di secoli e secoli di diaspora cinese nel mondo

EXPORT-M

1.4

MILIARDI DI DO

• agri
mine
• man

CHINA

ATTENTI AL MARCHI

CE

Ⓐ COMUNITÀ

CE

Ⓑ CHINA EXP

Il marchio della
europea e quell
sulle merci "Chi
differiscono sola
lo **spazio che s**
lettere. Ma solo
caso siamo sicu
i prodotti acquis
i nostri parame

Regno Unito 英國 500.000
利物浦 Liverpool
伦敦 Londra
Francia 法國 300.000
Germania 德國 110.000
柏林 Berlino
阿姆斯特丹 Amsterdam
Italia 意大利 160.000
巴黎 Parigi
米兰 Milano
普拉托 Prato
里斯本 Lisbona
Spagna 西班牙 135.000
Africa 非洲 600.000
杜拜 Dubai
孟買 Mumbai
India 印度 200.000
Russia 伊羅斯 700.000
GIAPPONE 日本 120 miliardi $
Giappone 日本 600.000
长崎 Nagasaki
Myanmar 緬甸 1.100.000
曼谷 Bangkok
Malesia 馬來西亞 2000.000
吉隆坡 Kuala Lumpur
Vietnam 越南 1200.000
胡志明市 Ho Chi Minh City
马尼拉 Manila
Filippine 菲律賓 8.500.000
Thailandia 泰国 7.000.000
Singapore 新加坡 2.500.000
新加坡 Singapore
Australia 澳大利亞 670.000

SUD AFRICA 36%
NAMIBIA 7%
ANGOLA 18%
ALGERIA 7%
CIAD 8%
NIGERIA 10%
ZAMBIA 14%

IN AFRICA
È l'ultima frontiera della penetrazione cinese nel mondo: circa 600mila persone si sono riversate in Africa a lavorare. La moneta di scambio del continente coincide con l'interesse nazionale di Pechino: materie prime preziosissime

EUROPA 欧洲 390 miliardi $

LEGENDA

PRINCIPALI CHINATOWN
城市
Città

FLUSSO DI EMIGRANTI
Milioni di cinesi
—10
—0

FLUSSO MERCANTILE
Miliardi di $
—100
—0

PING LINE

ATTENTI A QUESTO DRAGONE
Francesco Franchi
ATTENTI A QUESTO DRAGONE places the world on "red alert" with its decidedly non-combative depiction of Chinese trade and population distribution. Retracing trade routes and cultural spread, it also shows migratory flows and the world's biggest expatriate communities, i.e Chinatowns. / Ship Illustration: Danilo Agutoli /

NEXT PAGE
A NEW CARTOGRAPHY OF EUROPE DIFFUSION AND TECHNOLOGY IMPACT IN THE EU27
DensityDesign
Visualising statistics can be a dry business. Density Design put pertinent figures and design on the map with their investigation of the spread and impact of communication technologies among the 27 EU member states.   Based on two recent EU Commission surveys, the project overlays a contour map — to visualise the perceived impact of broadband and mobile phones in each country — with a cartogram of technological dispersal. From this arises a new geography — a re-imagined European landscape — that keeps its proportions but changes morphology.   Here, the tectonic shift in communications technology throws up new mountain ranges for a novel topology of interaction and a tangible, visual approximation of technological spread and acceptance. / Scientific supervisor: Paolo Ciuccarelli, Marco Fattore / Creative Direction: Donato Ricci / Code Development: Giorgio Caviglia, Michele Mauri / Designer: Lorenzo Fernandez, Luca Masud, Mario Porpora /

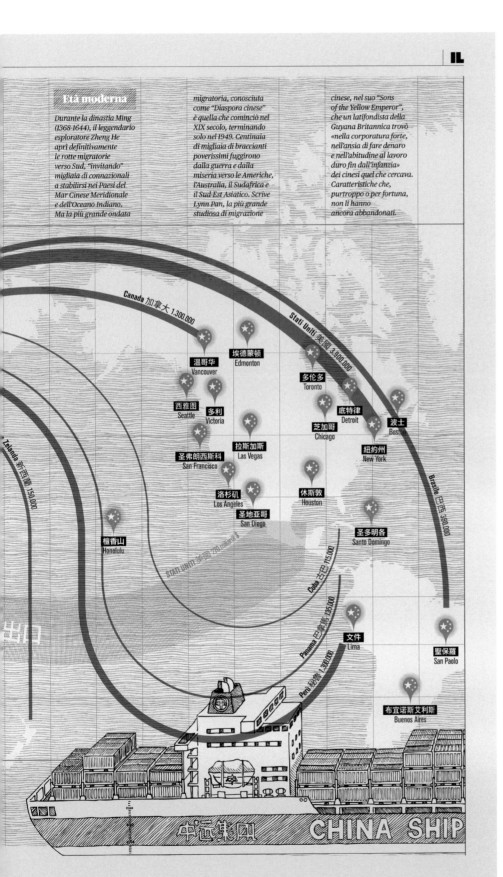

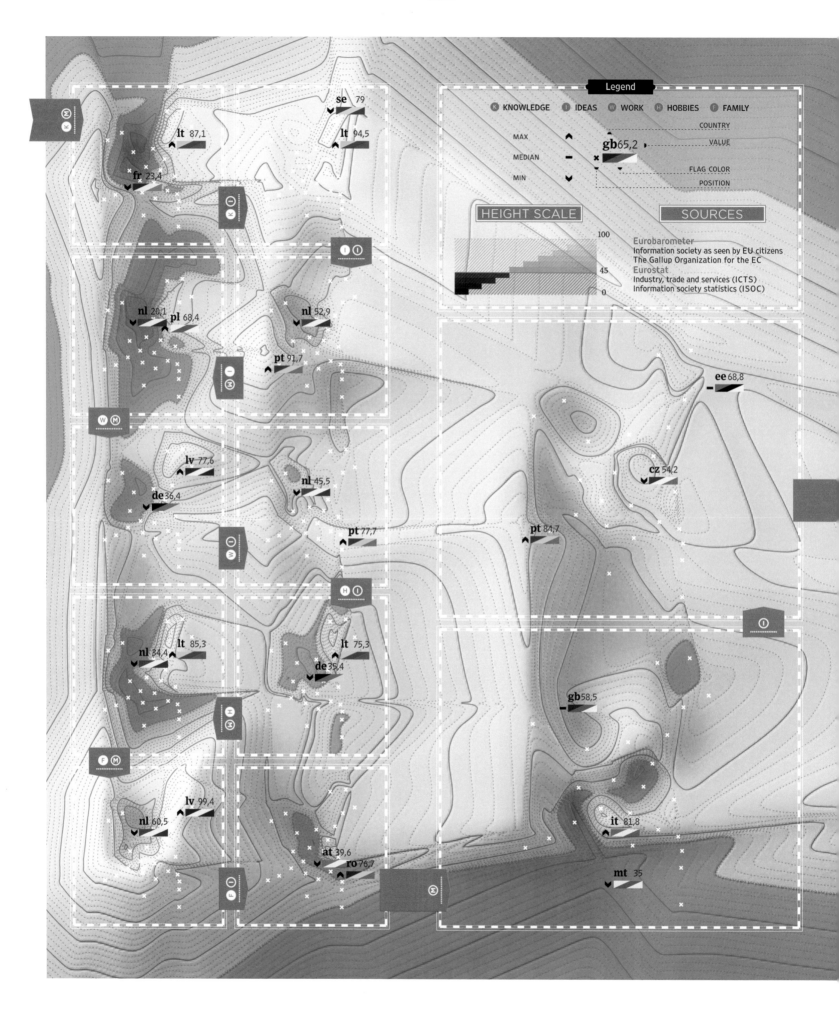

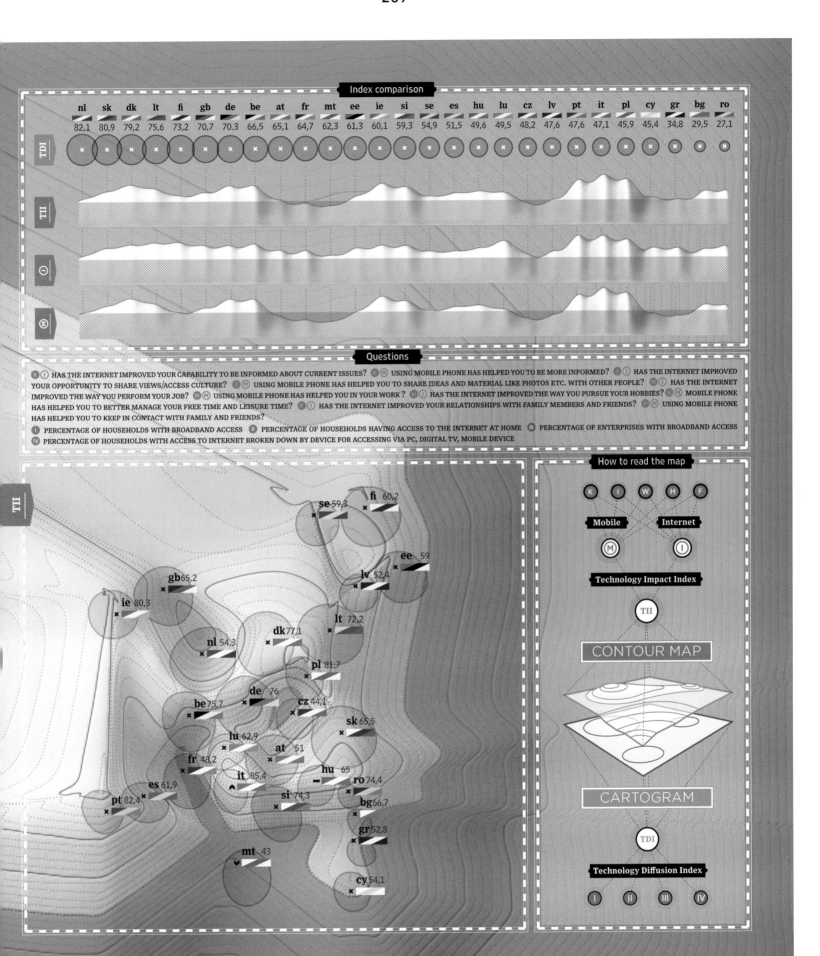

THROUGH 150 DRY WELLBORES
(№ 3)
Torgeir Husevaag

Oil and gas underpin Norway's economy: Most of the country's relative wealth is based on these finite offshore resources.

A celebration of frontier spirit and exploration, but also a timely reminder of the precious resources' ephemeral nature, Torgeir Husevaag's WELLBORES map every dry, i.e. unsuccessful, bore well drilled between the start of Norwegian oil exploitation in 1967 and August 1984, when the SNOWHITE gas field was discovered. While bore hole numbers (from 1 to 150) and colour codes retrace the timeline, water depth and the depth of deep-sea drilling, the overall picture underscores the expanding search for natural resources — pushing ever north and further down. A beautiful record of things past, of progress and pioneering, but also a hint of things to come, of future boundaries to exploration and exploitation; this commission for one of the fleet's active tankers is a welcome reminder of human ingenuity — and its natural limits. / THROUGH 150 DRY WELLBORES (№ 3) / 2005 / Ink on paper / 84 × 80 cm /

2
MAPS OF SECRET FISHING LOCATIONS
(№ 5)
3
MAPS OF SECRET FISHING LOCATIONS
(№ 3)
Torgeir Husevaag

A treasure chest of public information on all things maritime, the Norwegian Coastal Administration seems to have it all, and yet there are still blind spots in their archives. Norwegian artist Torgeir Husevaag decided to fill some of the gaps with a thoughtful gift: a series of drawings that reflect local lore and individual knowledge of "secret" fishing spots with exceptionally promising yields. More a riddle than a set of directions, these artworks are not straightforward maps. Although they show each location and how to take the right bearings (without GPS), it is precisely their level of loving detail that prevents them from being effective navigational aids. Close up — and devoid of further points of reference such as latitude or longitude — these tantalising gems become isolated islands and thus keep the local fishermen's secrets safe after all. / Photo: Werner Zellien / MAPS OF SECRET FISHING LOCATIONS (№ 5) / 2004 / Ink on paper / 76 × 84 cm / MAPS OF SECRET FISHING LOCATIONS (№ 3) / 2004 / Ink on paper /

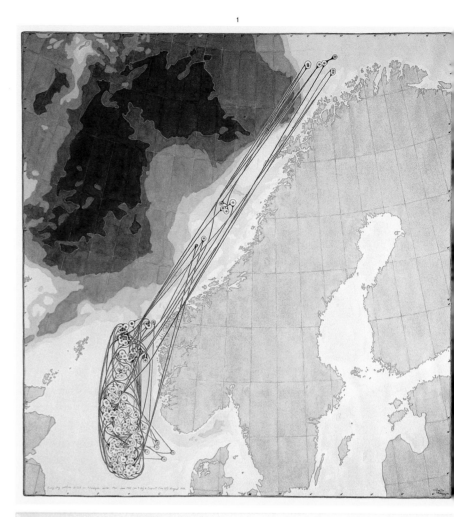

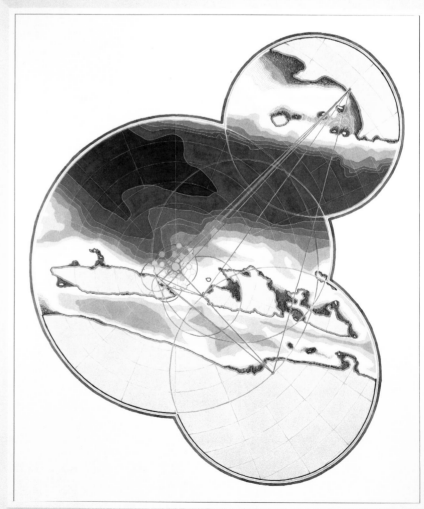

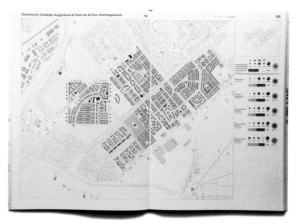

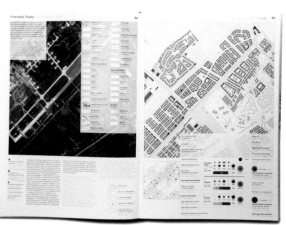

4
VINEX ATLAS
Joost Grootens
The first in-depth account of the Netherland's notorious state-planned Vinex settlements documents 52 sample districts via plans, site data and aerial views from the mid-nineties and more recent onsite photography. / Design book and maps: Studio Joost Grootens (Joost Grootens with Tine van Wel, Jim Biekmann and Anna Iwansson) /

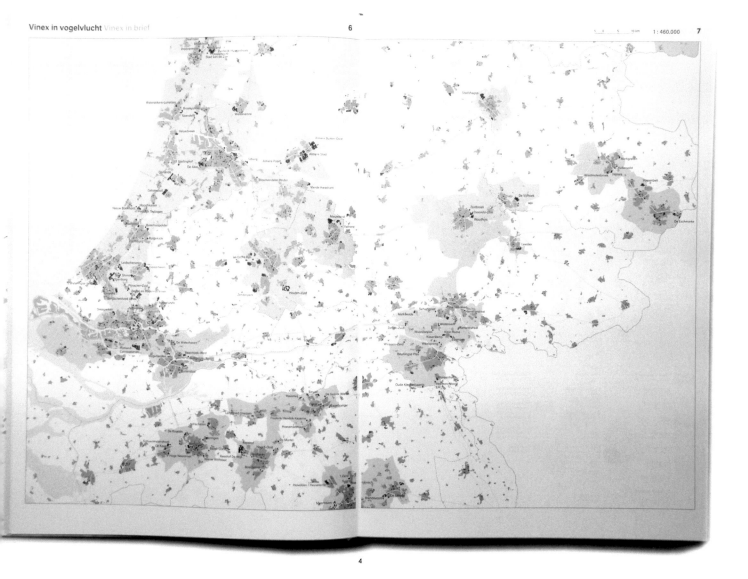

1

1
ATLAS OF SHRINKING CITIES
1kilo
THE ATLAS OF SHRINKING CITIES exposes
the reasons behind urban shrinkage, from
demographic developments and migration
patterns to scarce resources, destruction of
nature and settlement transformations. As
part of the accompanying exhibition, Berlin
maps from the atlas were transformed into
objects in space. / Photo: Christoph Petras /

2
WORLD CONSPIRACY
Tim Schwartz
Time to dust off those conspiracy theories
for a fascinatingly skewed peek at the world
as we know it.   Akin to the self-portraits
presented in DATALOGY, WORLD CON-
SPIRACY paints a distorted — but in itself
logical — picture of the world viewed through
the eyes of one individual. How much weight
and import do we assign to particular issues
or certain nations? What are our personal
political hobbyhorses?   Pieced together
and reshaped according to data harvested
from more than 10,000 documents collected
by an anonymous conspiracy theorist between September 19, 2001 and January
15, 2009, Tim Schwartz adjusted the world
map to the number of mentions each country warranted — thus visualising both the
paranoia of one individual and the latest
political hotspots.

2

3

3
JUST LANDED
Jer Thorp
In a variation of epidemiological disease transmissions models, JUST LANDED plots social network movements. Based on tweets containing the phrases "just landed in ..." or "just arrived in ..." the resulting travel destinations were mapped via MetaCarta's LOCATION FINDER API and cross-referenced against the tweeter's home location to plot relevant routes.

4
GEOHISTORIOGRAPHY
Tim Schwartz
In a slightly different iteration of his conspiracy theme, Schwartz expands his redrawn maps from the view of one person to that of America as a whole.   For this world according to one US newspaper, the digital media artist scanned the archives of for the number of articles written on each country and then expanded or contracted their physical appearance accordingly.
In its animated version, GEOHISTORIOGRAPHY reveals how America's perspective has changed over the last 150 years and how red button topics and countries have shifted with time, e.g. from Iron Curtain to Islamic states.   With the disinterested distance of the scientific observer, Tim Schwartz dissects the human psyche and unveils our predominant interests and fears — more or less unchanged from prehistoric times: our home, our neighbours and those we perceive as an ominous threat.

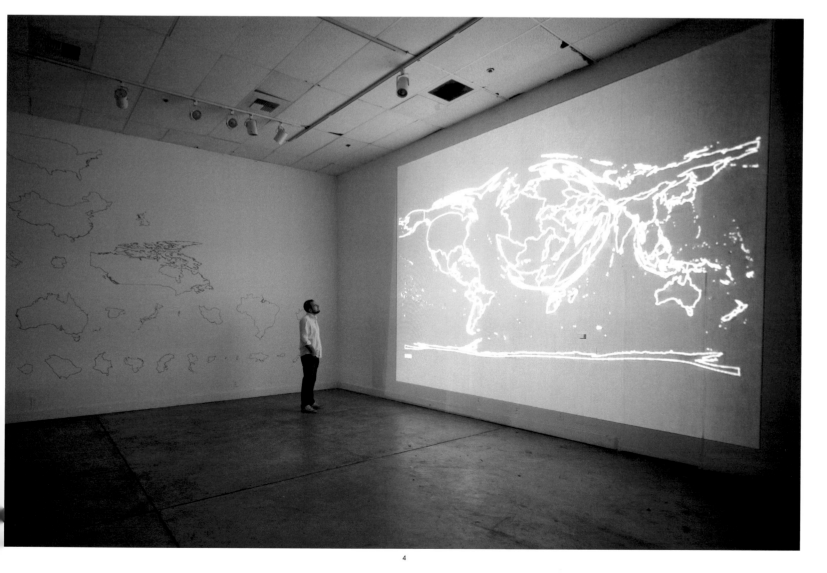

MENNO-JAN KRAAK

Professor Dr. Menno-Jan Kraak was born in 1958 at 52° 16' 59.79" N,
5° 57' 44.63" E. He is head of the Geo-Information Processing
Department at the International Institute for Geo-Information Science and Earth Observation (ITC) in Enschede,
Netherlands.
Author of over 200 publications on cartography and
geographic information systems, speaker at numerous engagements and holder of key positions
in cartographic societies and journals, he is
one of the most passionate and reputable
protagonists in his field. MJ Kraak is a
true map aficionado and his interest is
not just limited to his busy professional life, as his impressive col-
lection of "carto-philatelics"
(stamps with cartographic
motifs) proves.

•

Cartography was never so popular and ubiquitous in its long history as it is now. Our cell
phones record GPS data, we have Google maps
at our fingertips, and a friendly voice tells us
if we have to turn left or right at the next intersection. But at the same time, working with

geospatial data is not limited to professionals
anymore. Every tech-savvy person can create
their own "map-mashups." Are these good or
bad times for your discipline? /MJK/
Good times! However, you might have different
perspectives on what is good. But the overall

positive message is that everybody seems to love maps. More maps are being produced and used than ever before. Internet companies like Google and manufacturers of navigation systems contribute to this. Then there are all those web 2.0 trends like neogeography, open street maps, etc. Those maps are generated by the user, utilizing systems that define the final look and feel. Some frameworks however, allow much more freedom, often resulting in poorly designed maps. This might be considered a negative aspect, but as long as those maps are not used in serious decision making, it is not too bad.

So cartographers won't be out of work any time soon? /MJK/ If we look at the work professionals do, there isn't necessarily less work. But other professions are now also involved in map making. Those people might need some extra training.

Could the same thing be said the other way around? Must cartographers also learn from those people to evolve their profession? /MJK/ I certainly believe cartographers should look at and learn from other disciplines. Actually it happens. There is an active scientific geo-visualization / information visualization/(geo)visual analytics community where knowledge is exchanged in multiple directions.

And what about graphic designers? /MJK/ When it comes to design and aesthetics, the creativity from graphic and media designers is a good source of inspiration. But these ideas have to be channeled into cartographic guidelines to let maps do their task. In their basic format, that is either to present information, as a tool to explore, or as an interface displaying geodata sets.

Tell us a bit more about those rules and guidelines. What sets cartography apart from just illustrating a map? /MJK/ Maps have the ability to present, synthesize, analyze and explore the real world. Maps do this well because they only present a part of the complex reality and visualize it in an abstract way. The cartographic discipline has developed a whole set of design guidelines to realize the most suitable map that offers insight in spatial patterns and relations. Some of these guidelines are conventions – the sea is blue, sand is yellow – as we see mostly on topographic maps. Others are based on perception – large symbols stand for big

> WHEN IT COMES TO DESIGN AND AESTHETICS, THE CREATIVITY FROM GRAPHIC AND MEDIA DESIGNERS IS A GOOD SOURCE OF INSPIRATION. BUT THESE IDEAS HAVE TO BE CHANNELED INTO CARTOGRAPHIC GUIDELINES TO LET MAPS DO THEIR TASK.

> EVERY MAP DESIGN IS STRONGLY INFLUENCED BY THE NATURE OF THE DATA. BEFORE VISUALIZATION COMES DATA ANALYSIS.

amounts, dark tints for high values – and are mostly used in thematic maps. However, these are mainly for maps that have to present a message. Today, maps should also be considered as flexible interfaces to – often web-based – geospatial data and offer interaction with the data behind the visual representation. Maps are also instruments to encourage exploration. Therefore they can be used to stimulate (visual) thinking about geospatial patterns and relationships.

How much creative design should be allowed in a map? /MJK/ Maps should have a design flavor, otherwise they are sterile. Many "artistic maps" however, have the right look, but apply the guidelines incorrectly. One example is wrong usage of color ramps, where the darkest tint is in the middle of a range instead of at the end. So if there is a message at all, it does not come across. And that is what maps are about: helping to solve a problem and being the basis for decision making, like finding your way from A to B.

Can you tell us how a cartographer deals with data? How much does the available data determine a map? /MJK/ Every map design is strongly influenced by the nature of the data. Before visualization comes data analysis. For this, we have a whole set of guidelines to assure the best possible outcome. Here is a simple example: assume we want to display the number of people in a country's municipalities. The basic question we have to ask is what is the measurement scale? Is the data qualitative – nominal values like a list of categories? Or is it quantitative – numeric values using an ordinal, interval, or ratio scale? In our example the data is quantitative and we need to use the ratio scale. From our graphic tools box we know how we can express these characteristics: symbols that vary in size will be best to display the amount of people. In other words, based on the data analysis, the best graphical variables will be selected to create a correct map.

Finally, a more personal question: when did you discover your love of maps? What's the fascination of cartography? /MJK/ Maps came into my life as a kid, sitting on the lap of my grandfather during our armchair travels. I was attracted to maps and started to draw them. It fascinates me that maps can capture parts of reality in their design. They can be a message and a tool for thinking, especially in today's interactive web-mapping environments.

1

2

1
REFLECTION
Andreas Nicolas Fischer
and Benjamin Maus
/ 2008 / Material CNC-milled MDF Dimensions
900×720×120mm /

2
EARTH BOWL PINSTRIPE
Fluid Forms
The EARTH BOWL PINSTRIPE invites design
fans to pick the perfect spot for their new
home accessory: to customise their personal
bowl, customers choose a location on an
interactive map. Fluid Forms then transforms
the selected topography into production
data and mills it into the required shape.
/ Photocredits: Günther Kubizer /

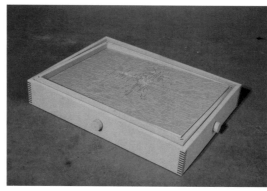

3

4

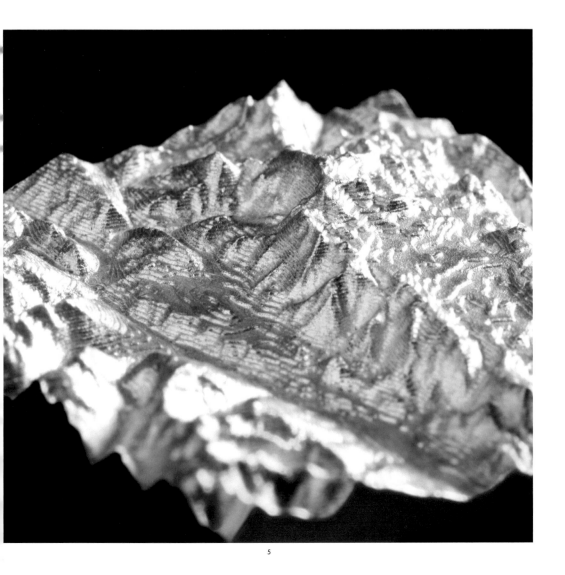

3
GUIDED
R. Justin Stewart
An exercise in patience and skill, popular childhood staple Labyrinth requires players to navigate a marble through an obstacle course. GUIDED applies this principle to the Twin Cities map, with streets carved at a depth of 1/16" and public transport routes at 1/8", allowing marbles to travel the transit routes but not the streets. In this, GUIDED underscores the duality of any transit system, which simultaneously provides and denies access to a city. / 2008 / MDF, hardware, steel ball /

4
SÈ SAN DIEGO HOTEL CITY WALL
Ball Nogues Studio
Sculptural wall map of San Diego for the upscale Se San Diego Hotel. Working from aerial photography, Ball Nogues Studio created a model for a three-dimensional bas-relief. The resulting CNC-milled wall sculpture was finished with polymer resin impregnated with bronze powder. / 2008 / Principals in Charge: Benjamin Ball, Gaston Nogues / Project Manager: Ben Dean / Project Design and Development: Benjamin Ball, Gaston Nogues, Ben Dean, Andrew Lyon / Custom Software Development: Pylon / Technical Photography: Ramona d'Viola, ilumus photography / Interior Design: Dodd Mitchell Design /

5
EARTH BROOCH SILVER
Fluid Forms
Akin to the EARTH BOWL PINSTRIPE, its brooch equivalent adds shape to personal contours. Consumers select their favourite coordinates to be transformed into a decorative silver landscape. / Photocredits: Karin Lernbeiß, www.lupispuma.at /

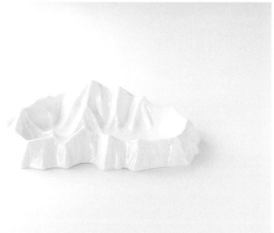

1

TOPOGRAPHY PLATE
kyouei design
Kouichi Okamoto
The latest kitchen helper for alpinists invites us to give chocolates or biscuits a peek of the peak with this miniature mountain range.

2

MAPA TUR'STICO — LEIRIA
Rodrigo Machado
Interactive map of the tourist highlights in the Portuguese region of Leiria. Small 3D icons indicate sights of interest; a click on the icons reveals further information. /Lu's Correia: involved in the creation of 3D icons/

3

**IF THE WORLD
WERE A VILLAGE OF 100 PEOPLE**
Hyebin PARK
According to the principle IF THE WORLD WERE A VILLAGE OF 100 PEOPLE, Hyebin Park's imaginary online community — populated by small, three-dimensional characters and buildings — tackles fundamental global statistics in friendly and familiar surroundings. /Teammate: Jhoo-Youn Cha /Tutor: Juhyun Eune/

4

CARPET
Laurens van Wieringen
Studio Laurens van Wieringen put a spring in our step with the staggered layers and extra-thick ranges of their expansive topography carpet. The resulting relief consists of more than 10,000 individual foam bars of different height and colour, assembled by a total of 52 hands.

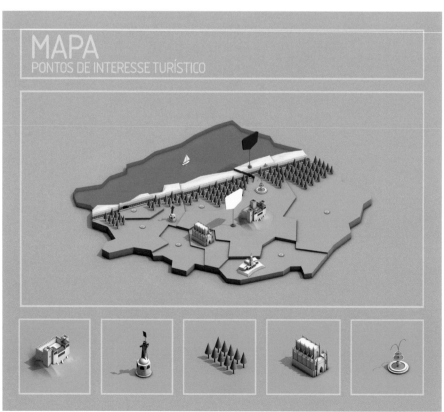

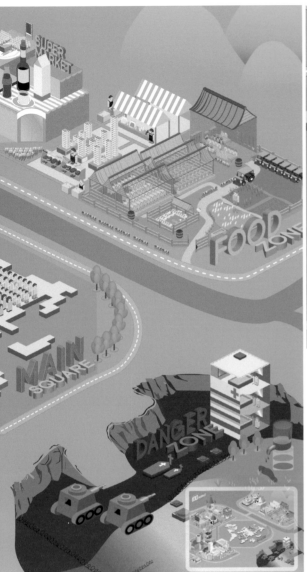

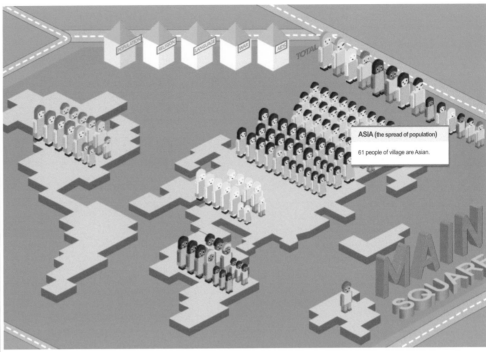

ASIA (the spread of population)

61 people of village are Asian.

3

4

FALTJAHR 2010
Johann Volkmer

Snap, crackle and pop-(up)! Johann Volkmer's FALTJAHR 2010 calendar provides an immediate reminder of the seasons. Each month, a separate paper module unfolds into an A3 feat of paper engineering, jutting out into the room.   Although abstract in nature, each sculpture reveals different pleats and folds, from the brisk angularity of January to the softly blossoming curves of July. /Photo: Kristian Barthen/

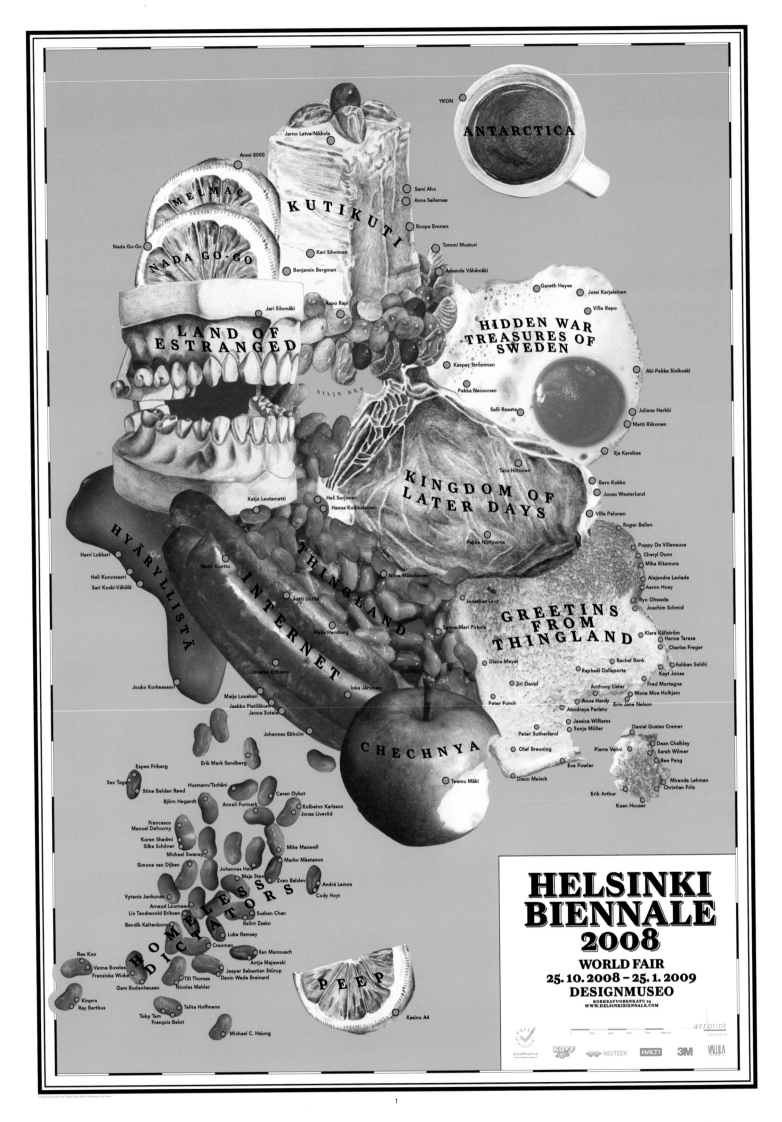

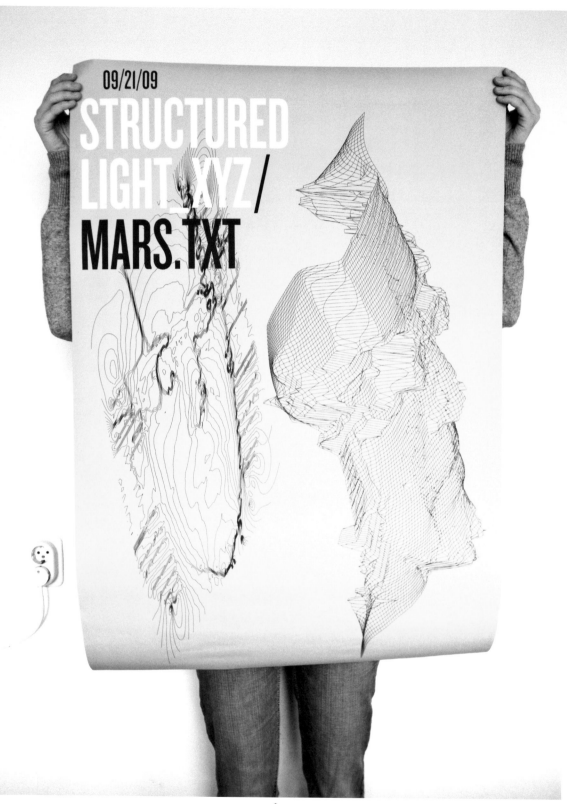

2

1
HELSINKI BIENNALE
Stine Belden Røed
Helsinki Biennale 2008 assembled installations, drawings, paintings, photographs,
video and audio works by almost 150 artists. Instead of printing a straightforward list,
the event's promotional poster portrayed the
site's 13 pavilions as discrete countries populated by several cities (individual artists). / With
Blank Blank & Korea / Design: Petri Henriksson / Art Direction:
Aki-Pekka Sinikoski / Illustrations: Stine Belden Røed /

2
STRUCTURED LIGHT
Catalogtree
Catalogtree's light experiments put the pho-
tons through their paces.   Here, they use
STRUCTURED LIGHT to project patterns onto
a scene. The resulting isoline deformations
reveal the scanned object's 3D properties,
making the invisible visible in a tightly
controlled grid of light. / Plaatsmaken Arnhem, The
Netherlands /

FLOCKING DIPLOMATS NEW YORK

SAME PLACE, MULTIPLE TIMES
Parking Violations by Diplomats in 1999 shown as treemap. The Top 100 of addresses with most violations is used, the surface of the image is related to the number of violations committed at that place.

Top 5: 307 E 44 ST (2014 violations), 310 E 44 ST (1896 violations), 304 E 45 ST (1407 violations), 333 E 38 ST (1152 violations) and 866 UN PLAZA (835 violations).

SOURCES
Based by kind permission on data from: Ray Fisman and Edward Miguel, "Corruption, Norms and Legal Enforcement: Evidence from Diplomatic Parking Tickets", December 2007, Journal of Political Economy.

DESIGN
Catalogtree, June 2008

PHOTOGRAPHY
Mikhail Illatov, New York City

printed by Plaatsmaken, Arnhem, NL

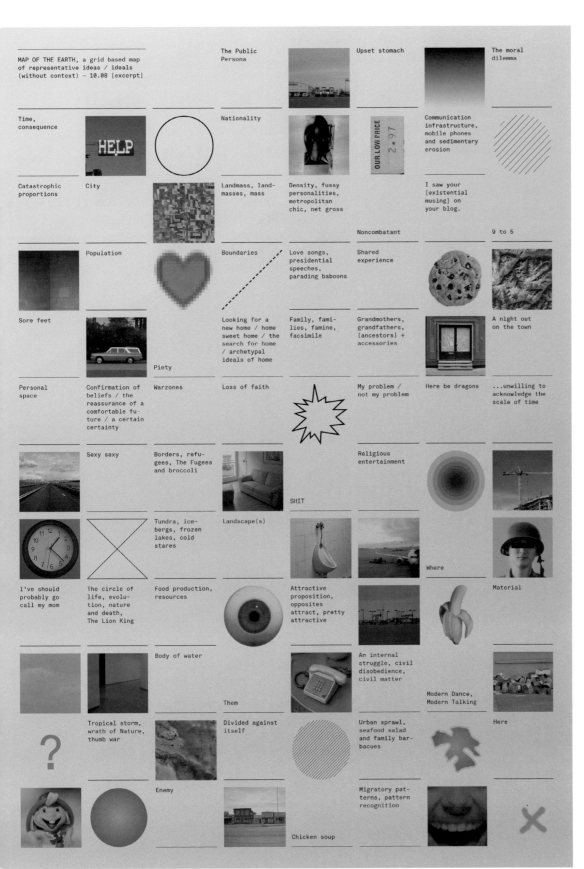

MAP OF THE EARTH, a grid based map
of representative ideas / ideals
(without context) – 10.08 [excerpt]

The Public Persona

Upset stomach

The moral dilemma

Time, consequence

Nationality

Communication infrastructure, mobile phones and sedimentary erosion

OUR LOW PRICE 2.97

Catastrophic proportions

City

Landmass, landmasses, mass

Density, fussy personalities, metropolitan chic, net gross

I saw your [existential musing] on your blog.

Noncombatant

9 to 5

Population

Boundaries

Love songs, presidential speeches, parading baboons

Shared experience

Sore feet

Looking for a new home / home sweet home / the search for home / archetypal ideals of home

Family, families, famine, facsimile

Grandmothers, grandfathers, [ancestors] + accessories

A night out on the town

Piety

Personal space

Confirmation of beliefs / the reassurance of a comfortable future / a certain certainty

Warzones

Loss of faith

My problem / not my problem

Here be dragons

...unwilling to acknowledge the scale of time

Sexy sexy

Borders, refugees, The Fugees and broccoli

Religious entertainment

SHIT

Tundra, icebergs, frozen lakes, cold stares

Landscape(s)

Where

I've should probably go call my mom

The circle of life, evolution, nature and death, The Lion King

Food production, resources

Attractive proposition, opposites attract, pretty attractive

Material

Body of water

An internal struggle, civil disobedience, civil matter

Them

Modern Dance, Modern Talking

Tropical storm, wrath of Nature, thumb war

Divided against itself

Urban sprawl, seafood salad and family barbacues

Here

Enemy

Migratory patterns, pattern recognition

Chicken soup

2

1
FLOCKING DIPLOMATS 4
Catalogtree

Protected by diplomatic immunity — and thus exempt from prosecution — diplomatic staff around the world show remarkable disdain for "petty" local regulations. Unauthorised parking tends to top their list of violations. To this end, FLOCKING DIPLOMATS IN NEW YORK charts the worst-hit spots in a graphic reconstruction of the top 100 NYC locations; the respective image size indicates the volume and frequency of illegal parking.   Documenting a stunning 2000+ violations at just one address, the map not only underscores the principle of "repeat offenders" who find themselves lured back to the scene of their (unpunished) crimes, but also becomes a coincidental map of the city's most desirable locations, where the global elite congregates. /Pictures: Mikhail Iliatov/

2
EARTH MAP (EXCERPT)
abiabiabi

What is the opposite of a map? Abi Huynh's EARTH MAP (here shown as a small excerpt) is an ambitious undertaking. Doing away with context and geography, with discernible hierarchies or anchors in space, his anti-map relies solely on associative positioning to visualise his train of thought.   A meta-map of sorts, Huynh's EARTH MAP questions the scale, content and methodology of mapping itself. By forcing non-hierarchical connections and associations, it rewires connections into a new mind map with different outcomes for observer and creator.   In its grid-based approach to representative ideas and ideals, the EARTH MAP becomes a search for home and identity, for the familial and familiar, for heads of state and states of being, for the banal and decidedly alien in a public/personal document that blurs the boundaries between the mapping and mapped.

NEXT PAGE
JOUR 1
rollergirl

Why live dangerously when you could live vicariously? In 16 days of intense Internet travel, Rollergirl recreates the perfect — and perfectly average — trip to a string of US West Coast highlights.   L.A., Grand Canyon, Las Vegas, San Francisco: planned, assembled and documented via virtual means — with information harvested from personal trip planning site MAPPY.COM, publicly available webcams and accounts by some of the seven million people who follow this route every year — the fictitious journey becomes a hyper-real amalgamation of the accumulated knowledge and experiences of those who actually took the trip.

Akin to Flaubert's spoof DICTIONARY OF RECEIVED IDEAS, the documentation of well-travelled clichés is never authentic, but in its distillate of lowest common denominators it becomes "more true" than each of the individual journeys.

```
7:02    0,06    Prendre à gauche la rue de Genève [520m]
7:02            Sortir de Lausanne et continuer sur 1 [3.1km]
7:05    4       Prendre la E23 [3.1km] en direction de Genève Morges
7:07    7       Continuer sur l'A1/E62 [51.5km] en direction de Morges-Ouest
7:35    59      Sortir et prendre la E21 [1.9km]
7:37    61      Entrer dans Cointrin [1.5km] en direction de Aéroport
7:40    62      Arrivée Aéroport Genève-Cointrin
```

```
4:00    0,0     Depart Los Angeles International Airport on Local road(s) (East) for 98 y
4:00    0,1     Turn RIGHT (South) onto Departures Acc [World Way S] for 0,6 mi
4:02    0,6     Continue (East) on Ramp for 0,4 mi
4:03    1,0     Bear RIGHT (East) onto W Century Blvd for 1,5mi
4:06    2,5     Bear RIGHT (East) onto Ramp for 0,7 mi
4:08    3,2     Merge onto I-405 [San Diego Fwy] (North) for 16,0 mi
4:27    19,1    Turn off onto Ramp for 0,2 mi
4:28    19,4    Bear LEFT (North-East) onto Sepulveda Blvd for 0,5 mi
4:29    19,9    Turn RIGHT (East) onto Ramp for 0,2 mi
4:38    20,1    Continue (South) on US-101 [Ventura Fwy] for 5,5 mi
4:38    25,6    Continue (South-East) on Ramp for 0,2 mi
4:39    25,8    Turn RIGHT (South) onto Vineland Ave for 87 yds
4:39    25,8    Arrive Holiday Inn-Beverly Garland's
                [4222 Vineland Ave, North Hollywood, CA 91602, Tel: (818) 980-8000]
```

réveil à 06 h 10. Contrôler les robinets
les fenêtres. Vider le frigo. Arroser les plantes
rifier deux fois la poignée de la porte. Mettre

```
0,0
```

Ford Mustang Convertible
- 2 Adults, 2 Children
- 1 Large Suitcase, 2 Small Suitcases
- Automatic Transmission
- Air Conditioning
- Dual Airbags
- ABS
- AM/FM,
- Cassette
- CD
- Power Brakes
- Power Steering
- Power Windows
- Central Locking
- Tilt Steering
- Dual Mirrors
- Cruise Control
- V6 Engine
- Bucket Seats
- Power Mirrors

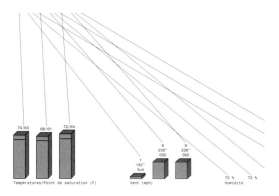

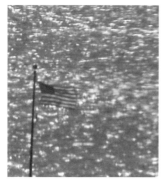

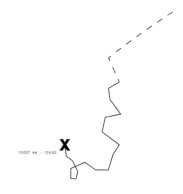

10037 km - 13h52   X

5:48:03   Jul 13 04 15:49:11

harmacie.

. Could you recommend something for a bad cold?
oi, pourriez-vous me recommander quelque chose contre un gros rhume?
ds. Is it just a simple head cold?
. Est-ce seulement un simple rhume de cerveau?
ave a headache, a sore throat? a slight cough, and I ache all over.
i en effet une migraine, mal à la gorge, je tousse un peu et j'ai des douleurs partout.
ainly sounds like the flu that's going around. Everyones got it. I can give you a cold capsule that'll relieve the runny nose and so
tout l'air de la grippe qui circule, tout le monde l'a. Je peux vous donner une gélule contre le rhume qui soulagera le nez et
n't knock me out, because I've gotta go to leave tomorrow.
ue ça ne vas pas m'assommer, parce que demain il faudra que je parte.
make you drowsy, but it'll get you over the worst part fast. How about some vitamin C tablets? They won't do you any harm.
va vous rendre somnolent, mais ça va vous soulager rapidement. Que diriez-vous de comprimés de vitamine C? Ça ne vo
. I've got plenty.
. J'ai tout ce qu'il faut.
re. This ought to do the trick, but if you're not better in a couple of days, you should see a doctor.
evrait faire l'affaire, mais si vous n'allez pas mieux d'ici deux, trois jours, vous devriez voir un médecin.
. Bye now.
ue je ferai. Bon eh bien au revoir.

er les pastilles.

seoir sur un banc. Regarder les passants.
ndre à l'agence de location de véhicules

Lick Observatory
Jul 27 04 09:50:07

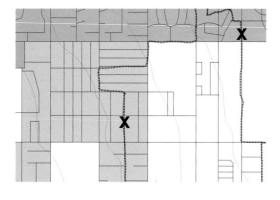

La route qui a des bosses.
Tout droit.
Les nuages qui se précisent.
Le soleil dans le rétroviseur.
Le panneau 60.
La climatisation sur 22°.
Le volume sur 12.

Riders on the s
There's a killer

West

```
00    1294,8    Depart Goulding's Monument Valley RV Park [PO Box 360001, Monument Valley
                UT 84536, Tel: (435) 727-3235] on Local road(s) (South) for 54 yds
00    1294,8    Turn LEFT (East) onto Gouldings Hospital Rd for 0,8 mi
03    1295,5    Bear RIGHT (East) onto Monument Valley Rd for 1,8 mi
09    1297,3    Bear RIGHT (South) onto SR-163 for 23,7 mi
09    1297,7    Entering Arizona
38    1321,0    Turn RIGHT (West) onto US-160 for 31,9 mi
16    1352,9    Turn RIGHT (North) onto SR-98 for 9,4 mi
33    1362,3    Bear LEFT (West) onto SR-98 [BIA-22] for 3,0 mi
38    1365,3    Continue (West) on SR-98 for 1,2 mi
40    1366,5    Bear LEFT (West) onto SR-98 [BIA-22] for 0,3 mi
40    1366,8    Continue (West) on SR-98 for 0,5 mi
41    1367,4    Bear LEFT (West) onto SR-98 [BIA-22] for 2,2 mi
45    1369,6    Continue (North-West) on SR-98 for 12,1 mi
06    1381,6    Bear LEFT (South-West) onto SR-98 [BIA-22] for 3,1 mi
11    1384,7    Bear LEFT (West) onto SR-98 for 34,0 mi
10    1418,7    Turn RIGHT (East) onto US-89 [Lake Powell Blvd] for 3,2 mi
16    1421,9    Bear RIGHT (North) onto Lakeshore Dr for 0,7 mi
17    1422,6    Turn LEFT (West) onto Local road(s) for 109 yds
17    1422,7    Arrive Wahweap/Lake Powell RV Park
                [PO Box 1597, Page, AZ 86040, Tel: (520) 645-1004]
```

rd. Include Choice of Soup du Jour or
sings: Italian, Roquefort, Sherry Wine,
Vegetables, Potato, Garlic Bread.

Chicken Marsala_17.00
Chicken Breast Chez Jay_17.00
Chicken Curry_17.00
Swordfish Béarnaise Seasonal_21.95 **X**
Swordfish "Roti" au Poivre_21.95
Sand Dabs Sauté Almondine_17.00

ori

igh

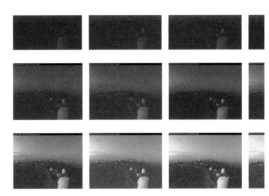

igressive. Le nœud dans les cheveux longs.
Les cheveux humides. Les lunettes Gucci avec
liamant incrusté incrustés dans les cheveux. I
strings jaunes. Les strings bleus. Les strings a
rés. Les strings rouges. Les strings violets. Le
strings roses fluo. Le clip R n' B. Les blondes
ines. Les bombes latines. Les 2 filles joujouta
lans les éclaboussures du bassin. Le plongeon
lans l'eau. La douzaine de brasses jusqu'au r
ord. Remonter sur les dalles. Se rasseoir dan
chaise longue. Les nœuds fragiles. Les discuss

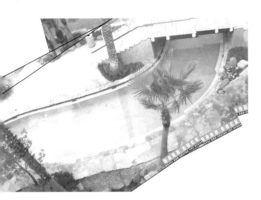

e knows I'm goin
alifornia dreamin
winter's day.
ll the leaves are l
e sky is gray. I'v
walk on a winter

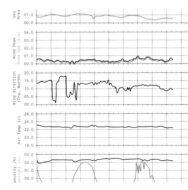

680 Southbound between 242 and NORTH MAIN ST
Heavy traffic

2:02 PM 09/02/04 Conditions
ACE TRAIN
No problems to report: #3 AND # 5 ON TIME...

2:02 PM 09/02/04 Conditions
BART
No problems to report: 62 TRAINS ON TIME...

2:02 PM 09/02/04 Conditions
880 Southbound between 238 and THORNTON AV/84 EAST
No problems to report: no delays on the nimitz freeway... between hayward and the DUMBARTON BRIDGE...

2:01 PM 09/02/04 Conditions
WINSTON BRIDGE
No problems to report: TRAFFIC AT THE LIMIT_ NO FOG...

2:01 PM 09/02/04 Conditions
SAN MATEO BRIDGE
No problems to report: no delays at the toll plaza...

2:01 PM 09/02/04 Conditions
BAY BRIDGE
No problems to report: METERING LIGHTS_ ARE NOW ON_ TOLL PLAZA BACKED UP TO WEST GRAND...

1:59 PM 09/02/04 Congestion
238 Northbound between 580 and 880
Heavy traffic

1:58 PM 09/02/04 Information
LOS ANGELES
Police directing traffic: POLICE STAND-OFF GOING ON, ON THE 500 BLOCK OF LINDEN ST @ LAGUNA. LAGUNA & BU
CLOSED BETWEEN FELL & HAYES. MUNI ROUTE 21re-ROUTED... (ALL OF THIS IS FOUR BLOCKS EAST OF ALAMO SQUARE PA
ADDITION). (SINCE 11: 30PM)

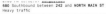

DATAESTHETIC

This last chapter differs from the ones before, because the primary goal of these visualizations is not to inform. At least, not in the way the previous examples do. We enter the world of information art, where data is a means to express personal feelings and to create works that reach out to our senses and emotions. Here, the aesthetic dimension of data is explored.

•

It was probably the *Matrix* Trilogy that introduced "data aesthetic" to the mainstream. Sure, the image of illegible green code fragments trickling down on

PREVIOUS PAGE
THE GOOD-TIME MIX MACHINE:
SCRAMBLER DRAWINGS
Rosemarie Fiore
/ › P. 252 / 2004 / Acrylic paint on vinyl, 60 × 60 ft. (18 × 18 m),
Installation at the Queens Museum, Flushing, NY /
Photo: Stefan Hagan / Courtesy of Priska C. Juschka Fine Art /

a black surface was quite clichéd (hey, it's a Holly-
wood blockbuster!) but it was a powerful metaphor
of the movie's theme.

Since Neo's battles we have seen a lot
more visualizations of abstract data. They have
become part of our daily life. We have gotten used
to the visual language that comes with it. Certain
aesthetic characteristics let us immediately think
of a representation of information. An intricate
structure with lots of nodes and interconnections:
might be a network representation. Colored bars
in different heights: probably a statistic. Curved or
zigzaging lines: could be data recorded over a certain period of time. Chad Hagen plays with these
expectations. His images /1/ have everything
a data visualization needs – except data. Their use
of form and color, their grids and layout, trick us
into thinking of it as an info-graphic, but there is
no meaning whatsoever.

Ross Racine's images mislead us too. What
look like aerial photos or renderings from an urban
planner /2/ are actually made-up freehand
drawings. No data involved, just imagination.

Our (mis-)interpretations reveal that
data visualization has developed a very diverse,
but distinct aesthetic. This aesthetic is a result
of the data itself, but also of how it is shaped.
Data becomes material. How much it is compa-
rable with physical matter is debatable – media
artist Joachim Sauter /see interview ›PP.250,251/ dismisses this
analogy – still, data is subject matter. And like
any other material, we can turn it into a commodity or a work of art. While most projects in this
book use data to convey "useful" information,
this last chapter presents examples where data
is employed for artistic purposes. For example
ART+COM's installation for the BMW museum:
 /3/ the design process of a car is not explained, but interpreted in a metaphorical, emotional way.

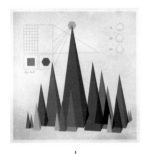

1
NONSENSICAL INFOGRAPHICS
Chad M. Hagen
/›PP.236,237/

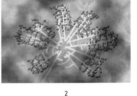

2
SUBDIVISION:
EVERGREEN PARK
Ross Racine
/›P.240/

3
KINETIC SCULPTURE
ART+COM AG
/›PP.256,257/

An experimental series on basic geometry, primary colours and their multifarious applications in graphic design.

The joy of tinkering — Max Frey's spinning, colourful circles of light disclose the gears and levers underneath. Here, etched drawings on a programme disc determine the final visual outcome. / 2007 / Bycicle rims, ciruit board, motor, LED lamps / 91 × 73 × 28 cm / Edition 3/10 / Photo: Carolina Frank /

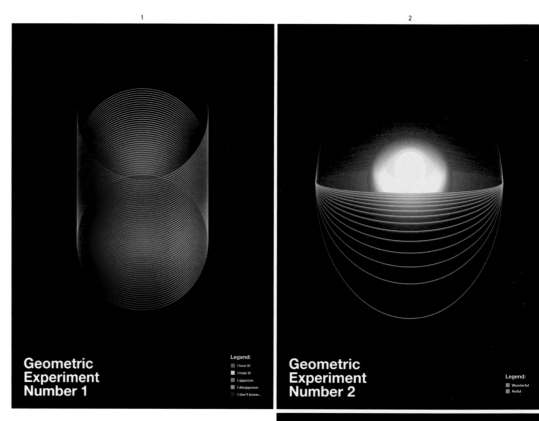

Geometric Experiment Number 1

Legend:
I love it!
I hate it!
I approve.
I disapprove.
I don't know..

Geometric Experiment Number 2

Legend:
Wonderful
Awful

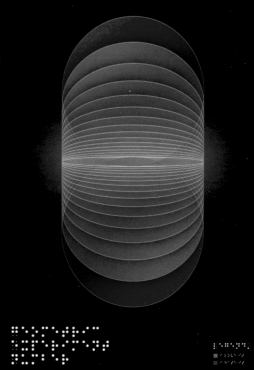

3

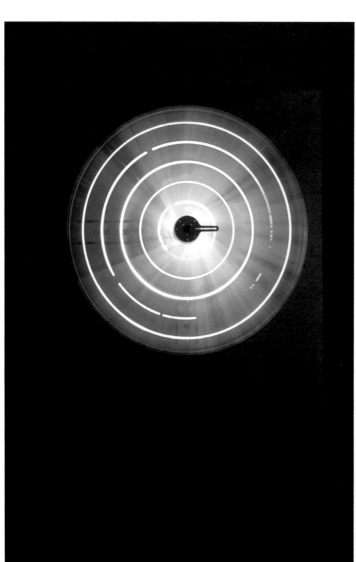

5

6

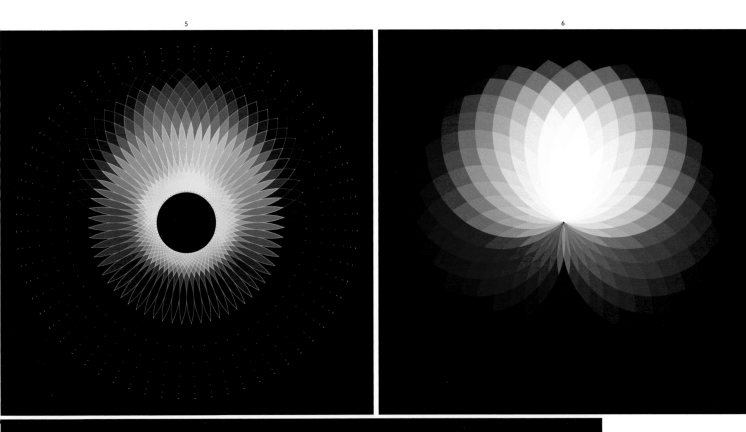

7

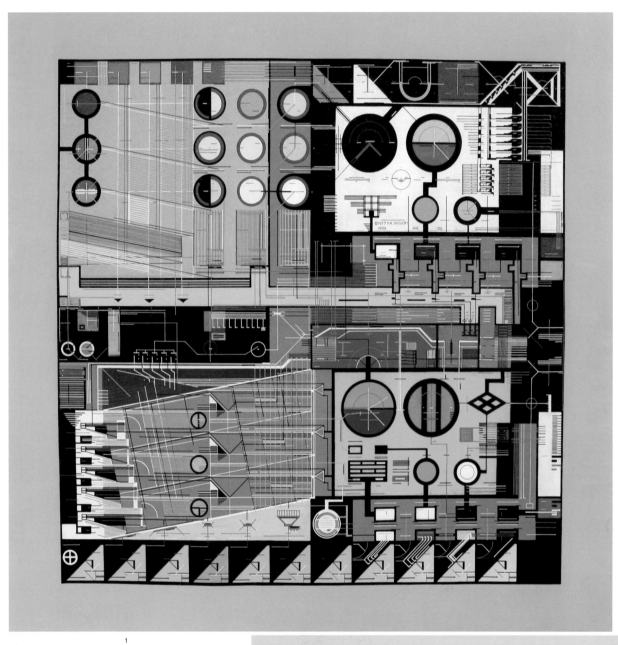

1
GREEN PAINTING
2
POSTCARD PAINTING 2
Mark Wilson
This one's from the vaults! Dating back to the
late 1970s — when diagrams and technology
equalled the way forward — Mark Wilson's
paintings exhort the beauty of networks and
electric circuitry. / GREEN PAINTING / 1977 / Acrylic on
linen / 76×76 cm / POSTCARD PAINTING 2 / 1978 / Acrylic on
paper / 10×15 cm /

1

2

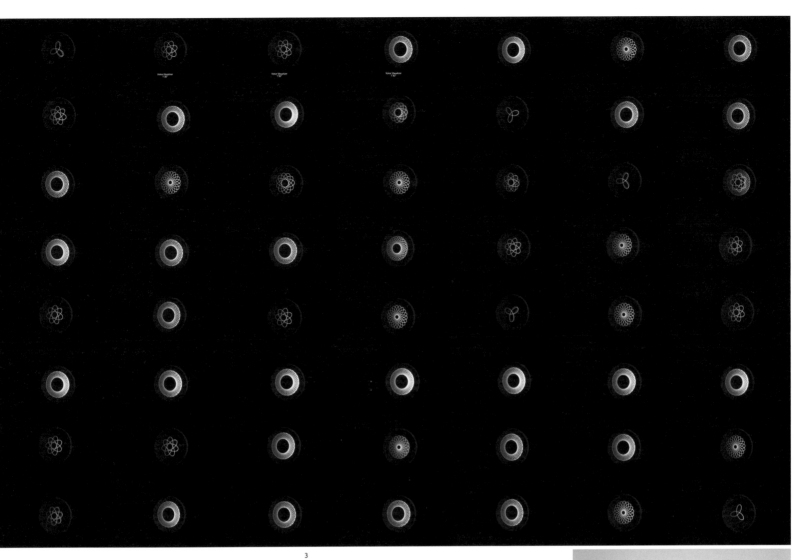

3

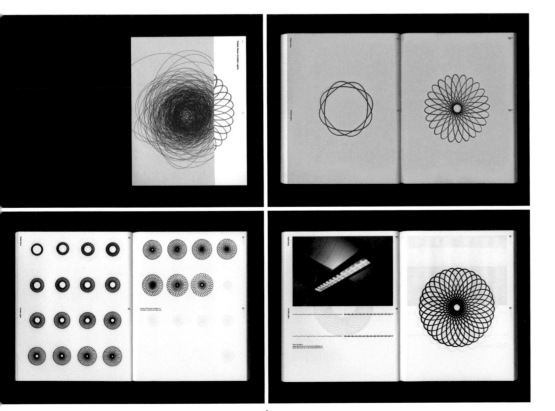

4

3
VOICE VISUALIZER
why not smile
Hoon Kim
VOICE VISUALIZER aims to improve the quality of communication in the public sphere. A loudhailer with kaleidoscopic results, the real-time device translates voices into pixels, spirograph patterns or colour spectra according to their volume and pitch.

4
VISIBLE NOISE / INVISIBLE LIGHTS
why not smile
Hoon Kim
VISIBLE NOISE / INVISIBLE LIGHTS explores the white noise generated by light sources. Using a spirograph in an experimental studio set-up, the artist investigated the relationships between 25 different types of light. All lights were photographed and their sounds recorded, both on and off. Kim then analysed the differences in repetition, volume and frequency between the emitted sound waves.

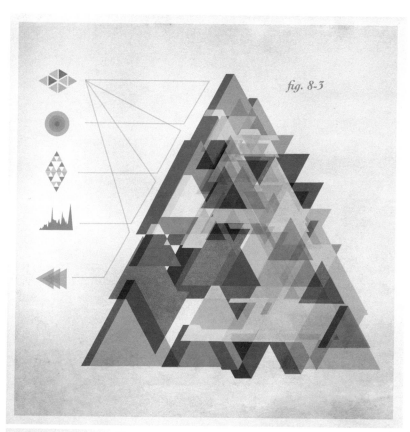

fig. 8-3

NONSENSICAL INFOGRAPHICS
Chad M. Hagen
In a graphic take on THE EMPEROR'S NEW CLOTHES parable, Chad M. Hagen's NON-SENSICAL INFOGRAPHICS expose what information graphics look like without any true data or statistics to substantiate their visual structure.

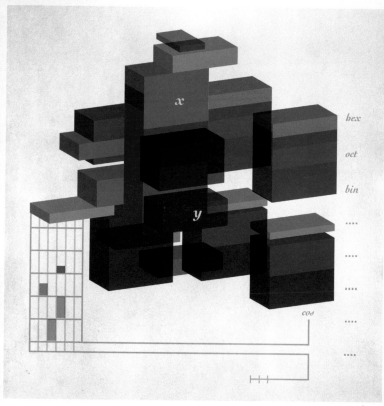

hex

oct

bin

cos

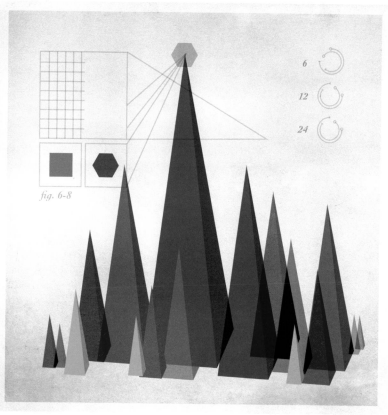

fig. 6-8

6

12

24

The encyclopedia was viewing the events on the other pages with immense satisfaction and decided to introduce some facts to Jack from Jack and the Beanstalk. Almost immediately the golden goose keeled over. Next to the bird's lifeless body was a group of words claiming 'no animal is able to sustain metal ore in its digestive tract'. Jack spun round to see more words declare, 'a garden beanstalk is unable to grow beyond 13 feet'. Suddenly all his words were swamped with explanations.

And so, like the beast's enforced timeline, Jack's tale was now inhabited with the encyclopedia's 'facts'. Jack's Bean was looking considerably less Magic

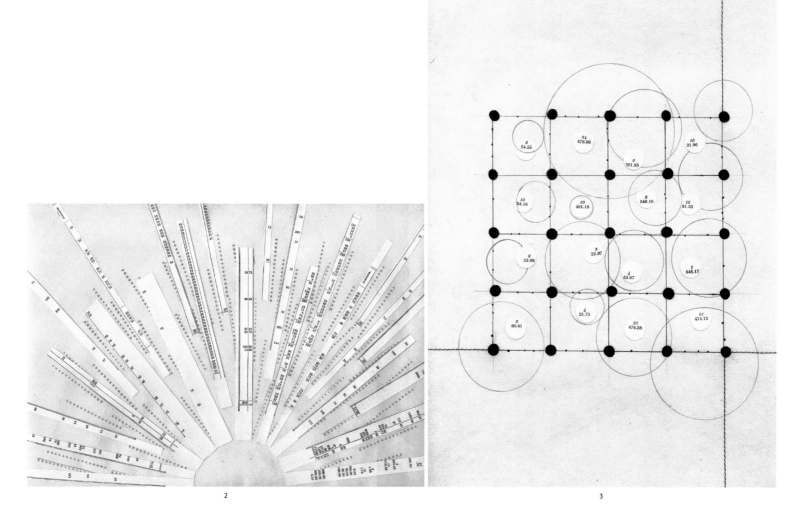

1

2   3

1

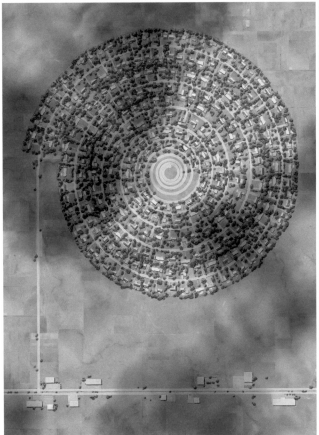

2

3

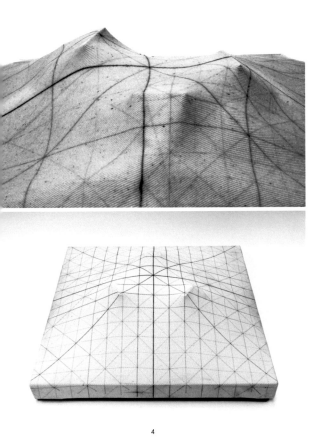

4

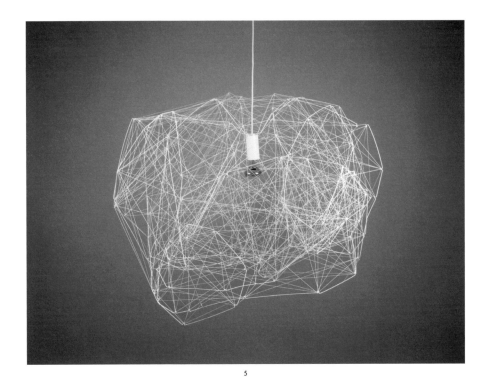

5

6

1
SUBDIVISION: EVERGREEN PARK
2
SUBDIVISION: GREENFIELD LAKES
3
SUBDIVISION: BEACHVIEW BLUFFS
Ross Racine
A graphic, stern look at the world below, at
human organisation, cities and suburbs; Ross
Racine's fictional aerial views of metropoli-
tan and rural realities are drawn freehand
on the computer.

4
SURFACE MODULATION
Richard Sweeney
In his SURFACE MODULATION series, maths
experimentalist Sweeney puts design on the
grid. Here, wooden formers — clamped behind a stretched canvas — push the taut
material outwards. The resulting shape is
painted with epoxy resin that leaves a permanent impression, even after the former's
removal. /2009 /Graphite on canvas, wooden former /Art-
work and photography by Richard Sweeney/

5
DRAWING LIGHT — CUMULUS
Sara Ivanyi
DRAWING LIGHT is a series of lampshades
that emphasise the spatial quality of light.
Spinning their web across the walls, they
translate great volumes of light with little
mass. /2009 /metal, treated rubber wire 110 cm diam-
eter×70 cm h/

6
FRED AND ME
Matt Shlian
/›P.232 /2009 /Ball point pen 19×24 inches/

1

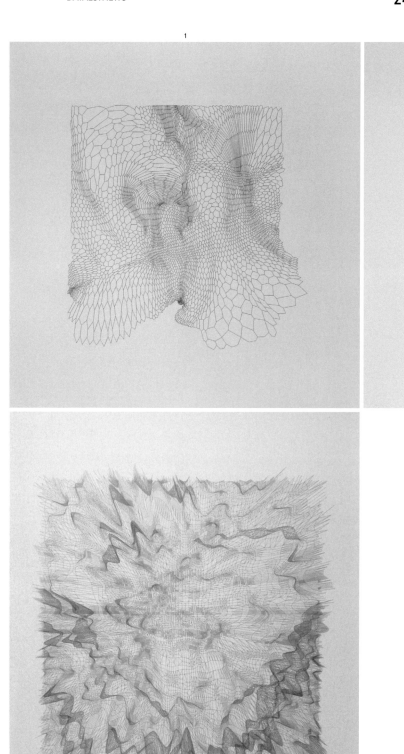

2

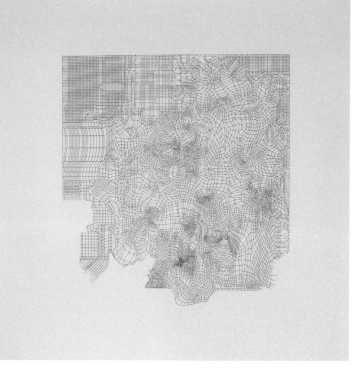

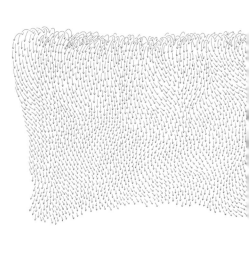

3

1
6
2
4
3
12 MORNING GLORY LANE
Matt Shlian
In this play on mistranslated information — think a game of telephone or Chinese whispers — Matt Shlian explores the way software can fracture or compound input on its way through different digital formats. Often bearing little resemblance to the original text or image, the new, warped information is rendered by a pen plotter. / 6 / 2008 / ball point pen on arches 19 × 25 inches / 4 / 2008 / ball point pen on arches 19 × 25 inches / 12 MORNING GLORY LANE / 2007 / / ball point pen on 19 × 24 inches /

4
O.T. (PFEILE 4)
Jorinde Voigt
/ Berlin / 2006 / Ink on Paper / 150 × 300 cm / Unique /

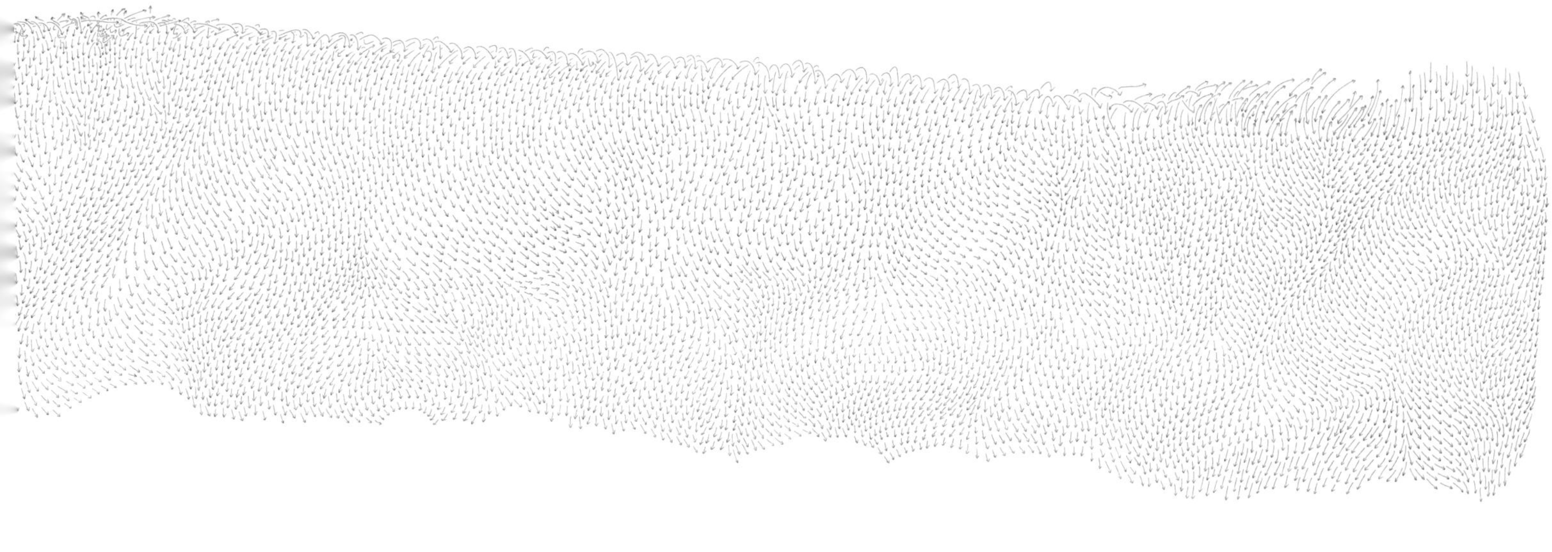

1
RANDOMIZER 4
Zalibarek

Zalibarek's RANDOMIZER 4 scales the dizzying heights of landscaped prose. / 2009 / pencil, ink on paper /

2
TEST AUDIENCE DRAWINGS
(RED REJECT, 7TH GENERATION)
3
TEST AUDIENCE DRAWINGS
(ORANGE REJECT, 1ST GENERATION)
Torgeir Husevaag

An example of generative ink sketches executed according to pre-defined rules, Husevaag's TEST AUDIENCE DRAWINGS thrive on the tension between method and play, between attention to detail and deliberate flaws.   In order to test his own skill and concentration, this particular exercise requires the artist to draw circles around each other — as close to each other and as fast as possible. According to the experimental framework, none of the lines should ever touch — mistakes are marked with a "punishment circle" to exaggerate the original flaw.   For a further twist, all drawings run through several "generations". After each round, a test audience picks their favourite from a set of four to serve as a starting point for the next batch, further reinforcing Husevaag's kinks and deviations.   An exercise in skill and perceptions, it is precisely these imperfections that add interest and structure to the streamlined setup. Akin to the principles of evolution, tiny mutations can trigger huge change. Over the course of several generations, minute mistakes spawn astonishing diversity. / TEST AUDIENCE DRAWINGS (RED REJECT, 7TH GENERATION) / 2002 / Ink on paper / TEST AUDIENCE DRAWINGS (ORANGE REJECT, 1ST GENERATION) / 2001 / Ink on paper /

1

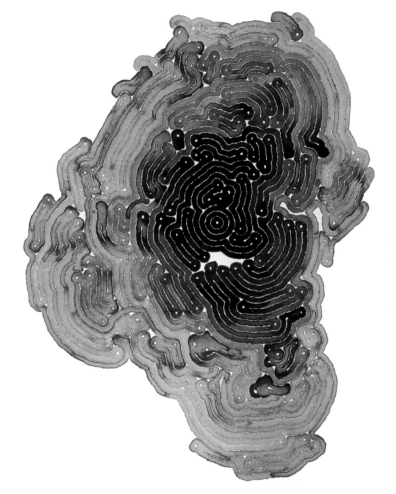

2

3

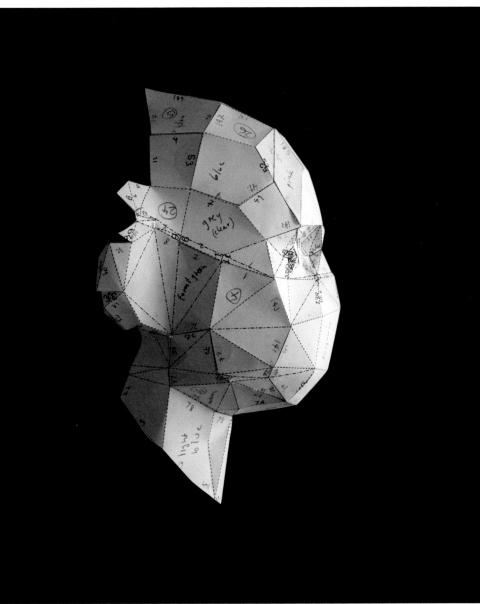

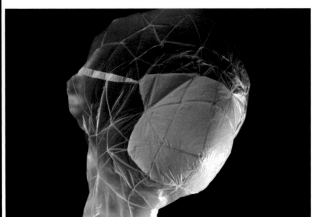

4

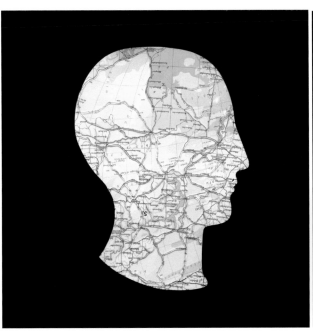

5

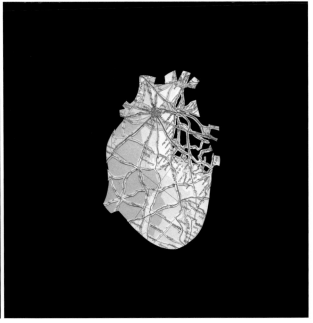

6

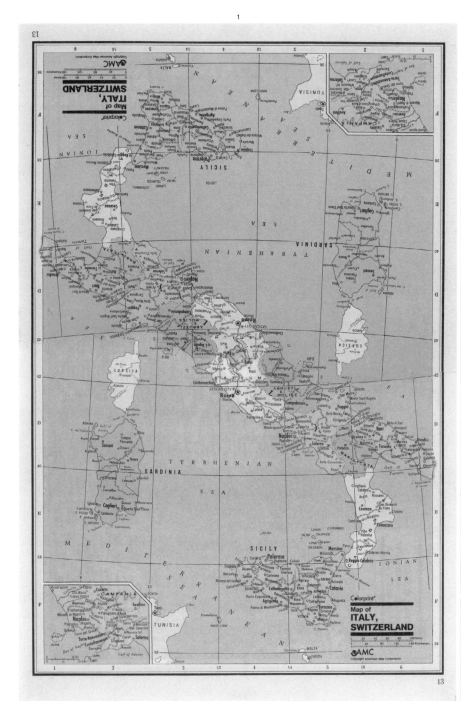

1
ITALY
from the GEOGRAPHIC PATHOLOGIES series
2
SOUTH AMERICA
from the GEOGRAPHIC PATHOLOGIES series
3
NORTH AMERICA
from the GEOGRAPHIC PATHOLOGIES series
Nina Katchadourian
Where is up and where is down? Nina
Katchadourian's GEOGRAPHIC PATHOLO-
GIES change the map of the world as we
know it. By simple inversion and reflection,
she achieves a sense of instant alienation —
and enforces a new point of view. /1996/
Courtesy of the artist, Sara Meltzer gallery (New York) and
Catharine Clark gallery (San Francisco)/

4
CIRCLE SERIES (VENTS 02)
5
UNCHARTED SERIES — FRACTURE
6
CIRCLE SERIES (MIGRATION)
7
UNCHARTED SERIES — BASIN
Shannon Rankin
/ 2009 / map on paper /

4

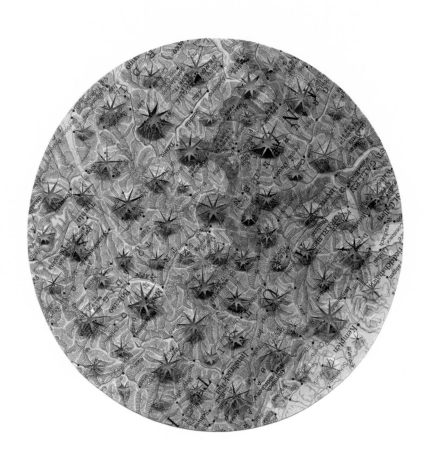

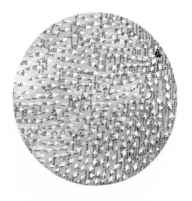

5

6

7

1

1
HIGH ALTITUDE/hangseng_80—09
2
HIGH ALTITUDE/dax_80—09
3
HIGH ALTITUDE/nasdaq_80—09
Michael Najjar
Photographic material gathered near Mount
Aconcagua — at 6,962 meters the highest
mountain on the American continent —
forms the basis of HIGH ALTITUDE, a series
visualising the development of the leading
global stock market indices over the past
20—30 years./2008—2009/Courtesy by the artist and
Galería Juan Silió/

2

JOACHIM SAUTER

Joachim Sauter is a co-founder of ART+COM, one of world's leading agencies for spatial solutions created with new media. The
company has been a pioneer in this field for over 20 years and is
still setting the standard of excellence in the development of
projects at the intersection of art, media, design and the
communication of information. ART+COM is particularly skilled at presenting brands and content both
effectively and playfully so that they resonate on
an emotional level. Today, Sauter still works as
head of its creative department, but he also
makes time to pass his experience and
knowledge on to students. Since 1991
he has been professor of new media
art and design at Berlin's University of the Arts. In 2001 he was
appointed as an adjunct
professor at UCLA.

•

You work in both fields of art and design. What is the difference between approaching a visualization project in an art versus design context? /IS/ In short: the result of design work has to be understood immediate-ly and should be directly legible by as many as possible. This means it has to be told in a lan-guage everyone understands. Artwork how-ever is produced using an individual and per-sonal language and it is mainly not meant to be understood immediately or by everyone. The process of understanding artwork by deci-phering is very important. It forces one into a much deeper dialogue with what is presented.

In design work it is the opposite – if there is a fire, you don't want to decipher an exit sign. It goes without saying that the borders are blurry and that you find both approaches in both fields.

In the domain of data there is on one hand information visualization. Here, the goal is to inform someone about something in a legible way, or to make them understand what's behind a data set. On the other hand there is data visualization where data is used as a form-finding factor to create a visual/aesthetic/experiential sensation. In a design project it's all about the information you want to communicate. The designer has to find the right way to translate this data into information. In a data-based art project it is more about the formal and aesthetic quality than the content.

> IN A DATA-BASED ART PROJECT IT IS MORE ABOUT THE FORMAL AND AESTHETIC QUALITY THAN THE CONTENT.

To what extent do you let the data influence the outcome? How much does the data determine the aesthetic? /IS/ In a design project it is all about what you want to communicate with the data or how to make the data legible. So never let the data dictate to you – but "listen" carefully to it. On the other hand if you go for a purely aesthetic outcome you can play with data and go into a mutual dialogue with it until a visually satisfying result appears. Again, the borders are blurry.

> IF YOU GO FOR A PURELY AESTHETIC OUTCOME, YOU CAN PLAY WITH DATA AND GO INTO A MUTUAL DIALOGUE WITH IT UNTIL A VISUALLY SATISFYING RESULT APPEARS.

Do you consider data your "material"? Similar to how paint is the material of a painter, or stone, metal or wood that of a sculptor? /IS/ No, it is not material to me. It is either content or the basis for a form-finding process. If you want to compare it with the traditional painting process, then it is rather the motif or subject than the paint.

Your work is often very experimental. Do you think we underestimate the receptivity of our audience? Should we challenge them more? /IS/ My process of designing might be experimental and the outcome unconventional. But usually it is legible and I make sure that the audience understands the information which is communicated. I would say the audience is cleverer than many think. You have to challenge people – if you don't, they are not interested in what you want to tell them. You have to do it in a clever and intelligent way though.

How important is interactivity in conveying information? /IS/ Interactivity means that you design a mutual dialogue between the audience and the subject. In information visualization it is often helpful to see data from different angles, compare it with other information, update it, network it, give a personalized view of something, go to deeper levels and so on. All of this can be best provided with interactivity.

You often work with quite impressive set-ups, sophisticated software and the latest technology. How do you make sure that the medium doesn't become the message? /IS/ The stories always have to be more interesting and more in the foreground than the narrator. So I try to write the stories in an appropriate and interesting way and choose the appropriate storyteller, or even hide them.

We always talk about information "visualization." Aren't we missing out on our other senses? /IS/ The visual sense is the one with which we can understand, perceive and handle information in the best way. But there is also good data sonification work out there. In some cases it is even better than visualization, especially when our visual sense is occupied by other tasks.

For decades information visualization was mainly static, printed in books or newspapers. Today we see lots of interactive solutions, mostly on the internet. More and more people, including yourself, start to work with space and objects. What will be the next frontier? In which domain will we see more visualizations in the future? /IS/ In the last decade we observed a data visualization hype. This has a lot to do with the new field of computational design. Both screen-based media – the internet and the television – have passed the print medium. But we also see a renaissance of the physical world. We see an increasing number of people leaving the isolated situation in front of a computer, going into a museum to experience information in a physical environment with other people. I think that information and narration in space will be-

> I THINK THAT INFORMATION AND NARRATION IN SPACE WILL BECOME A DOMAIN WHERE WE WILL SEE AN INCREASING NUMBER OF PHYSICALLY STATIC AND MECHATRONIC INFORMATION INSTALLATIONS.

come a domain where we will see an increasing number of physically static and mechatronic information installations.

1

THE GOOD-TIME MIX MACHINE:
SCRAMBLER DRAWINGS
(PROCESS PHOTOGRAPH)
Rosemarie Fiore

For THE GOOD-TIME MIX MACHINE: SCRAMBLER DRAWINGS, Fiore transformed a 1964 Eli Bridge Scrambler into a painting machine. The resulting (remote) controlled graffiti on vinyl tarps can extend to 18×18m and resemble giant spirographs. / 2004 / 1964 Eli Bridge Scrambler ride, generator, compressor, bucket, acrylic paint on vinyl, video camera / 60×60 ft. (18×18 m) / Photo Credit: E.G. / Courtesy of Priska C. Juschka Fine Art /

2

SPHERE
Eva Schindling

/ Produced for Amy Cheung while employed at Handkerchief Productions, Hong Kong / 2008 / Processing, P5Sunflow library /

RIGHT PAGE
ASHES UNTO PEARL
Amy Cheung

Installation at the Third Guangzhou Triennial, September—November 2008. / Charcoal, wood, control units, speakers, incense / Computerization design: Eva Schindling / People: Miya Zhao, David Lo, Edwin Law, Joseph Chan, Qiqi and Vasco / Company credit: Handkerchief Production and Yuco Lab / Sponsored by the Hong Kong Arts Development Council, Guangdong Museum of Art and the 3rd Guangzhou Triennale, China /

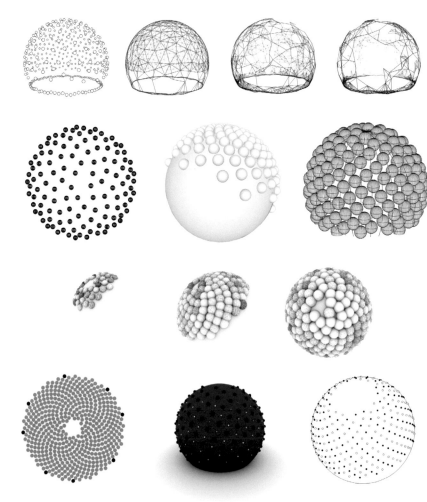

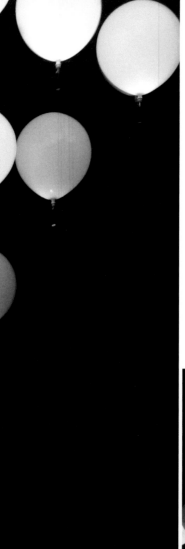

ATOM
WHITEvoid interactive art & design
An eight-by-eight array of white, self-illu-
minated spheres floats in space like a complex molecule. Carefully elevated and reined
back in by computer-controlled cables, the
gas-filled bubbles are lit from within via dim-
mable super-bright LEDs, each constituting
a single pixel in this spatial matrix.
A dynamic sculpture of physical objects, light
patterns and synchronous rhythmic and tex-
tural sounds, the ATOM sets out to explore
the interstices between interaction design,
media design, product design, interior architecture and electronic engineering.   The
resulting pitter-patter(n) of light, movement
and sound is subject to real-time manipulation as part of a 60-minute performance by
"balloonist" Christopher Bauder (WHITEvoid)
and experimental electronic sound designer
Robert Henke (Monolake). ∕ATOM ∕ Performance:
Christopher Bauder, Robert Henke ∕ Photo: Justine Lera ∕

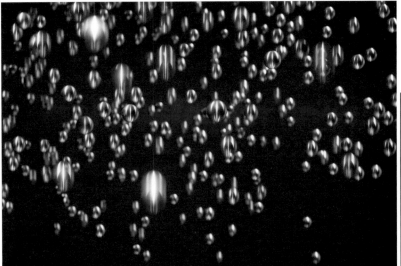

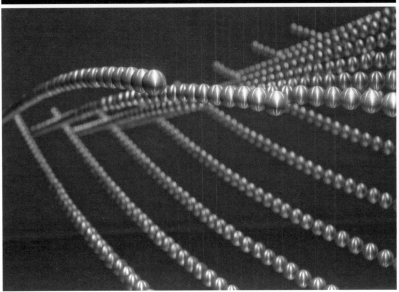

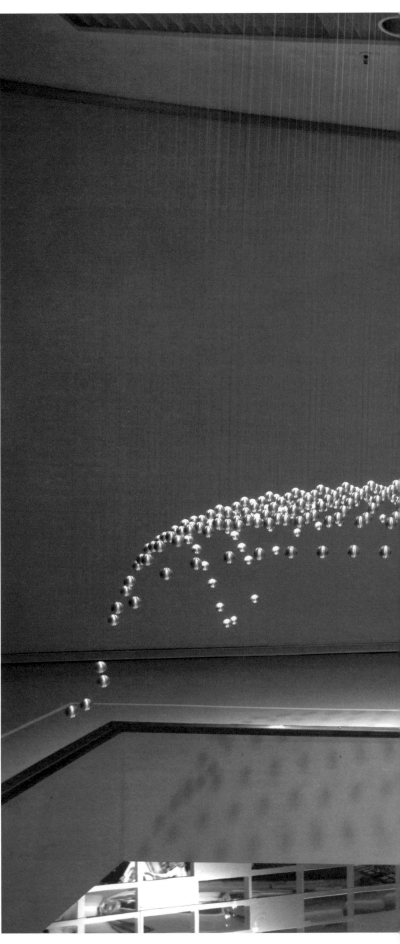

KINETIC SCULPTURE
ART+COM AG

Tasked with creating a metaphorical visualisation of the design process for BMW's new
museum in Munich, ART+COM decided to
put poetry in motion with a kinetic sculpture
that epitomises the promise and potential
of high-precision engineering.   Here, 714
metal spheres — attached to individually
controlled stepper motors — come together
in complex 3D shape animations that reflect
the car industry's precise interplay between
a great number of single elements and the
subsequent coherent shape.   During
the seven minute choreography, the osten-
sible chaos of randomly moving spheres
— a cloud of infinite ideas — gradually co-
alesces into abstract shapes and finally the
contours of recognisable car models.
Analogous to the fluidity of thought, creativity and design, the sculpture becomes
a neutral blank slate for infinite potential
and pays homage to the concepts of motion,
transience and flexibility.

1

MOVEABLE TYPE
EAR Studio
Mark Hansen and Ben Rubin
In this media artwork, installed in the ground-floor lobby of THE NEW YORK TIMES Building, two grids of 560 small digital screens translate the daily output of THE NEW YORK TIMES (news, features, opinion, blogs) as well as THE TIMES' 150-year archive and user comments into a series of fragmented, re-combined and ever-changing kinetic compositions. / 2007 / The artwork is located in the lobby of the New York Times Building in New York City /

1

2
BASF-BESUCHERZENTRUM
flying saucer
Exploring the Manhattan-sized BASF production plant in Ludwigshafen on an interactive media table, remains one of the highlights at the multinational visitor centre. The display allows up to six visitors to explore several layers of information projected onto a relief model of the entire site. / Software development: deux:luxe GbR, Muskelfisch Entertainment / Construction Management: R&F Logistik GmbH / Show Systems Integration: project syntropy GmbH /

2

1

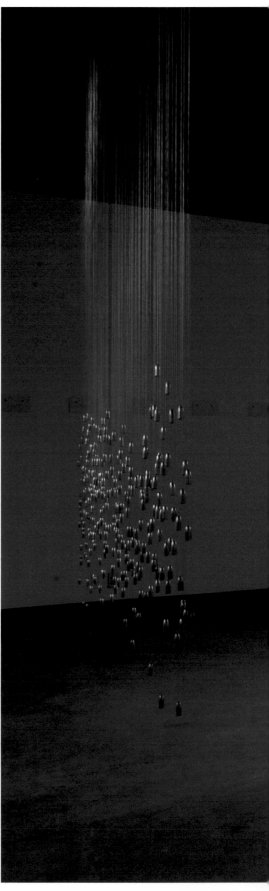

1
DIVIDED TIME (1999—2009)
R. Justin Stewart
History repeats itself: in a world where fast-paced stock quotes have started to govern the rhythm of everyday life, DIVIDED TIME serves as a 10-year portrait of the United States or to be more precise, its intrinsic and extrinsic value in business terms — its business success.   A tight tangle of thin blue lines and small, lightweight steel spheres, each day is represented by a single thread, its length corresponding to the day's Dow Jones closing value.   Faced with this blur of information, it soon becomes clear that no single day carries that much weight in the overall whole, within the stock market's circular and unpredictable nature. / 2009 / Thread, 1/8 oz steel weights /

2
2AM-2PM
R. Justin Stewart
2AM-2PM explores the ramifications of trying to parse the everyday onslaught of visual information. In order to make sense of it all, we tend to filter out non-essential data by means of abstraction, abbreviation and categorisation.   A prime example of visual simplification would be the map of a transit system; complex routes are boiled down to basic schematics and thousands of scheduled stops are organised into a navigable matrix.   2AM-2PM removes these filters and rekindles the bewildering complexity involved in the citywide choreography of public transport in several three-dimensional models of the Sunday Minneapolis / St. Paul transit system.   In these new, three-dimensional "maps", horizontal axes represent directional movement, while vertical axes indicate time. A total of 47 horizontal layers show the bus routes running during a given interval and within each of these layers, active transit routes are represented by wood balls placed at the scheduled stops. / 2008 / copper, wood, thread, steel /

1

1
TOMMY STØCKEL'S ART OF TOMORROW
Tommy Støckel
In his abstract representation of future endeavours, of things to come and what might be, Tommy Støckel tries to predict his own artistic future in a sculptural visualisation of prospective tendencies and aesthetics. / 2009 / Paper, inkjet print, cardboard, wood, polystyrene / Copyright Tommy Støckel and VG Bild-Kunst, Bonn / Photo: Carl Newland /

2
CARD CATALOG
Tim Schwartz
Only a decade or so ago, around 20 songs was considered the limit for on-the-go listening on a portable CD, MiniDisk or cassette player. In the meantime, digital technology has advanced in leaps and bounds and music collections have kept pace with the exponential growth of portable storage media. To drive this particular message home, Tim Schwartz's CARD CATALOG holds all 7,390 songs of the artist's iPod, organised in reverse chronological order.

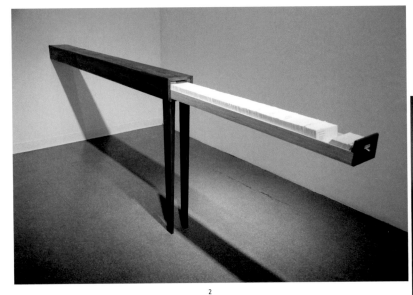

2

3
SYSTEM OF KNOWING 02
(RED CAPS)
4
SYSTEM OF KNOWING 05
(ORANGE RINGS)
R. Justin Stewart

Inspired by the evolving interpretation of ideas, SYSTEM OF KNOWING investigates how information is translated, transformed and conveyed across time and space. A combination of drawing and sculpture made from Teflon o-rings and zip ties, neither sculpture nor drawing forms the beginning: both are equal representations of the same information displayed through different frameworks. / SYSTEM OF KNOWING 02 (RED CAPS) / 2009 / teflon o-rings, zip ties, pencil and ink on paper, wood, paint / SYSTEM OF KNOWING 05 (ORANGE RINGS) / 2009 / teflon o-rings, zip ties, pencil and ink on paper, wood, paint /

4

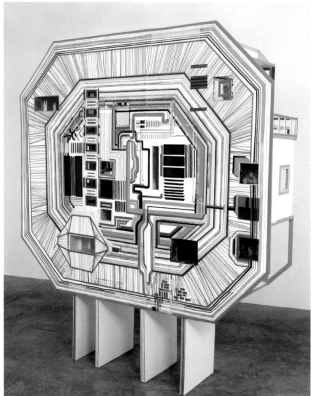

1

1
SPEEDWAY
Diana Cooper
Installation at the Postmasters Gallery, NYC.
/2000–2002/foam core, ink, acrylic, felt tip marker, acetate,
foam, photographs, pom poms and wood/77×69.5×14.5
inches/Photographed by Bill Orcutt at Postmasters Gallery, NYC/

2
EMERGER
Diana Cooper
Installation at the Whitney Museum of Art,
New York./2005–2007/Acrylic, ink, acetate, felt, foam-
core, map pins, wood, Velcro, and paper/165×144×36
inches/Photographed by Allison Wermager at The Whitney
Museum of Art, Altria, NYC/

2

1
URBAN WEATHER PRAIRIES
SYMPHONIC STUDIES IN D
Nathalie Miebach
URBAN WEATHER PRAIRIES likens data collected in Omaha, Nebraska (May/June 2008) to a symphonic orchestration. Akin to an instrument — playing one part of the overall score — each sculpture and wall piece evokes a particular aspect of the data. All pieces are brought together in an informational symphony of larger behavioural patterns that slowly emerge over time. / 2009 / reed, wood, chipboard, origami, data /

2
TWILIGHT, TIDES AND WHALES
Nathalie Miebach
TWILIGHT, TIDES AND WHALES investigates the relationship between the rising and setting of moon and sun as well as tidal and twilight readings (Provincetown, MA) and whale sightings along the New England Coast in February and March 2006.

3
ANTARCTIC TIDAL RHYTHMS
Nathalie Miebach
ANTARCTIC TIDAL RHYTHMS translates a wealth of tide-related data (collected between January and December 2005) into a multi-faceted data construct. While the inner structure converts sunrise/sunset and moonrise/moonset information into the woven structure, additional markers integrate tidal readings, moon phases, solar noon readings and the molecular structure of ice. / 2006 / Reed, wood, styrofoam, data /

3

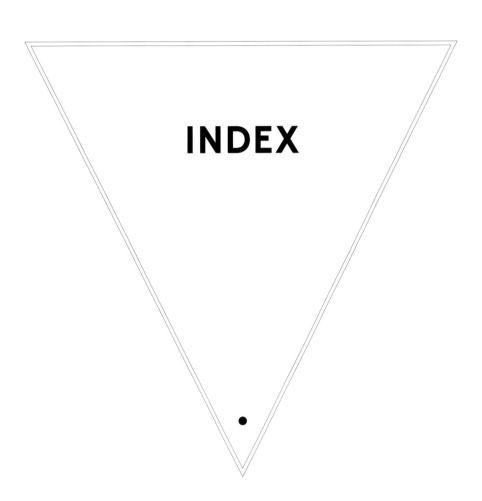

INDEX

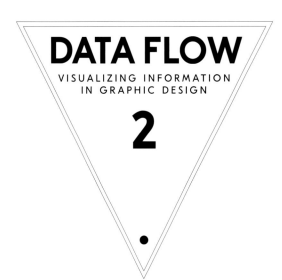

DATA FLOW

VISUALIZING INFORMATION IN GRAPHIC DESIGN

2

Edited by Robert Klanten, Sven Ehmann, Nicolas Bourquin, Thibaud Tissot
Preface, Chapter Introductions and Interviews by Johannes Schardt
Project Descriptions by Sonja Commentz

Cover by onlab, Thibaud Tissot and Johanna Klein
Cover Photography by Michael Najjar, high altitude / lehman_92–89, 2008–2009,
Courtesy of the artist and Galería Juan Silió
Layout by onlab, Thibaud Tissot and Johanna Klein
Typefaces: Eesti by Reto Moser and Tobias Rechsteiner (www.grotesk.cc) and
Farnham by The Font Bureau

Project Management by Julian Sorge for Gestalten
Production Management by Vinzenz Geppert for Gestalten
Proofreading by Lyndsey Cockwell
Printed by Eberl Print GmbH, Immenstadt im Allgäu
Made in Germany

Published by Gestalten, Berlin 2010
ISBN 978-3-89955-278-2

For more information, please check www.gestalten.com

Bibliographic information published by the Deutsche Nationalbibliothek.
The Deutsche Nationalbibliothek lists this publication in the Deutsche Nationalbibliografie;
detailed bibliographic data is available on the internet at http://dnb.d-nb.de.

None of the content in this book was published in exchange for payment by commercial parties or designers; Gestalten selected all included work based solely on its artistic merit.

This book was printed according to the internationally accepted FSC standard for environmental protection, which specify requirements for an environmental management system.

Mixed Sources
Product group from well-managed forests, controlled sources and recycled wood or fiber
www.fsc.org Cert no. GFA-COC-001446
© 1996 Forest Stewardship Council

Gestalten is a climate neutral company and so are our products. We collaborate with the non-profit carbon offset provider myclimate (www.myclimate.org) to neutralize the company's carbon footprint produced through our worldwide business activities by investing in projects that reduce CO_2 emissions:
www.gestalten.com/myclimate

myclimate
Protect our planet